THE LONG
LONELINESS

THE LONG
LONELINESS

The Autobiography of the Legendary
Catholic Social Activist

DOROTHY DAY

ILLUSTRATED BY FRITZ EICHENBERG

HarperOne
An Imprint of HarperCollinsPublishers

I think, dear child, the trouble and the long loneliness you hear me speak of is not far from me, which whensoever it is, happy success will follow. . . . The pain is great, but very endurable, because He who lays on the burden also carries it.

MARY WARD, English Nun (1585–1645)

HarperOne

HarperCollins books may be purchased for educational, business, or sales promotional use. For information, please e-mail the Special Markets Department at SPsales@harpercollins.com.

HarperCollins Web Site: http://www.harpercollins.com

HarperCollins®, 📖®, and HarperOne™ are trademarks of HarperCollins Publishers.

Library of Congress Cataloging in Publication Data

Day, Dorothy
  The long loneliness.
  Reprint. Originally published in 1952 by Harper, New York.
  Includes index.
  1. Day, Dorothy. 2. Converts, Catholic—United States—
Biography. I. Title.
BX4668.D3A33 1981   282'092'4 [B]   81–47427
ISBN 978–0–06–061751–6
AACR2

17 18   RRD(C) 70

CONTENTS

INTRODUCTION

In the mid-1970s I took a freshman seminar I taught at Harvard College to New York City. We had been reading about the life of poor people in the early decades of this century, as described by writers such as James Agee and George Orwell, and we were lucky to be invited to meet with another writer who had spent years documenting the experiences of hard-pressed people, down on their luck, in the urban precincts of America. Dorothy Day was then in her seventies, and ailing with congenitive heart disease— yet she was more than willing to converse with us, tell us of her experiences as someone who had observed the poor and struggled on their behalf for over half a century.

We met her in St. Joseph's House, on 36 East First Street, in Manhattan's Lower East Side, at the edge of what used to be the Bowery. Her home was a "hospitality house" that belonged to the Catholic Worker, a social, religious, cultural, and political movement that she and Peter Maurin founded in 1933, at the height of the Great Depression. In that building she occupied one small room, most modestly furnished. We met her in a downstairs kitchen, where every day the poor were served a free hot lunch. Over mugs of coffee these young students, the whole world before them, posed questions to and listened to a woman who had been, in her twenties, a well-known journalist and essayist, a novelist, a close friend of writers such as Eugene O'Neill, Mike Gold, John Dos Passos, and Malcolm Cowley—but who had become, in her early thirties, a Catholic convert who took the Church's teachings to heart and embarked on a lifelong effort to live up to them.

The students knew all of that—they had read *The Long Loneliness*, as well as copies of *The Catholic Worker*, a monthly newspaper that Dorothy Day and Peter Maurin first started selling in New York City during early May of 1933. They knew the biographical facts: the story of a middle-class woman born to Protestant parents (her father was a journalist) who became a suffragette, a social and political writer, a Greenwich Village intellectual, and, eventually, a lay activist within the Catholic Church—a founder, really, of a twentieth-century spiritual movement of sorts, a network of hospitality houses and newspapers across the land whose purpose is to feed the hungry and attend the poor, the vulnerable, the sick, the needy in the spirit of Christian caring.

Still, those young men and women wanted to move from abstract knowledge to a concrete consideration of what Dorothy Day held high and dear (her values, her assumptions, her commitments) and how she believed this life ought to be lived (under what circumstances, and with what purposes in mind). Moreover, they were at pains to indicate their specific, unashamed interest in her, in how she lived, but also in how she regarded her life—its achievements, its significance. How well I remember my embarrassment at such a curiosity—an unseemly interest, I thought, and an ironic one, given the well-known efforts of the person in question to draw attention away from herself and toward the people whose interests, whose material and spiritual causes, she had so insistently championed. But Dorothy Day had never stopped being a hard-working, shrewd newspaper woman, and she rather enjoyed these practical-minded youths, as they tried hard to figure out her life, its contours, its blind alleys, its overall direction.

"I've always worried about unfairness, injustice—going back to when I was your age, and was in college [at the University of Illinois, Urbana]," so she told one of the students, who had asked for a summing up, a connection between her life's origins and its eventual outcome. She amplified in this manner: "When I was your age women couldn't vote—and the poor could fall back on nothing but the charity of the rich. I remember as a girl asking my mother *why*—why things weren't better for people, why a few owned so much and many had little or nothing. She kept on telling me that 'there's no accounting for injustice, it just *is*.' I guess I've spent my life trying to 'account' for it, and trying to change things, just a little—and that is what I believe people like me ought try to do: we've been given a leg up in the world, so why not try to help others get a bit of a break, too!"

There was no arguing with such a modestly put, quietly stated proposal; but the students wanted more, wanted, really, to hear about her ideas, the books that mattered to her, and, yes, her political struggles. She had, after all, been in prison many times for the street battles she had helped wage, and she had led a vigorous, somewhat idiosyncratic intellectual and spiritual life—she had expressed in her articles and books her deep love of novelists such as Dickens, Dostoevski, Tolstoi, and her strong sense of connection to the Church's late nineteenth-century social teachings, as embedded in such important documents as the papal encyclical *Rerum Novarum* and, later, *Quadrigessimo Anno*, bold efforts on the part of the Vatican to spell out the moral and social obligations of Christians in the contemporary industrial order.

Soon enough, we were witness to that side of her; we were hearing a very well-read, articulate *reader* discourse with evident passion on the singular virtues of, say, Dickens's *David Copperfield*, or Dostoevski's *The Brothers Karamazov*, or Tolstoi's *War and Peace* and *Anna Karenina*, or his extraordinary short fiction, such as "The Death of Ivan Ilych," "Master and Man," and "How Much Land Does a Man Need?"

Indeed, though I had known her for a long time—since 1952, when (as a medical student) I lived and worked in one of her hospitality houses—I had never heard her tell quite so much about her rock-bottom convictions as she did when she stopped what seemed like a pleasantly casual discussion of books in order to point out the moral seriousness that informed her reading: "You ask me what I'd like to be remembered for—well, I hope for some of the talks here [a gesture of her hand toward the kitchen tables, now empty] with our guests; and I hope they will remember that I tried to make good coffee for them, and good soup! I've enjoyed getting to know them—they have been good teachers. You listen to them, hear of the troubles they've faced, and you realize how much courage they have needed, to go from one week to the next. I've met some truly remarkable people, sipping soup or coffee here—and I hope I have earned their respect!

"Another thing—I'd like people to say that 'she really did love those books!' You know, I'm always telling people to read Dickens or Tolstoi, or read Orwell, or read Silone. I could be one of your teachers—though I'm not a great one for analyzing those novels; I want to *live* by them! That's the 'meaning of my life' [a student had asked]—to live up to the moral vision of the Church, and of some of my favorite writers. This would have been a far lonelier life for me, if I hadn't 'met' Mr. Dickens or Mr. Tolstoi, and some others [whose books have influenced her so much]. I have had *David Copperfield* as a companion—over half a century of going back to certain chapters, passages; and the same with the books of Dostoevski and Tolstoi, and certain Chekhov stories.

"Now don't think that I've lost my mind—but I'll tell you, I'll look at some of the cards I have, some of Van Gogh's pictures of the poor, the coal miners, or Daumier's, and I talk to those pictures! I look, and I speak. I get strength from the way those writers and artists portrayed the poor, that's how I've kept going all these years: I pray to God and go visit Him in churches; and I have my conversational time with Van Gogh or with Dickens—I mean, I'll look at a painting reproduced on a postcard, that I use as a bookmark, or I read one of those underlined pages in one of my old books, and Lord, I've got my strength to get through the morning or afternoon! When I die, I hope people will say that I tried to be mindful of what Jesus told us—His wonderful stories—and I tried my best to live up to His example (we fall flat on our faces all the time, though!) and I tried to take those artists and novelists to heart, and live up to *their* wisdom (a lot of it came from Jesus, as you [students] probably know, because Dickens and Dostoevski and Tolstoi kept thinking of Jesus themselves all through their lives)."

She had told us so very much, despite the apologies she proceeded to offer for her "rambling, disconnected thinking." In fact, she had been altogether precise, pointed, and lucid. She had let us know what mattered to her, and why—a long-standing devotion to spiritual introspection, with the help of the Bible and a daily church attendance, and a similarly prolonged reliance upon the wisdom to be found in the great masters of nineteenth-century fiction, as well as some of their twentieth-century heirs. For her, literature or art were no mere opportunity for entertainment, no mere occasions for aesthetic satisfaction or self-enhancing erudition. She hungered for answers to the big questions—how ought one live this life, where, in what manner, and for what purpose? She found answers to such a kind of self-addressed inquiry in novels and paintings, and, most of all, in Holy Scripture, in the life of an itinerant preacher and healer who died on a cross, a thief on either side of Him, almost two thousand years ago in Roman-controlled Palestine. She drew inspiration from this century's poor—descendants, she never forgot, of the humble folk Jesus attended, the insulted and humiliated whom her dear novelist and artist friends kept evoking. She chose to spend her life with such people, trying to be of help to them, learning from them. Hers was a hands-on, a localist and personalist politics—she had little use for the bureaucracy of the modern state. She sought to live in a community of people devoted to the moral teachings of the Hebrew prophets (Isaiah, Jeremiah, Amos, Micah) and, of course, those of Jesus of Nazareth. She wanted to be remembered not institutionally (she laughed at the notion of herself as a "saint") but as a humble person of faith who tried her best to live in accordance with the biblical teachings she kept pondering—the Sermon on the Mount, for instance.

All of the above can be gleaned from her various writings—though it was a privilege, certainly, to hear her speak so pointedly on these matters so close to the end of her life. In *The Long Loneliness*, especially, she makes clear her passionate devotion to those who have not had the easiest time of it. She also makes clear how tirelessly she has given herself to her various loves—the love of literature and writing, the love of Jesus and His church, the love, again, of the Hebrew prophets, whom I know she constantly attended in her well-thumbed Bible, the love of ordinary men and women whose empty stomachs she worked so hard to fill, and, not least, the constant love she experienced for what might be called "the things of this world," the small gifts each morning or evening brings to us, even in a crowded, noisy city such as New York: a graceful tree here, a stand of birds perched on a wire there, the East River moving along, always moving along, an elderly woman taking good care of her wares in a food shop, a man selling his newspapers at a local convenience store. In truth, Dorothy Day loved her fellow human creatures and the world they inhabited, as the good Lord had told her she should, and if there always had to be "the long loneliness" (an aspect of our "existential" situation) there were for her, most certainly, many soul mates to keep her company on her spiritual pilgrimage, and many who still hold her close, cherish her memory, and thank the good Lord for her presence among us.

Robert Coles
July 1996

THE LONG
LONELINESS

CONFESSION

WHEN you go to confession on a Saturday night, you go into a warm, dimly lit vastness, with the smell of wax and incense in the air, the smell of burning candles, and if it is a hot summer night there is the sound of a great electric fan, and the noise of the streets coming in to emphasize the stillness. There is another sound too, besides that of the quiet movements of the people from pew to confession to altar rail; there is the sliding of the shutters of the little window between you and the priest in his "box."

Some confessionals are large and roomy—plenty of space for the knees, and breathing space in the thick darkness that seems to pulse with your own heart. In some poor churches, many of the ledges are narrow and worn, so your knees almost slip off the kneeling bench, and your feet protrude outside the curtain which shields you from the others who are waiting. Some churches have netting, or screens, between you and priest and you can see the outline of his face inclined toward you, quiet, impersonal, patient. Some have a piece of material covering the screen, so you can see nothing. Some priests leave their lights on in their boxes so they can read their breviaries between confessions. The light does not bother you if that piece of material is there so you cannot see or be seen, but if it is only a grating so that he can see your face, it is embarrassing and you do not go back to that priest again.

Going to confession is hard—hard when you have sins to confess, hard when you haven't, and you rack your brain for even the beginnings of sins against charity, chastity, sins of detraction, sloth or gluttony. You do not want to make too much of your constant imperfections and venial sins, but you want to drag them out to the light of day as the first step in getting rid of them. The just man falls seven times daily.

"Bless me, Father, for I have sinned," is the way you begin. "I made my last confession a week ago, and since then . . ."

Properly, one should say the *Confiteor*, but the priest has no time for that, what with the long lines of penitents on a Saturday night, so you are supposed to say it outside the confessional as you kneel in a pew, or as you stand in line with others.

"I have sinned. These are my sins." That is all you are supposed to tell; not the sins of others, or your own virtues, but only your ugly, gray, drab, monotonous sins.

When one writes the story of his life and the work he has been engaged in, it is a confession too, in a way. When I wrote the story of my conversion twelve years ago, I left out all my sins but told of all the things which had brought me to God, all the beautiful things, all the remembrances of God that had haunted me, pursued me over the years so that when my daughter was born, in grateful joy I turned to God and became a Catholic. I could worship, adore, praise and thank Him in the company of others. It is difficult to do that without a ritual, without a body with which to love and move, love and praise. I found faith. I became a member of the Mystical Body of Christ.

Going to confession is hard. Writing a book is hard, because you are "giving yourself away." But if you love, you want to give yourself. You write as you are impelled to write, about man and his problems, his relation to God and his fellows. You write about yourself because in the long run all man's problems are the same, his human needs of sustenance and love. "What is man that Thou art mindful of him?" the Psalmist asks, and he indicates man's immense dignity when he says, "Thou hast made him a little less than the angels." He is made in the image and likeness of God, he is a temple of the Holy Spirit. He is of tremendous importance. What is man, where is he going, what is his destiny? It is a mystery. We are sons of God, and "it is a terrible thing to fall into the hands of the living God."

I can write only of myself, what I know of myself, and I pray with St. Augustine, "Lord, that I may know myself, in order to know Thee." I could write long chapters about my daughter, about my early associates, about the men and women I have been working with these last eighteen years. Probably I have been unfair not to have written more about them, but if I started to tell about all the saints and sinners among us and the fascinating account of their lives, I would never end. Moreover, I feel hesitant to go too deeply in writing of other lives. It is hard enough to write about my own. I do feel, however, that I have a right to give an account of myself, a reason for the faith that is in me. But I have not that right to discuss others. Just the same, if I have slighted anyone, if I have failed to give credit where credit is due, if I have neglected some aspects of the work in stressing others, I beg pardon of my readers. I am a journalist, not a biographer, not a *book* writer. The sustained effort of writing, of putting pen to paper so many hours a day when there are human beings around who need me, when there is sickness, and hunger, and sorrow, is a harrowingly painful job. I feel that I have done nothing well. But I have done what I could.

I have not always felt the richness of life, its sacredness. I do not see how people can, without a religious faith. Children have a sense of joy in life but that soon wears away. One hears adolescents say, "I did not ask to be born." Rebellion has started.

My life has been divided into two parts. The first twenty-five years were floundering, years of joy and sorrow, it is true, but certainly with a sense of that insecurity one hears so much about these days. I did not know in what I believed, though I tried to serve a cause. Five years after I became a Catholic I met Peter Maurin and his story must play a great part in this work because he was my master and I was his disciple; he gave me "a way of life and instruction," and to explain what has come to be known as "The Catholic Worker Movement" in the Church throughout the world, I must write of him.

But I will begin with my own story. "All my life I have been haunted by God," as Kiriloff said in *The Possessed*. This must indeed be so, as former friends and comrades have said this of me. Not long ago when I was visiting a patient at Bellevue, I again met someone whom I had known casually at the University of Illinois and in Chicago in the early days of the Communist party there.

"I remember you," she said, "because Fred Ellis' mother-in-law did a painting of you which they still have." Fred is a *Daily Worker* cartoonist. "The last time I saw you, years ago, you were talking to me of God."

A Cleveland Communist said once, "Dorothy was never a Communist. She was too religious."

How much did I hear of religion as a child? Very little, and yet my heart leaped when I heard the name of God. I do believe every soul has a tendency toward God. "As soon as man recalls the Godhead, a certain sweet movement fills his heart. . . . Our understanding has never such great joy as when thinking of God," St. Francis de Sales writes.

Part One

SEARCHING

THE GENERATIONS BEFORE

WHEN we were little children, my brothers and sister and I, we used to sit around the supper table at night and listen to our mother talk about "when I was a little girl." Our father worked nights on a morning newspaper, so we seldom saw him and our evening meals were leisurely. We never learned much about his family from mother except that he was from Cleveland, Tennessee, and that his people despised her because she was a Northerner.

Cleveland is a small town just over the border from Rome, Georgia, where my grandmother, Mary Mee, was born. She married Dr. Sam Houston Day who was a surgeon and served in the Confederate army. My mother's father, Napoleon Bonaparte Satterlee, was from Marlboro, New York, a chairmaker, who went to war very young, was taken prisoner and came home with tuberculosis of the larynx, which made him speak, the remaining years of his life, in a hoarse whisper. My mother recalls bringing him eggnog with whiskey and sipping it on the way, and he used to reward her for her service by gay flattery, calling her Graceful. Her name was Grace.

That house in Marlboro still stands on Route 9, and I have driven past it often and past the Episcopal church where my mother was baptized and the churchyard where doubtless my forebears are buried. If I wish to go back still further, on Charity Hummel's side (she was my mother's grandmother), I could go to the cemetery at New Paltz, and on the Washburn side to the Massachusetts branch of the family, since tradition has it that there were nine brothers, all of them captains of whalers, and all lost at sea save a Christian Washburn who married Charity.

Tradition! How rich a word that is. To a thinking child it

15

means a great deal. Children all love to hear stories of when their parents were young, and of their parents before them. It gives the child a sense of continuity.

Aunt Cassie, my mother's aunt, used to skate down the river from Poughkeepsie to Marlboro to bake a batch of bread and cookies and then skate back again. Was she in love then? And did love give strength to her limbs and wings to her feet? It was a sad love story, the story of her affair with one of the engineers who built the railroad bridge over the Hudson. But Aunt Del was a telegrapher in Baltimore, a Russellite or a Bible Christian, and helped support the family, and Anna, my grandmother, had enough to do with her five children and her invalid husband. So Aunt Cassie had to stay unmarried to take care of her mother, Charity Hummel Washburn, who had been married herself at fourteen and borne eighteen children of whom only six lived.

Charity's husband had been captain of a whaler which sailed up the Hudson with a cargo of whale oil. He fell from a mast and cracked his head and was never quite right after that, running down Delafield Street in his night shirt and finally drowning in a brook.

How we loved to hear these stories and how welcome our warm house was as we heard of terrible winters with the Hudson freezing over so that skating and ice-boating were commonplace.

Tradition! We scarcely know the word any more. We are afraid to be either proud of our ancestors or ashamed of them. We scorn nobility in name and in fact. We cling to a bourgeois mediocrity which would make it appear we are all Americans, made in the image and likeness of George Washington, all of a pattern, all prospering if we are good, and going down in the world if we are bad. These are attitudes the Irish, the Italian, the Lithuanian, the Slovak and all races begin to acquire in school. So they change their names, forget their birthplace, their language, and no longer listen to their mothers when they say, "When I was a little girl in Russia, or Hungary, or Sicily." They lose their cult and their culture and their skills, and leave their faith and folk songs and costumes and handcrafts, and try to be something which they call "an American."

"Tradition," G. K. Chesterton says, "is democracy extended through time. Tradition means giving the vote to that most obscure of all classes, our ancestors. Tradition is the democracy of the dead. Tradition refuses to submit to the small and arrogant oligarchy of those who are walking about."

I wonder if those stories of our ancestors took away the fear of death that comes to us all, or whether it mitigated it.

Aunt Cassie is by now united to her love. Grandfather Napoleon is now young and dashing once more and free from all pain. But their tragedy, their pain made their lives a rich and colorful tapestry for us to gaze at, a Berlioz requiem with its glory and mourning to listen to.

Did they believe? What did they believe? We never asked these questions. Do happy children ask these questions? Ecclesiastes said, "Only this I have found, that God made man right and he hath entangled himself with an infinity of questions."

"WHAT ABOUT GOD?"

WE DID not search for God when we were children. We took Him for granted. We were at some time taught to say our evening prayers. "Now I lay me," and "Bless my father and mother." This done, we prayed no more unless a thunderstorm made us hide our heads under the covers and propitiate the Deity by promising to be good.

Very early we had a sense of right and wrong, good and evil. My conscience was very active. There were ethical concepts and religious concepts. To steal cucumbers from Miss Lynch's garden on Cropsey Avenue was wrong. It was also wrong to take money from my mother, without her knowledge, for a soda. What a sense of property rights we had as children! Mine and yours! It begins in us as infants. "This is mine." When we are very young just taking makes it mine. Possession is nine points of the law. As infants squabbling in the nursery we were strong in this possessive sense. In the nursery might made right. We had not reached the age of reason. But at the age of four I knew it was wrong to steal.

Morality lay in the realm of property and sex. Violence, murder, all had to do with our relations with one another over property.

Sex was a deeper matter, and in some obscure way had a connection with the supernatural law and God Himself. Sex and religion! It was immodest to talk of either. People were uncomfortable and embarrassed in talking about God.

Modesty at first had to do with our bodies. We used to dress around the big kitchen range down at Bath Beach and if anyone came in, the grocer, the laundry boy, we would *back out of* the room to hide our nakedness. We did not know why and whatever obscure sense of shame we had may have been connected with that part of our anatomy which was seriously smacked for punishment.

We did not learn shame as children until we learned about sex. The dark fascination of this knowledge, incomplete, legendary and instinctive, struck deep into our inmost parts. A shuddering pleasure accompanied the contemplation of it, a pleasure which we knew was *evil*, but did not know why.

Later we were confused in our adolescence, as to why such a consciousness linked up in some obscure way with beauty and love, could be evil.

Still later we understood the social attitude too. If a girl had a baby out of wedlock, she sinned against God and society. Society would have to support it, and that was wrong. The child had no father. That was a sin. So a stigma fell upon her. She was deprived of the baby, which was put in an orphanage, and she herself was left to starve to death. This was the classic picture in our twelve-year-old minds. It was simple. It was bad enough. It was the warp and woof of all tragedy to us little women. We imagined ourselves in the place of these tragic heroines, these Hester Prynnes, mainly I suppose because they had reached a peak of existence; then, before love had time to grow old and stale and cold, as doubtless our parents' had (we saw no signs of passionate, romantic love between them, and that is what we ourselves wanted), they were held in that state, solidified in a state of ecstasy as it were, forever noble and sad, a picture enlarged by love.

I do not remember going to church in those years, but Mary Manley, the girl who worked for us, was a Catholic, and she told me years afterward that she took me once to Mass and I stood in the pew looking all around and she did not take me again. I slept in the same room with Mary and I must have seen her saying her prayers but I do not remember it. We were living in Bath Beach, in Brooklyn, where I was born November 8, 1897, and I had two older brothers and a baby sister. We lived there until I was six and had started school. We prayed at school every morning, bowing our heads on our desks and saying the Our Father, and I can still smell the varnish, and see the round circle of moisture left by my mouth on the varnish as I bent close to the desk.

In trying to remember my religious experiences, that is all I can recall of formal prayer during those years.

I can remember well the happy hours on the beach with my brothers, and fishing in a creek for eels, and running away with a younger cousin to an abandoned shack in a waste of swamp around Fort Hamilton, and pretending we were going to live there all by ourselves. I wanted adventure; on one occasion I went away alone, spending what I felt to be long hours one sunny afternoon, blissful enchanted hours until the sudden realization came over me that I was alone, that the world was vast and that there were evil forces therein. I can remember on the one hand my bliss—it was almost a state of natural contemplation—and then suddenly the black fear that overwhelmed me at being alone, so that I ran all the way home.

It seems to me I spent much time alone in spite of the fact that I had two brothers and a sister. There was joy in being alone, and I can remember happy hours after we moved to California. We lived in Berkeley, and later in Oakland. There were hours working in the garden, playing with dolls made of calla lilies with roses for heads, making perfume by crushing flowers and putting them in bottles with water, playing with dirt and sand, watching anthills, gopher holes, sitting and listening to a brook, smelling geranium leaves. There is a great rich sense of joy in these childish memories.

In Berkeley we lived in a house with an attic and I spent hours one rainy Sunday afternoon reading the Bible. I remember nothing that I read, just the sense of holiness in holding the book in my hands. I did not know then that the Word in the Book and the Word in the flesh of Christ's humanity were the same, but I felt I was handling something holy.

In Oakland (I was eight then) we lived next door to a Methodist family who had a little store with a tiny apartment in back. The entire place smelled of fresh shingles. Birdie, my neighbor, took me to Sunday school and church with her, and then I began to experience real piety, in the sense of the sweetness of faith. I believed, but I did not know in what I believed. I became disgustingly, proudly pious. I sang hymns with the family next door. I prayed on my knees beside my bed. I asked my mother why we did not pray and sing hymns and got no satisfactory answer. No one went to church but me. I was alternately lonely and smug. At the same time, I began to be afraid of God, of death, of eternity. As soon as I closed my eyes at night the blackness of death surrounded me. I believed and yet was afraid of nothingness. What would it be like to sink into that immensity? If I fell asleep God became in my ears a great noise that became louder and louder, and approached nearer and nearer to me until I woke up sweating with fear and shrieking for my mother. I fell asleep with her hand in mine, her warm presence by my bed. If she connected my fears with my religious attitude, she never spoke of it.

Even as I write this I am wondering if I had these nightmares before the San Francisco earthquake or afterward. The very remembrance of the noise which kept getting louder and louder, and the keen fear of death, makes me think now that it might have been due only to the earthquake. And yet we left Oakland almost at once afterward, since my father's newspaper job was gone when the plant went up in flames; we were on our way to Chicago within a week to a new life in another city. I remember these dreams only in connection with California and they were linked up with my idea of God as a tremendous Force, a frightening impersonal God, a Voice, a Hand stretched out to seize me, His child, and not in love. Christ was the Saviour, meek and humble of heart, Jesus, the Good Shepherd. But I did not think of Jesus as God. I had no one to teach me, as my parents had no one to teach them.

Another thing I remember about California was the joy of doing good, of sharing whatever we had with others after the earthquake, an event which threw us out of our complacent happiness into a world of catastrophe.

It happened early in the morning and it lasted two minutes and twenty seconds, as I heard everyone say afterward. My father was sports editor of one of the San Francisco papers. There was a racetrack near our bungalow and stables where my father kept a horse. He said that the night before had been a sultry one and the horses were restless, neighing and stamping in their stalls, becoming increasingly nervous and panicky. The earthquake started with a deep rumbling and the convulsions of the earth started afterward, so that the earth became a sea which rocked our house in a most tumultuous manner. There was a large windmill and water tank in back of the house and I can remember the splashing of the water from the tank on the top of our roof. My father took my brothers from their beds and rushed to the front door, where my mother stood with my sister, whom she had snatched from beside me. I was left in a big brass bed, which rolled back and forth on a polished floor. Whether I realized what was happening I do not know, but I do know that the whole event was confused in my mind with something which might have occurred a few nights earlier, my mother fainting on the floor of my room on her way to the bathroom, and my father carrying her back to bed. The illness of my usually strong and cheerful mother and the earthquake were both part of the world's tragedy to me.

When the earth settled, the house was a shambles, dishes broken all over the floor, books out of their bookcases, chandeliers down, chimneys fallen, the house cracked from roof to ground. But there was no fire in Oakland. The flames and cloud bank of smoke could be seen across the bay and all the next day the refugees poured over by ferry and boat. Idora Park and the racetrack made camping grounds for them. All the neighbors joined my mother in serving the homeless. Every stitch of available clothes was given away. All the day following the disaster there were more tremblings of the earth and there was fear in the air. We had always been considered Easterners by our neighbors and one of them told my mother he would rather have San Francisco's earthquakes than our eastern thunder and lightning storms any day!

ON THIRTY-SEVENTH STREET

As soon as possible we pulled out for the East. Of course the Red Cross was providing aid and offered free transportation to refugees but my father would not take this help. We had no trouble selling our household furnishings for just enough to get us to Chicago, where we stayed for a while in a hotel, the Briggs House. Mother soon found us an apartment. We went first to the South Side, Thirty-seventh Street and Cottage Grove Avenue, to a flat over a tavern. It had a window in the dining room facing Lake Michigan two blocks away, which was on the other side of a stone wall separating the gardens of a very fine street from the railroad tracks along the lake.

Why is it that the river, lake and ocean fronts of our country are overrun with railroads and factories and polluted by the waste of industry and home? Chicago, amazing city, made land on the other side of the tracks, in later years, by filling in the lake for miles, and turned the waters of the Chicago River backward to keep the lake from being polluted. When we lived on Thirty-seventh Street we could see the mountainous waves in winter which built up hills of ice like dunes all along the shore.

There was a breakwater along the lake, filled with huge yellow slabs of Indiana limestone, but the water seeped through, forming treacherous pools in which two children from our street were drowned. My brothers used to swim "inside the breakwater" they always said, seeking to reassure my mother as to their safety, and I remember the grim sunny day we went down to watch the dynamiting for the bodies of another brother and sister who had been drowned. The little boy had found himself beyond his depth and his sister, leaning over from the breakwater, had taken off her dress to twist into a rope for him to catch hold of; instead he had dragged her in too and they had drowned in each other's arms. Here was death in the concrete and yet it did not touch me so nearly as those forebodings of death which came to me at night after I had closed my eyes in the dark room and the universe began to spin around me in space.

I remember the vast sunny lake, calm and treacherous, the weeds and grasses among the sands where little children played while older ones stood in awe close to their parents, that long quiet afternoon. When the bodies were found, we did not run to the spot, but mother hurried us home and doubtless there was panic in her heart.

Mother must have been around thirty-five and there were four of us then. She lived in a dingy, six-room flat, whereas before she had lived in a bungalow surrounded by trees and flowers and looking off to the soft slopes of the hills. Now she had to do all her own work, washing for six in a large common basement which stretched almost the length of the block and was like a series of caverns where the children played on rainy days. Outside was a cement-paved yard with neither tree nor blade of grass. The nearest green was that of a vacant lot on the corner, where I wheeled my doll carriage and smelled the sweet clover, gathering sheaves of it for mother to dry in pillowcases and put in linen chests. There were long porches that stretched the whole length of the tenement and there were other children to play with, including Mary Harrington, who told me about the saints, of whom I had never heard before.

There were nine children in that family and Mary was the oldest, a hard-working child of twelve. I had the greatest admiration for her, because of the rigorous life she led.

My sister and I had begun to help my mother with the dishes and housecleaning for the first time, and we felt important indeed having a part in the family concerns, having mother depend on us for help. We had never had to do without a servant before, and the household tasks, the washing and cooking, were too much for my mother, who after her four children had a series of miscarriages. I took my dishwashing very seriously and I remember scouring faucets until they shone. The work grew wearisome of course; it did not always have the aspect of a game. But it had to be done, and after some months of it I was well used to doing my share. Without knowing it, I had imbibed a "philosophy of work," enjoying the creative aspect of it as well as getting satisfaction from a hard and necessary job well done.

I had a great amount of liberty compared to Mary Harrington, who was my senior by four years. It was not until after the dishes were done at night that she could come out on the porches to play. Often she was so tired that we stretched out on the long back porch, open to the sky, and lay there, gazing at the stars and clouds, the only beauty the city had to offer us, and talked and dreamed.

I don't remember what we talked about, but I do remember one particular occasion when she talked to me about the life of some saint. I do not know what saint it was, and I cannot remember any of the incidents of the life; I only remember my feeling of lofty enthusiasm, and how my heart almost burst with desire to take part in such high endeavor. One verse of the Psalms often comes to my mind, "Enlarge Thou my heart, O Lord, that Thou mayst enter in." This was one of those occasions when my small heart was enlarged and I could feel it swelling in love and gratitude to such a good God, for a friend like Mary, for conversation such as ours; I was filled with a natural striving, a thrilling recognition of the possibilities of spiritual adventure.

I wanted to do penance for my own sins and for the sins of the whole world, for I had a keen sense of natural imperfections and earthiness.

And yet as I think back I realize that it was Mrs. Barrett, another neighbor, who gave me my first impulse toward Catholicism. It was already late in the morning that I went to Kathryn's to call her out to play. There was no one on the porch or in the kitchen. The breakfast dishes had long been washed. The flats were known as railroad flats, that is, one room connected with another. Thinking the children must be in the front room, I burst in and ran through the bedrooms.

In the front bedroom Mrs. Barrett was down on her knees, saying her prayers. She turned to tell me that Kathryn and the children had all gone to the store and then went on with her praying. I felt a burst of love toward Mrs. Barrett that I have never forgotten, a feeling of gratitude and happiness that warmed my heart.

It was she who taught me what to do. For many a night after that, I used to plague my sister with my long prayers. I would kneel until my knees ached and I was cold and stiff. She would beg me to come into bed and tell her a story. I, in turn, would insist on her joining in. So we began to practice being saints—it was a game with us.

HOME

THANKS to my father I was treated like a child until I finished high school at sixteen. Perhaps because of the fact that he was a newspaperman and saw much of the tragedy of the world, he had the old-fashioned and beautiful impulse to protect innocence, and he believed that the place for women and children was in the home. There was no blaring radio, bringing in the news every hour on the hour so that you heard about the latest murder, train wreck, plane disaster and political coup twelve times a day. There were no picture books, detective stories or what father termed "trash" around the house. We had Scott, Hugo, Dickens, Stevenson, Cooper and Poe. I can remember sneaking romances into the house, lent me by friends at school, but I saw to it that they did not reach my father's eyes. My brothers brought in "dime novels," of which they were also very careful. I can remember one with a lurid cover of ten robed and hooded men walking in a single file along a mountain path with a boa constrictor gliding along beside them. I wonder what that story was about.

We were seldom allowed to have friends in the house because it interfered with my father's privacy. Because he worked at night and slept in the morning, often we did not see him until the week end, but we felt his influence at every moment. We children did not know him very well, so stood in awe of him, only learning to talk to him after we had left home and he began to treat us as friends—casual friends it is true, since he was always impatient with our ideas and hated the radical movement which both my sister and I were involved in later. Being from Tennessee, he had the prevalent attitude of the South toward the Negro. He distrusted all "foreigners" and "agitators." But he was a good man and a happy man in his own circle and he enjoyed life greatly. Probably his greatest unhappiness came from us whose ideas he did not understand and which he thought were subversive and dangerous to the peace of the country. He wanted to keep things as they were. He carried a Bible around with him and he read Shakespeare; his writing about racing and racetracks was filled with Biblical and Shakespearean allusions. He was one of the founders of the Hialeah racetrack in Florida, and was very proud to have "made" the *Saturday Evening Post* before he died.

My mother had a temperament which helped her through much hardship and uncertainty. She refused to worry when things were going badly and when the family had its periods of poverty. After the earthquake, when we were settled in Chicago, my father decided to write a book and also try his hand at short stories. He spent day after day in a smoke-filled room, sitting in a Morris chair with a table leaf over the arms to hold his type-writer, working over a novel of adventure, only pausing between chapters to run off a "potboiler" to keep food on the table and the rent paid. The novel of course was to be a best seller.

Mother hung living-room and dining-room curtains over fish-ing rods, made a bookcase out of the mantelpiece and orange crates, and kitchen stools out of nail kegs. But even so, the collector from the installment-plan house where we bought what new furniture we had, came often and threatened to take our beds if the payments were not made on time.

Whenever mother had extra troubles or a specially hard day's work behind her, she used to bathe and dress with particular care as though she were going to a dinner party. She reigned over the supper table as a queen and had as much interest in entertaining her four children as if we were all adult friends in for a party. When she felt especially low she used to spend ten cents carfare to go downtown to the Loop to window-shop or perhaps find a bargain in a new hat or a piece of material to sew on, never forgetting to bring home a gift of salted peanuts and pattern books for Della, my sister, and me to make paper dolls from. In a day when there were no washing machines, electric irons, vacuum cleaners and electric sewing machines, she made shirts for my father and two brothers and all the dresses for my sister and me. I can still see the sheen of our ginghams, pale blue and pink, and feel the flowered challis. Linen, wool and cotton were the only things in "good taste" for little girls, and all our clothes were beautifully made and laundered no matter how poor we were.

Childhood was a happy time for me, in spite of moods of uncertainty and even of hopelessness and sadness. The latter mood only accentuated the joys that were truly there. It seems to me we had much time to ourselves, much time alone. The fact that father kept us from going out, and did not want company to come in, saved us from the busy existence that most persons had. Even education at that time was not so crowded. We had many study periods and high school was over at two-thirty in the afternoon.

There were long hours when I had nothing to do except what I chose. I can remember interminable Sunday afternoons when cold or illness kept us in the house. My sister and I spent hours those afternoons with our noses pressed to the pane of glass, watching a man making and selling popcorn at a bright-colored stand under an umbrella on the corner. We watched every

motion, beginning with the popping of the corn, with the cage
suspended on a wire and shaken back and forth; we watched him
fill each bag and pour in a little melted butter from a white
coffee pot, and shake in some salt, and we could smell it and
taste it as we watched him.

I remember even sad summer afternoons when there was
nothing to do, and suddenly everything palled and life was dull
and uninteresting. Our parents did nothing to offer us distrac-
tion and entertainment. We were forced to meet our moods and
overcome them. There were times when my sister and I turned
to housework from sheer boredom.

The Psalms became part of my childhood. There was a small
Episcopal church on Thirty-fifth Street and Cottage Grove Avenue. Dr. Wilson, the rector, called on my father when he was
writing his book. Father was embarrassed because of the highball
and plate of cigarette stubs by his side. Dr. Wilson was making
a door-to-door visit in his parish, and when he heard my mother
had been brought up in the Episcopal Church, he persuaded her
to send the boys to sing in the choir and play in the gymnasium.
I went to church too every Sunday and admired my brothers in
their cassocks and surplices, and was much attracted to a blond
boy soprano soloist named Russell. I loved the Psalms and the
Collect prayers and learned many of them by heart, and the
anthems filled me with joy. I had never heard anything so
beautiful as the *Benedicite* and the *Te Deum*. The words have
remained with me ever since:

> We praise Thee, O God—
> We acknowledge Thee to be the Lord.
> All the earth doth worship Thee
> The Father Everlasting. . . .

> All ye works of the Lord, bless ye the Lord
> Praise Him and glorify Him forever.
> O ye sun and moon, O ye stars in the sky,
> O ye winds and hoarfrosts, ye rain and dew,
> Bless ye the Lord, praise Him and glorify Him forever.
> O ye trees and flowers, O ye beasts of the field,
> O ye fish in the sea. . . .

The song thrilled in my heart, and though I was only ten years old, through these Psalms and canticles I called on all creation to join with me in blessing the Lord. I thanked Him for creating me, saving me from all evils, filling me with all good things.

Whenever I felt the beauty of the world in song or story, in the material universe around me, or glimpsed it in human love, I wanted to cry out with joy. The Psalms were an outlet for this enthusiasm of joy or grief—and I suppose my writing was also an outlet. After all, one must communicate ideas. I always felt the common unity of our humanity; the longing of the human heart is for this communion. If only I could sing, I thought, I would shout before the Lord, and call upon the world to shout with me, "All ye works of the Lord, bless ye the Lord, praise Him and glorify Him forever." My idea of heaven became one of fields and meadows, sweet with flowers and songs and melodies unutterable, in which even the laughing gull and the waves on the shore would play their part.

When we moved to the North Side I went to the Episcopal Church of Our Saviour, on Fullerton Avenue, and studied the catechism so that I could be baptized and confirmed. There too I learned the formal prayer of the Church in her Psalms.

ADOLESCENCE

WHAT other religious influences were in my life then? I remember coming across a volume of John Wesley's sermons when I was thirteen and being strongly attracted to his evangelical piety. Later when a series of blinding headaches made my mother call in the services of a Christian Science practitioner, I read *Science and Health* and the Bible passages in the lessons that are marked out for daily reading.

Our poverty did not last long. My father soon took a job as sports editor on *The Inter Ocean,* and we moved from our

Thirty-seventh Street flat first to Oakwood Boulevard and then to a house on the North Side.

There was one especially happy year when we were living on Webster Avenue near Lincoln Park, in a house where there was privacy for all. There were fireplaces in my mother's bedroom and in the library, and in the center of that room there was a large round table with a green cover and a lamp in the middle, a gas lamp, green-shaded, with a long green hose that always smelled slightly of gas. There were five comfortable chairs in the room and we could arrange ourselves around the table in a circle, each with his back to the other so that the light came over our left shoulders, with plates of apples to eat as we read. I had a little desk in the corner of the room. Mother had her sewing box. Often we made hot cocoa over the fire before we went to bed. We burned huge lumps of soft coal that hissed and sputtered and sent out blue and rose flames. To draw the curtains at night on a street where people bent against the wind, and where a steady whirl of snowflakes blurred the outlines of trees and shrubs, and made the trees black against the heavy gray sky, and to turn to a room where a fire glowed in the basket grate and a smell of fresh bread filled the house—this was comfort, security, peace, community.

There was a new baby that year, born in May. I fell in love that year too—I was fourteen years old—and first love is sweet. He was a musician who lived down the street, and since I spent much of the day during those vacation months wheeling the new baby, I met him several times a day as he went to afternoon or evening engagements. We never exchanged a word, but I hungered for his look! He must have been conscious of my adoration because he never failed to dart at me that glance which was a recognition of something between us. He led the band in Lincoln Park on Sunday afternoons and Wednesday nights, and my sister and I never missed a concert that summer. Sundays were hot, crowded days and there were picnickers everywhere. Sometimes the three-months-old baby fretted and we had to leave our position of vantage, where I could see my love, to go walking again. But Wednesday nights there was the delicious feeling that the trees were breathing all around us and there was fragrance in the air. Sometimes, when it rained so that we were fearful there would be no concert that evening, and then it cleared—our joy would be beyond endurance as we hastened through the park, under still-dripping leaves, skirting puddles and finding little toads in our path. The jeweled beauty of those little toads put the fringe on my happiness. At the concert stand, early comers would be spreading papers on the seats, and rarely were we disappointed in our concert.

The love for my baby brother was as profound and never-to-be-forgotten as that first love. The two seemed to go together. Early every morning the next two school years, long before dawn, my mother used to bring him in to my bed. Since my father did not get to bed until two in the morning, it was very important that the baby be kept quiet so that his sleep should be undisturbed. The child was difficult to put to bed, and every night I rocked him to sleep, singing hymns to him from my Episcopal hymnbook. Sometimes my back and shoulders ached long before he went to sleep, and it was an endurance feat between the baby and me as to who could hold out longer. But the very hardship of taking care of him, the hours I put in with him, made me love him the more.

About four in the morning mother put him in a crib in my room, and for a while he was content to make earthquake changes in the mountains and valleys of the bedclothes. Toes were fascinating if he could extricate them from the jungle, and there were noises to make at the flicker of a street lamp on the ceiling and the brass corner knob of his crib. Steadfast gazing at the knob reminded him that here was another toy, and in making his way down the crib in pursuit of his object, there was always the discovery—new every morning it would seem from the surprised way he stopped—of a singsong creaking of the spring. For a moment there were a few little songs to make by jumping up and down, songs interspersed with delighted chuckles and delicious crowings. And then he would reach the brass knob and start to rattle it as loud as he could. Sometimes I would be able to tuck him in firmly and keep him there for a while longer until the outside noises began which he delighted to imitate. He would peep with the birds and wait for them to answer back. Then he would stop to listen to the milk wagon coming over the cobbles in the back alley, the metallic sound of bottles being deposited, the sound of the milkman's footsteps, the jingle of the horses' harness. All these sounds I too would be delighting in at the beginning of the new day.

In winter it was always hard to get up in the house because the fires were low. By four-thirty I was usually downstairs, looking for a gleam from the grate fire of the night before, throwing on a lump of soft coal which caught easily, before I made haste out to the kitchen where the fire had been banked. There was always a hot kettle in which to warm the baby's bottle. As soon as the child was changed and fed, he was perfectly willing to go back to sleep again, and that left me free to do my homework, Latin and Greek, history and English composition. I loved languages, but history was dull to me. Often the night before I had made some attempt at translating Vergil and Xenophon, but never did too thorough a job. I always found that by morning I was able to translate freely and easily. Our teacher, Mr. Matheson, at Waller High School, was so good that he taught us Greek after school, on his own time and ours. His delight in our interest in Latin was so great (our interest was a response to his own enthusiasm) that of our own accord we went on to the Georgics and Bucolics of Vergil though they were not a part of the course.

Only recently in an old story of mine I found a copy of a letter I wrote at that time to a school friend. I was fifteen and a high school senior.

We went to the park Friday, [the letter began abruptly] and Della and I went on the merri-go-round and the lake boat. We each had fifty cents and it was with regret that I saw the money go. It seemed a shameless waste, but then I realized there was more for God's children and it will come to them when they need it. "Be careful for nothing. . . ." "Take no thought for the morrow." So I just spent it with the others and enjoyed myself very much. Today my brother gave me money again and I'm going downtown to the second-hand bookstores some day next week after school.

Yesterday I took the baby to the park. He was sweet and good, and the sky was a dark, deep blue, all flecked with purplish clouds. The trees were rustling and the sun flickered on my book. I was happy but not in the right way. I did not have the spiritual happiness that I crave, only a wicked thrilling feeling at my heart.

Remember in Tennyson?—

> "Dear as remembered kisses after death
> Or sweet as those by hopeless fancy feigned
> On lips that are for others.
> Deep as love, deep as first love
> And wild with all regret,
> O death in life, the days that are no more!"

But I could not give way to my sinful thoughts because the baby yelled for candy, soda, sandwich and to see the animals, and my thoughts were taken away from myself. It's a good thing. Such a foolish pining. I forgot all about "God's silent messengers, the winged thoughts of love," and just wanted to think of my troubles. How weak I am. My pride forbids me to write this and to put it down on paper makes me blush, but all the old love comes back to me. It is a lust of the flesh and I know that unless I forsake all sin, I will not gain the kingdom of heaven. [I had confessed my summer passion to my friend and it was a great joy to write about it. She in turn had similar confidences to give me.]

My letter went on:

Della and I have been following an exciting serial in the movies and father lets us go only on Sunday afternoons when it's rainy, but never at any other time during the week. My ideas have changed about Sunday. I have learned that it is rather hypocritical to be so strict on Sunday and not on every other day of the week. Every day belongs to God and every day we are to serve Him doing His pleasure. And "as every good gift is prepared for them that love God," and moving pictures are a good thing, if you stop to think of the educational advantages of them, therefore, I can see nothing wrong in going to a show and pleasing Della and incidently myself.

This afternoon it took us two hours to do the dishes and now that they are done, I suppose I'll have to take the baby out for a long walk in the park. How I love the park in winter! So solitary and awful in the truest meaning of the word. God is there. Of course, He is everywhere but under the trees and looking over the wide expanse of lake He communicates Himself to me and fills me with a deep quiet peace. I need those hours alone in the afternoon with the baby and I feel as though the troubles of life are lifted until I return to the house and it all comes back to me.

Maybe if I stayed away from books more this restlessness would pass. I am reading Dostoevski and last night I stayed up late and this morning I had to get up early and I feel that my soul is like lead.

I am sitting in my bedroom in my comfortable chair by the window. The wind is cold and seeps in around the glass so that I have to wrap my bathrobe around me as I write. I should be reading the Bible because it is Sunday afternoon, but I don't want to. I'd rather write to you. I'm still in the Acts. I never went over it so thoroughly before and now I find much more in it. Isn't it queer how the same verses will strike you at different times? "We must through much tribulation enter into the Kingdom of God." How true that is! Only after a hard bitter struggle with sin and only after we have overcome it, do we experience blessed joy and peace. The tears come to my eyes, when I think how often I have gone through the bitter struggles and then succumbed to sin while peace was in sight. And after I fell how far away it fled. Poor weak creatures we are, yet God is our Father and God is love, ever present, ready to enfold us and comfort us and hold us up.

I have so much work to do to overcome my sins. I am working always, always on guard, praying without ceasing to overcome all physical sensations and be purely spiritual.

It is wrong to think so much about human love. All those feelings and cravings that come to us are sexual desires. We are prone to have them at this age, I suppose, but I think they are impure. It is sensual and God is spiritual. We must harden ourselves to these feelings, for God is love and God is all, so the only love is of God and is spiritual without taint of earthliness. I am afraid I have never really experienced this love or I would never crave the sensual love or the thrill that comes with the meeting of lips.

I know it seems foolish to try to be so Christlike—but God says we can—why else His command, "Be ye therefore perfect."

Oh, surely it is a continual strife and my spirit is weary.

Written when I was fifteen, this letter was filled with pomp and vanity and piety. I was writing of what interested me most, the conflict of flesh and spirit, but I was writing self-consciously and trying to pretend to myself I was being literary and pleasing Henrietta, my school friend, who was deeply religious and very sentimental. I enjoyed our correspondence but I did not want anyone else to see it. Once when I left an undelivered letter in my apron pocket, a letter in which the arms and lips of my beloved were mentioned, I was as stricken with shame as though I had been guilty of pornography. What if my mother had read it? I was sure she had—it was a common apron hanging on the pantry door—but in all delicacy she never indicated by word or attitude that she had seen these written thoughts.

Henrietta was not self-conscious at all. She was a little round dumpling of a girl, with blond curly hair and blue eyes, a lush little creature who was frankly sensual and very good. She kissed and hugged her friends with great abandon, clinging to them, and I was repelled by her soft arms and growing breasts pressed against me. There was never any kissing in my family, and never a close embrace. There was only a firm, austere kiss from my mother every night. My sister and I took out our desire for physical expression of affection on our baby brother. We kept ourselves to ourselves, as the saying is, but I don't see any particular virtue in that attitude. It is the way we were as a family; and we were like most Anglo-Saxons. It made us, I am sure, more intense, more sensual, more conscious of the flesh which we continually denied. We could never be free with others, never put our arms around them casually, lean against others companionably as I see Italian boys doing in this neighborhood where we live. We were never handholders. We were always withdrawn and alone, unlike Italians, Poles, Jews, and other friends I had who were fresh and spontaneous in their affection. But when I read in my Bible, in St. James, "Pure religion and undefiled . . . is this, To visit the fatherless and widows in their affliction and to keep himself unspotted from the world," to me the world meant the flesh and the lure of the flesh, the pride of life one felt when in love. This conflict was to go on for years.

All beauty, all joy, all music thrilled my heart and my flesh, so that they cried out for fulfillment, for union.

"I have loved, O Lord, the beauty of thy house," my heart used to sing out, "and the place where thy glory dwelleth." "My heart and my flesh crieth out for the living God." But probably I sensed that "it is a fearful thing to fall into the hands of the living God" and I di dnot want to face the issue.

All those years I believed. I had faith. The argument of authority, of conscience, of creation—I felt the validity of these. It is hard to see how I could fling my convictions from me a few years later; it is hard to understand unless it was because of the turbulent life that was in me.

I read St. Augustine at this time and he spoke also of this love.

What is it that I love when I love you? Not the beauty of any bodily thing, nor the order of seasons, not the brightness of the light that rejoices the eye, nor the sweet melodies of all songs, nor the sweet fragrance of flowers, herbs and ointments and spices, nor manna, nor honey, not the limbs which carnal love embraces. None of these things I love in loving my God.

Yet in a sense I do love light and melody and fragrance and food and embrace when I love my God—the light and the voice and the fragrance and the food and embrace in the soul which no place can contain, that voice sounds which no tongue can take from me, I breathe that fragrance which no wind scatters, I eat that food which is not lessened by eating, and I lie in that embrace which satiety never comes to sunder. This is that I love when I love my God.

UNIVERSITY

THEN it was September and school began again. There were no more concerts, and although I continued my walks after school my interest turned to books again and my reading began to be socially conscious. My brother Donald began his newspaper career on a paper called *The Day Book.* (The name had nothing to do with my own newspaper family but as I recall it was an experiment of Scripps-Howard.) It was the size of the dime novels we used to read, but it was lurid in another way. It told of the struggles in the labor movement and especially in Chicago. There were no advertisements, so working conditions in department stores, in factories and workshops were exposed with no fear of losing revenue. Carl Sandburg was one of the writers and this poet of the people sat on the copy desk and inspired my brother to look on the people as he did, with love and hope of great accomplishment. Through the paper I learned of Eugene Debs, a great and noble labor leader of inspired utterance. There were also accounts of the leaders of the Industrial Workers of the World who had been organizing in their one great union so that there were a quarter of a million members throughout the wheatfields, mines, and woods of the Northwest, as well as in the textile factories in the East.

I read Jack London's books, not only his tales of the North, his wonderful dog stories, but *Martin Eden,* and his essays on the class struggle, his journeys through America and England. When I read *The Jungle* by Upton Sinclair I began taking long walks toward the West Side rather than going to the park or lake.

I walked for miles, pushing my brother in his carriage, often with my sister at my side, she usually holding onto the carriage too. We explored until we were footsore, going up and down interminable gray streets, fascinating in their dreary sameness, past tavern after tavern, where I envisaged such scenes as that of the Polish wedding party in Sinclair's story, past houses which were sunk down a whole story below street level for block after block.

There were tiny flower gardens and vegetable patches in the yards. Often there were rows of corn, stunted but still recognizable, a few tomato plants, and always the vegetables were bordered by flowers, often grateful marigolds, all sizes and shades with their pungent odor. I collected odors in my memory, the one beauty in those drab streets. The odor of geranium leaves, tomato plants, marigolds; the smell of lumber, of tar, of roasting coffee; the smell of good bread and rolls and coffee cake coming from the small German bakeries. Here was enough beauty to satisfy me.

A strain of music coming from a home or a tavern, the music of a German band, or from the stringed instruments of some street players—these played too on the strings of my heart.

I read the life of one of the Haymarket anarchists, written by Frank Harris. Though I do not recall the name of its hero, I do remember that his work was to dig tunnels under rivers and that it was a dangerous work which exacted suffering from the men and sometimes life itself. He told of going through various compression chambers in getting down to his work under the great river, of the hours of work in a tank surrounded by tons of pressure, of the hours it took to come out through decompression chambers, and of the danger, even then with all these precautions, of suffering from a ghastly torture called the "bends" of which some men died.

Prince Peter Kropotkin and Vera Figner were also my companions at that time. When I was a senior in high school I wrote a story of Russian revolutionists and the martyrdom of one of them which must have surprised the staid little woman who taught us English composition and theme writing.

Kropotkin especially brought to my mind the plight of the poor, of the workers, and though my only experience of the destitute was in books, the very fact that *The Jungle* was about Chicago where I lived, whose streets I walked, made me feel that from then on my life was to be linked to theirs, their interests were to be mine; I had received a call, a vocation, a direction to my life.

I felt even at fifteen, that God meant man to be happy, that He meant to provide him with what he needed to maintain life in order to be happy, and that we did not need to have quite so much destitution and misery as I saw all around and read of in the daily press.

From my earliest remembrance the destitute were always looked upon as the shiftless, the worthless, those without talent of any kind, let alone the ability to make a living for themselves. They were that way because of their own fault. They chose their lot. They drank. They were the prodigal sons who were eating the swines' husks only because they had squandered their inheritance. Since it was in the Bible it must be so. Even Our Lord Himself said that the poor we would always have with us. When two brothers were quarreling over an inheritance and He was asked to settle it, He refused to enter into the dispute. He Himself lived a life of poverty and wandering, "with no place to lay His head." "My Kingdom is not of this world," He said. He evidently wanted people to remain as they were and not to concern themselves about the affairs of this world—that is, the great mass of poor, the workers, to whom He seemed especially to speak. They were to seek for PIE IN THE SKY.

This is the way my reasoning finally led me. On the one hand there were the religious people I had come up against in church, and they were few I must admit, a sparse congregation meeting on Sunday mornings and Wednesday evenings. They had enough money so that they did not have to bother about the things of this world.

There were also the worldlings, the tycoons, the people I read about who piled up fortunes and cornered wheat, and exploited the workers in the stockyards. I did not know such people myself, but I knew the rich were smiled at and fawned upon by churchgoers. This is all that I could see.

Children look at things very directly and simply. I did not see anyone taking off his coat and giving it to the poor. I didn't see anyone having a banquet and calling in the lame, the halt and the blind. And those who were doing it, like the Salvation Army, did not appeal to me. I wanted, though I did not know it then, a synthesis. I wanted life and I wanted the abundant life. I wanted it for others too. I did not want just the few, the missionary-minded people like the Salvation Army, to be kind to the poor, as the poor. I wanted everyone to be kind. I wanted every home to be open to the lame, the halt and the blind, the way it had been after the San Francisco earthquake. Only then did people really live, really love their brothers. In such love was the abundant life and I did not have the slightest idea how to find it.

One step I made toward it was joining the Socialist party when I went to the University of Illinois a year later.

As a result of my early morning hours of study I was able to pass an examination at the end of my high-school course, which brought me a three-hundred-dollar scholarship, enabling me to go to the university. The Hearst paper in Chicago sponsored an examination for three pupils from each high school in Cook County. The twenty highest of these were to receive cash scholarships, to be paid in installments, first a hundred dollars followed by ten dollars a week for twenty weeks. Thanks to my knowledge of Greek and Latin, I ranked fifteenth in the test and was announced as one of the winners. Out of my one-hundred-dollar check I was able to pay the matriculation fee of ten dollars and the twelve dollars a semester at the university. There were books to be bought, the cost of board and room to be considered, and lab fees and gym fees—all manner of expenses that I had not taken into account—but the nest egg I received made me feel rich indeed, and by working for my meals I was able to cover expenses.

The paper my father worked on, *The Inter Ocean*, failed that year, and had it not been for this scholarship, I would not have had two years at the university.

I was happy as a lark at leaving home. I was sixteen and filled with a sense of great independence. I was on my own, and no longer to be cared for by the family. The idea of earning my own living, by my own work, was more thrilling than the idea of an education. Since I did not intend to teach, I had no desire to follow any particular course or to work for a degree. It was experience in general that I wanted. I did not think in terms of philosophy or sociology. I continued the same course I had been taking, Latin, English, history and science. It was not until a few months later, when the novelty of my surroundings wore off, that I suffered from a terrible homesickness which made me go to bed weeping, wake up weeping, and which filled me with a sense of desolation and loneliness. I missed my baby brother, who was by that time two years old and at a most tender and responsive age. He loved me dearly; I had been a mother to him, so that he clung to me and was bone of my bone and flesh of my flesh. I had never loved anyone or anything as I loved him, with a love that was open and unreserved, entailing hardship but bringing also peace and joy. To know that this love was past, that John would grow up away from me, that I could not hold him, that I too had to go on, filled me with a sense of unutterable grief. I had a terrible sense of loss, and yet with it a sense of the inevitability of such losses in our lives. It never occurred to me to turn back, to try to hold onto him and to my life with him. It was a desolation to be worked through, lived through, and even while I suffered I knew that it would pass.

Fortunately I had much work to do. That first semester I worked for my board with a professor of romance languages. I had breakfast at the Y but at lunch time I went to Professor Fitzgerald and ate with the family that consisted of his wife, mother and three children. They were Methodists and delightful people. I used to talk about books with the professor and faith with the old lady as she washed the lunch dishes and prepared vegetables for the evening meal.

But even as I talked about religion I rejected religion. I had read Wesley's sermons and had been inspired by them. I had sung hymns from the Episcopalian hymnal to put little John to sleep. I had read the New Testament with fervor.

But that time was past. I felt so intensely alive that the importance of the here and now absorbed me. The radicalism which I absorbed from *The Day Book* and Jack London, from Upton Sinclair and from the sight of poverty was in conflict with religion, which preached peace and meekness and joy.

Remembering how much I liked the Fitzgeralds, I know I was happy in their religious atmosphere. And yet I scorned the students who were pious. Youth, I felt, should not be in a state of peace, but of war.

I was acutely conscious of the class war while I paid little attention to the war being fought in Europe. We were not yet involved in it. In my reading I must have absorbed a scorn of religion at that time, a consciously critical attitude toward religious people who were so comfortably happy in the face of the injustices in the world.

There was a real conflict going on in me at the time to overcome my religious sense.

As a matter of fact, I started to swear, quite consciously began to take God's name in vain, in order to shock my friends who were churchgoers. I shocked myself as I did it, but I felt that it was a strong gesture I was making to push religion from me. It certainly was a most conscious gesture. Because I was unhappy and rejoiced in my unhappiness, I felt harsh. Because I was hurt at being torn from my child, my baby brother, I had to turn away from home and faith and all the gentle things of life and seek the hard. In spite of my studies and my work, I had time to read, and the ugliness of life in a world which professed itself to be Christian appalled me.

I was tearing myself away from home, living my own life, and I had to choose the world to which I wanted to belong. I did not want to belong to the Epworth League which some of my classmates joined. As a little child the happy peace of the Methodists who lived next door appealed to me deeply. Now that same happiness seemed to be a disregard of the misery of the world.

While I was free to go to college, I was mindful of girls who worked in stores and factories through their youth and afterward married men who were slaves in those same factories.

The Marxist slogan, "Workers of the world, unite! You have nothing to lose but your chains," seemed to me a most stirring battle cry. It was a clarion call that made me feel one with the masses, apart from the bourgeoisie, the smug, and the satisfied.

The romanticism and the hardness of Jack London in his stories of the road appealed to me more at that time than the idealism of Upton Sinclair, though I still considered, and do to this day, that *The Jungle* was a great novel. But his romantic, realistic novel, *The Mystery of Love*, repelled me so that I discounted his other books. He had not yet written his other great labor novels. (Sinclair had been called the Dickens of the American scene, and he has always been more of a storyteller than a philosopher.)

The Russian writers appealed to me too, and I read everything of Dostoevski, as well as the stories of Gorki and Tolstoi. Both Dostoevski and Tolstoi made me cling to a faith in God, and yet I could not endure feeling an alien in it. I felt that my faith had nothing in common with that of Christians around me.

It seems to me that I was already shedding it when a professor whom I much admired made a statement in class—I shall always remember it—that religion was something which had brought great comfort to people throughout the ages, so that we ought not to criticize it. I do not remember his exact words, but from the way he spoke of religion the class could infer that the strong did not need such props. In my youthful arrogance, in my feeling that I was one of the strong, I felt then for the first time that religion was something that I must ruthlessly cut out of my life.

I felt at the time that religion would only impede my work. I wanted to have nothing to do with the religion of those whom I saw all about me. I felt that I must turn from it as from a drug. I felt it indeed to be an opiate of the people and not a very attractive one, so I hardened my heart. It was a conscious and deliberate process.

My work kept me from mingling much with other students the first five months I was at the university. I was greedy for books and I spent all my spare hours working to earn money to buy them. In addition to working for my board, I took jobs washing and ironing clothes and taking care of children. The latter job was easy because it meant long evening hours to read.

I don't recall putting in much time studying, but what I studied was not related to life as I saw it. Even history did not teach me to study past events in relation to present ones so that I could think in terms of shaping the present to mold the future. I was not interested in biology. I had loved the hours spent in reading Vergil in high school, but I lost interest in Latin in college. The only thing I was really interested in was reading the books I selected for myself, and, of course, in writing.

Many times before the two years were up I was out of work and money. To gain more time to read and write, I took a room in the home of a poverty-stricken instructor who had five children. I did not eat with them—they had scarcely enough for themselves—but I earned my room by doing the family washing on Saturdays. Many a time I scrubbed the skin off my knuckles, washing the baby clothes, and my back ached from the Saturday toil over the washtub and ironing board. To get money for my meals it was necessary to take at least a two-hour job that would bring me forty cents a day. This would suffice for food, I estimated at that time, if I bought it myself and cooked it over a one-burner stove. But my critical attitude toward the Y, which controlled the employment bureau, and my godless spirit, kept me from getting many jobs. Besides, I became immersed in writing and let days go by without working so that I went hungry.

Really I led a very shiftless life, doing for the first time exactly what I wanted to do, attending only those classes I wished to attend, coming and going at whatever hour of the night I pleased. My freedom intoxicated me. I felt it was worth going hungry for.

Writing on space rates for the little town paper brought me in some money and occasionally the paper published a column. Many of my columns were critical of the existing order and those were not published. Some of the columns merely criticized the working conditions of the students; these were published and got me into hot water.

I had joined a club for writers and the first story I turned in was on the experience of going hungry. It was not a bid for pity. I had taken a grim satisfaction in being made to pay the penalty for my own nonconformity, and I wrote with a great relish of three days without food other than salted peanuts. I knew of several jobs I could have taken, one of them with a bootlegger's family in Urbana (it was a dry town), caring for a howling troop of children, which would have brought me money for food. But I had spent a week there, and the sordid dreariness of the surroundings, the unattractive children, the unsavory character of my employer, had repelled me so that I left and took the room in the instructor's household.

The room was bare and carpetless. There was a bed, a table and chair, and a little stove to cook what food I had. My books were piled on the floor. It was so cold at night that it was hard to study. Even in bed it was impossible to keep warm. The winds from the prairies howled into the shabby old house, and the heavy snows and sleet beat against the window. In the evenings I could study in the university library. When I went back to my room I had to go to bed immediately, and when I was cold and hungry it was hard to get up in the morning. If it had not been for my English classes, which I really enjoyed, I would have given up classes and stayed in bed for days. I was seventeen, and I felt completely alone in the world, divorced from my family, from all security, even from God. I felt a sense of reckless arrogance and, with this recklesness, a sense of danger in which I rejoiced.

There was a great question in my mind. Why was so much done in remedying social evils instead of avoiding them in the first place? There were day nurseries for children, for instance, but why didn't fathers get money enough to take care of their families so that mothers would not have to go out to work? There were hospitals to take care of the sick and infirm, and of course doctors were doing much to prevent sickness, but what of occupational diseases, and the diseases which came from not enough food for the mother and children? What of the disabled workers who received no compensation but only charity for the remainder of their lives?

Disabled men, without arms and legs, blind men, consumptive men, exhausted men with all the manhood drained from them by industrialism; farmers gaunt and harried with debt; mothers weighed down with children at their skirts, in their arms, in their wombs, children ailing and rickety—all this long procession of desperate people called to me. Where were the saints to try to change the social order, not just to minister to the slaves but to do away with slavery?

I read in the New Testament—"Servants, be subject to your masters with all fear, not only to the good and gentle but also to the froward"; and on the other hand there was that call to action: "Workers of the world, unite! You have nothing to lose but your chains."

Jesus said, "Blessed are the meek," but I could not be meek at the thought of injustice. I wanted a Lord who would scourge the money-changers out of the temple, and I wanted to help all those who raised their hand against oppression.

For me Christ no longer walked the streets of this world. He was two thousand years dead and new prophets had risen up in His place.

I was in love now with the masses. I do not remember that I was articulate or reasoned about this love, but it warmed and filled my heart. The poor and oppressed were going to rise up, they were collectively the new Messiah, and they would release the captives. Already they had been persecuted, they had been scourged, they had been thrown into prison and put to death, not only in other parts of the world, but right around me in the United States.

There was Eugene Debs. There were the Haymarket martyrs who had been "framed" and put to death in Chicago in 1887. They were martyrs! They had died for a cause. Judge Gary in his charge to the jury had said, "The conviction had not gone on the ground that they did actually have any personal participation in that particular act, but the conviction proceeds upon the ground that they had generally by speech and spirit, advised large classes of people, not particular individuals but large classes, to commit murder—and in consequence of that advice and influenced by that advice, somebody not known did throw this bomb." The "advice," according to Lucy Parsons, widow of one of the martyrs, writing in a bitter letter to a labor newspaper years after, consisted in their appeal to workers to organize for the eight-hour day.

There had been in the past the so-called "Molly Maguires" in the coal fields, a terrorist organization, and the Knights of Labor, made up of union men working for the eight-hour day and the co-operative system. My heart thrilled at those unknown women in New England who led the first strike to liberate women and children from the cotton mills.

My mother, now that she saw my interest, told me how she had worked in a shirt factory in Poughkeepsie when she was a girl. She had seen no romance in those few hard years of her life until she saw them through my eyes. As a matter of fact, to her it was an episode to be forgotten.

Already in this year 1915 great strides had been taken. In some places the ten-hour day and increased wages had been won. But still only about 8 per cent of the workers were organized, and the great mass of workers throughout the country were ground down by poverty and insecurity. What work there was to be done!

There was a small group of Socialists in the town of Urbana and I joined the party, but the meetings were dull and I didn't attend very many. I was going to turn to larger fields as soon as I could get away from school. Marie Oberlander, a Jewish girl from New York who was ten years or so my senior, was the only other university student that I knew as a Socialist and we attended meetings together.

Then in the midst of the bare hardship of my days, a new love came into my life, a new love of friendship that was also as clear as a bell, crystal clear, with no stain of self-seeking, a give-and-take friendship that meant companionship and sharing.

On many occasions I had noticed a young girl, slight and bony, deliciously awkward and yet unself-conscious, alive and eager in her study. She had bright red curly hair. It was loose enough about her face to form an aureole, a flaming aureole, with sun and brightness in it. Her eyes were large, reddish brown and warm, with interest and laughter in them. There is a saying that the eyes conceal and the mouth reveals, but I remember that her eyes were always warm and loving and intensely interested. Her mouth was full and childlike and there were dimples in her cheeks. I can remember her face clearly. I remember one Sunday afternoon out on the prairie when she and the boy to whom she was engaged and I were having a picnic. We brought with us a phonograph and records and our books.

I can see Rayna lying on her side in a dull green dress, her cheek cupped in her hand, her eyes on the book she was reading, her mouth half open in her intent interest. Whatever she did she did with her whole heart. If she read, she read. If she was with you, all her attention was for you. She was single-minded, one of the pure of heart, and her interest in life was as intense as her interest in books.

I am not extravagant in making these statements about her. In Vincent Sheean's *Personal History*, in the section entitled "Revolution," there is the story of Rayna Prohme. Of all the people he wrote of, she stood out most clearly, beautiful and rare, a character one meets but once in a lifetime. She fascinated all who read the book.

I saw her first on my way to the university in September. She was the one person I remember on a train filled with students. She was like a flame with her red hair and vivid face. She had a clear, happy look, the look of a person who loved life. She was three years older than I, and entering her sophomore year. I was not to meet her until later that first year. Her name was Rayna Simons then.

Her father, I believe, had been at one time president of the Board of Trade in Chicago and her family was comfortably off. At that time, indeed, they were wealthy. The following summer I went with her to a farm outside of Chicago which her father had equipped with modern machinery and was running very efficiently and profitably as a hobby. She had fallen in love in high school with a young Jew from New York, Samson Raphaelson—we called him Raph—who was born on the East Side and was living with relatives in Chicago. Her family opposed their marriage because of her youth and his poverty. Wanting to be near him, she went to the university which is located in Urbana, several hours journey from Chicago, so that she could live away from the conflict in the family.

In spite of brilliant scholarship and an outstanding personality, good looks and wealth, she was not invited to join any sorority. It was my first contact with anti-Semitism.

Rayna and several other young women lived in a Jewish boarding house near the campus and Rayna insisted on my coming to live with her in my sophomore year. There should be no restraint between friends, she argued; they should share what each had, and I am surprised now at my childlike acceptance of her bounty. I had been ill that second winter with cold or influenza, and I was happy indeed to be cared for. As I look back on that first taste of hardship and voluntary poverty, and those months of friendship with Rayna, my heart swells with gratitude at her generosity, which never made me feel "beholden" to her. Raph, on the other hand, was jealous of our friendship and, acquainted with poverty himself and fiercely proud, was amazed at my ready acceptance of her help. He was too delicate to speak of it at the time, but wrote to me about it later, taking me to task for my readiness to lean on others. I did not take his letters too much to heart, as I remember. I loved them both and gave up my work gladly to be with them. I must have known that such friendships come only rarely in a lifetime and I treasured every hour we had together. Their other friends were seniors who edited the school paper. We wrote, we attended lectures, we listened together to the lectures of Rose Pastor Stokes and Scott Nearing, John Masefield and Edgar Lee Masters. We saw Shakespeare's *Twelfth Night* and listened to symphony orchestras; we walked and talked interminably. Even on those nights which we gave reluctantly to study, Raph would sometimes come to call beneath our window, to share some poem, some line he had just read which had fired him with enthusiasm.

I remember one such spring night, with Rayna leaning out of our window adoringly while Raph from the lawn below declaimed a last line of a *Saturday Evening Post* story:

". . . shall never die, shall never die, so long as I shall live. . . ."

At that time Rayna did not share my radical interests. She threw herself heart and soul into what she was doing at the time, her college classes, her studies, the work on the college paper, criticism of Raph's short stories.

It was a short story I had sent to the university paper that made me a part of Rayna's group. She became as enthusiastic about my writing as she was about Raph's and when I became moody and temperamental she drew me out of myself by her vivid interest in all that concerned me. I loved her and I loved Raph and wanted to be with them at all times. On one occasion when I slipped on the stairs and sprained an ankle she not only sat up with me, sympathizing and bathing my foot in hot water, but also read to me the diverting account of Tommy and Grizel, Barrie's immortal characters, and how he nicked his ankle in the door to get sympathy.

That last year at the university was an idyllic year; fall, winter and spring, glowing with health and youth, we enjoyed them all, the burning heat of the prairies, the dry cold of the winter snows, the smell of the upturned blue-black earth in spring. We enjoyed it all because of Rayna, who gave her loving heart to both of us, entering into all our plans and dreams and making us feel capable of great things.

Then in the summer of 1916 my father began to work for the *Morning Telegraph* in New York and the family moved back East. I had thought myself emancipated from "family" now that I had left home and attended the university. This new move made me realize that I was not as free as I thought. I could not bear to have them go so far without me. When I went home in June it was to move with them. I decided I was through with school. I wanted to go to work. Rayna had another year to go before graduation, and much as I hated to be parted from her, I looked forward to New York and new adventures.

THE EAST SIDE

MY FIRST job in New York was on the New York *Call*, a Socialist daily paper whose offices were on Pearl Street, just off Park Row. I had tried other newspapers but without success, in some cases because my father had told his city editor friends to lecture me on the subject of newspaper work for women.

During the months of job hunting, I walked the streets of New York as I had done in Chicago, exploring various neighborhoods, taking bus rides, subway rides, streetcar rides, walking over the bridges that were strung like jewels over the East River, walking along the waterfront (made more alive for me by reading Ernest Poole's *The Harbor*). Because I had determined not to go back to school but to find a newspaper job, I was released somewhat from the care of my brother, and my household tasks fell to my younger sister Della, who before I went to college had been my constant companion.

Two years' separation had made me a grownup and she was still a child. For a time there was a gap in our ages, and I felt alone. Those five months were months of great suffering in my life. During that time I felt the spell of the long loneliness descend on me. In all that great city of seven millions, I found no friends; I had no work; I was separated from my fellows. Silence in the midst of city noises oppressed me. My own silence, the feeling that I had no one to talk to overwhelmed me so that my very throat was constricted; my heart was heavy with unuttered thoughts; I wanted to weep my loneliness away.

The poverty of New York was appallingly different from that of Chicago. The very odors were different. The sight of homeless and workless men lounging on street corners or sleeping in doorways in broad sunlight appalled me. The sight of cheap lodging houses, dingy restaurants, the noise of subways and elevated railways, the clanging of streetcars jarred my senses. Above all the smell from the tenements, coming up from basements and areaways, from dank halls, horrified me. It is a smell like no other in the world and one never can become accustomed to it. I have lived with these smells now for many years, but they will always and ever affront me. I shall never cease to be indignant over the conditions which give rise to them. There is a smell in the walls of such tenements, a damp ooze coming from them in the halls. One's very clothes smell of it. It is not the smell of life, but the smell of the grave.

And yet, as I walked these streets back in 1917 I wanted to go and live among these surroundings; in some mysterious way I felt that I would never be freed from this burden of loneliness and sorrow unless I did.

Chester Wright was editor of the *Call* at that time, and they had so little money that he groaned as he thought of hiring me. There was a group of New York policemen who had constituted themselves a "diet squad" under the inspiration of some city publicity man, and every day one of the newspapers was carrying accounts of how little they could live on. It was the city's answer to the high cost of living complaints. Over thirty years later, Commissioner of Welware Hilliard publicized an experiment he and his family made. They lived on welfare rations for a month and "saved twenty-eight dollars!" What they were trying to demonstrate I do not know, except perhaps that even with the high cost of living, it was possible for the poor to live on a pittance. In my zeal for work, I offered to be a diet squad of one, demonstrating how one could live on five dollars a week, and Mr. Wright agreed to hire me.

The first thing I had to do was to find a room, as my father had made it plain that no daughter of his was going to work and live at home. My dear mother was easily persuaded (she had been delighted to leave home herself as a girl and come from Poughkeepsie to New York as a stenographer). I packed my suitcase, said good-by to my mother, sister and brothers, and went to the office for my first day's work.

What optimism and what courage! I left my suitcase in the office and walked along Cherry Street, under Manhattan Bridge, looking at the tenements that had "furnished rooms" signs outside. My guardian angel must have been leading me because I made a good choice in the first one I entered. Up three flights of bare dirty stairs, as dirty and smelly as any I have ever encountered, I knocked at the door of a front apartment (there were four four-room apartments on each floor). The door opened on a homelike scene. It was the kitchen, all painted white. There was cheap linoleum on the floor and fresh curtains at the windows. There were slate tubs by the kitchen sink and one window on an airshaft. Only the front room, which was the parlor and next to the kitchen, had windows on the street and they faced the river which could be glimpsed between several tenements. The kitchen was general living room; the parlor was used as a workroom by day and a bedroom by night. There was also a little bedroom off the kitchen, and in back of that still another, with a door on the hall. The toilet was outside the apartment in the hall, to be shared with the occupants of the rear apartment.

I always loved that little room of mine on Cherry Street, though I soon found out the discomforts which lurked behind that order and cleanliness. Under that warm feather bed there were always vermin, and nothing Mrs. Gottlieb could do eliminated them. They were in the walls. My room was cold and only the one-burner gas stove heated it. Wind came down that air-shaft around the loose panes of glass. The hall odor seeped in through the cracks and woke me with its stench. At night, cats prowled in the halls and their howls wakened me so that I sat up in bed wet with perspiration and trembling all over. Sometimes they shrieked with almost human voices as though that stairway were haunted by lost souls. One of the *Call* reporters who worked on the copy desk and ran a column called "The Guillotine," often quoted Baudelaire and one of his lines about "cats that crouch on pianos and howl with hoarse sweet voices like women" amused me by its inaptness.

Everyone on the city desk was writing a play or a book, and after the day's work was done we gathered together at Child's restaurant on Park Row and talked about them. It was against the law for women to smoke then in public restaurants and I used to practice smoking surreptitiously.

Although the *Call* was politically a Socialist paper there was a four-sided struggle going on among the men who made up the top staff. There were those who were in sympathy with the American Federation of Labor, opposing the Amalgamated Clothing Workers who were out of the Federation. There were those who favored the Industrial Workers of the World. The reporters on the *Call* were naturally attracted to the Wobblies, as the I.W.W.'s were called, because they believed in direct action and were impatient of the dialectic of the orthodox Marxist. The industrial workers opposed the craft workers of the old A. F. of L., calling the skilled workers of the federation the aristocrats of labor. The leadership was outstanding. Bill Haywood in the West, Joe Hill in the Southwest, and in the East Arturo Giovannitti and Joe Ettor, who led the strikes in the Lawrence and Paterson mills. These two men were arrested during the Lawrence strike and their places were taken by Carlo Tresca and Elizabeth Gurley Flynn. Both these strikes took place before I began to work on the *Call*, but I heard Gurley Flynn, as she was called, speak at meetings for the Mesabi Iron Range strikers and I was thrilled by her fire and vision. Later, after the Russian Revolution, she became a Communist as many of the I.W.W. members did, and right now at this writing she is under arrest with other leaders of the Communist party, for trying to do the same thing she was doing then, change the social order. Only now it is the Communist dictatorship she is working for, rather than a free society of decentralized and federated groups such as the I.W.W. envisaged.

Those I.W.W. workers who did not go over to the Communists were organized into the great industrial unions of the C.I.O., the Congress of Industrial Organizations. Today there is only a remnant left, and their weekly paper, *The Industrial Worker*, still published in Chicago, is placed on the subversive list.

At the time I worked for the *Call* there were also the small anarchist groups.

Anarchism, according to the American Encyclopedia, is a vaguely defined doctrine which would abolish the state "and other established social and economic institutions and establish a new order based on free and spontaneous co-operation among individuals, groups, regions and nations. Actually anarchism is not one doctrine but many; practically every theoretical Anarchist has had his own distinctive ideas."

Prince Kropotkin, for instance, was a scientist by avocation, who, after being trained in a military school as a personal aide to the Czar, chose a regiment going to Siberia so that he could engage in his scientific pursuits, work with the geographical society, and explore the natural resources of Russia. Later on in his explorations of Finland and Siberia, after active experience of co-operation, he pointed out that the voluntary association of

men on a scientific expedition worked out better than the regi-
mentation of military men. He lived and worked so closely with
peasants and artisans that his writings, *Fields, Factories and
Workshops, Mutual Aid*, and *The Conquest of Bread*, are practical handbooks.

Francisco Ferrer, the Spaniard, on the other hand, expended
all his energy and practical ability in the founding of free
schools, establishing hundreds of them in Spain. Sacco and
Vanzetti were syndicalists, engaged in organizing of workers and
calling for the abolition of the wage system.

Anarchism has been called an emotional state of mind, de-
nouncing injustice and extolling freedom, rather than a movement. There was anarchism in ancient Greece. Zeno believed
that freedom and equality would bring out the essential goodness of human nature. Kropotkin looked back to the guilds and
cities of the Middle Ages, and thought of the new society as
made up of federated associations, co-operating in the same way
as the railway companies of Europe or the postal departments of
various countries co-operate now.

William Godwin in England denounced government and the
accumulation of property, but modern anarchism stems from
Proudhon, who was a contemporary and an opponent of Karl
Marx. One book written by Proudhon called *A Philosophy of
Poverty* was countered by Marx with *The Poverty of Philosophy*.

Father de Lubac, the French Jesuit, has written a stimulating
book, *The Un-Marxian Socialist* about Proudhon. The term Socialist was a mild term for Communist then, and perhaps Proudhon was called Socialist because he wrote a book, *What Is Property*, and startled people by answering, Property is Theft.

Kropotkin and Tolstoi, the modern proponents of anarchism,
were sincere and peaceful men. Kropotkin's classic, *Memoirs of a
Revolutionist*, was published first in the *Atlantic Monthly* in
1898. After the Russian Revolution Kropotkin went back to
Russia and, revered by workers and scholars, lived in a country
place outside of Moscow until the early twenties. He in no way
sympathized with the revolution which had set up a dictatorship
in the name of the proletariat, which would bring about by

terroristic force what Kropotkin had hoped to attain through brotherly love, a society where "each worked according to his ability and received according to his need."

Kropotkin wanted much the same type of social order as Eric Gill, the artist, Father Vincent McNabb, the Dominican street preacher, G. K. Chesterton, Hilaire Belloc and other distributists advocated, though they would have revolted at the word anarchist, thinking it synonymous with chaos, not "self-government" as Proudhon defined it. Distributism is the English term for that society whereby man has sufficient of this world's goods to enable him to lead a good life. Other words have been used to describe this theory, mutualism, federalism, pluralism, regionalism; but anarchism—the word, first used as a taunt by its Marxist opponents, best brings to mind the tension always existing between the concept of authority and freedom which torments man to this day.

Emma Goldman and Alexander Berkman, both Russian Jews and both proponents of anarchism, spent most of their lives in America and so represented American thought on the subject. Both did much to help the I.W.W. I met Berkman briefly but I never met Emma though she lived in New York at the time I worked on the *Call* and edited a journal called *Mother Earth* which opposed conscription and the coming war.

Working on the New York *Call,* I had no time for membership in any organization and never went to Socialist meetings.

JOURNALISM

EVEN though I made fun of the "diet squad of one" in the column I wrote for the paper, I was surprised myself at how cheaply one person could live, once having given up the kind of standards set up by a family such as mine. If one lived in the slums, one didn't have so much of that race with the neighbors over kitchen appliances, upholstered furniture, lace curtains. I did not spend money on recreation, books, clothes, doctors (there were the free clinics). In the slums it was such a struggle for the family just to live that great emphasis was placed on food and sunshine. All the East Side mothers believed that the sun and the air were as important as food, so they kept their babies out all day in carriages, and while they lived in foul-smelling hovels, they countered the foul smells by delicate smells of baking, and roastings. They were artists in the kitchen, and the food which they bought was the best and the freshest.

I soon found that I could make a quick meal off a pushcart in the winter, by eating a few roasted sweet potatoes and a piece of fruit, and there were innumerable little restaurants, with sawdust on the floor, where one could get good bean soup and plenty of bread and butter for ten cents. Living within walking distance of the office I had no carfare to worry about, and being a reporter, I had an expense account which paid my fares around the city. I had enough clothes from home, though I soon began worrying about shoes and stockings. Reporters on other papers were always treating me to a dinner here and there, so I was able to keep my expenses down.

I satirized in my column the police diet squad, especially when the Russell Sage Foundation seriously asked me to send them the result of my findings for the benefit of the working girl. I emphasized the sordidness of slum living and wrote that as it was necessary to do something to lighten the gloom of the tenement, something to counter the harsh cries of the fighting cats on the stairs, I had bought a small phonograph for a dollar down and a dollar a week, plunging at once into installment buying, that plague of the poor, that dishonesty by which the poor are robbed of their meager earnings. I also wrote about the luncheons and dinners my fellow reporters treated me to.

My assignments took me to all kinds of strike meetings, picket lines, peace meetings. Many groups were working for peace, trying to prevent our entry into the war—the Emergency Peace Federation, the I.W.W., the Socialists, the anarchists, an anti-conscription group at Columbia University.

The *Call* didn't pay much attention to the anarchists and the meetings of their No-Conscription League. With the instinctive loyalty which the reporter has to his paper, I interested myself only in the meetings to which I was sent, in the unions whose struggles I covered. Actually the only anarchist I knew was a young fellow by the name of Louis Kramer, who had been arrested for distributing anticonscription leaflets and sentenced to two years in Atlanta Penitentiary. He was young, an unbalanced youth, who often escorted me home at night. We would sit for hours in one of the little East Side restaurants, but he talked so disjointedly, so incoherently, that it is impossible to remember now the point of his discourses.

With all my radicalism, I was extremely conventional, and disliked his long hair, his ragged clothes, his emotional speech. I only endured his company because I could not get away from him, and perhaps also I pitied him, his poverty and impending jail sentence. I know that I dreaded his constant telephone calls, and groaned at finding him waiting for me every night as I was about to go home. I got away from him as often as I could, to go with some of the men from the copy desk to the restaurant on Park Row where we sat over pancakes and applesauce and talked for hours.

Every Friday night there were dances at Webster Hall on Twelfth Street to raise money for some radical group. One night there was an Anarchist ball, probably to get funds for the defense of the half-dozen anarchists who were being tried for obstructing the draft, and Louis Kramer was at the dance waiting for me. When he saw me come in he rushed to embrace me and, taken aback, I pushed him, or slapped him, I don't recall which. Thereupon he slapped me back. Altogether it was a childish affair that I was much ashamed of afterward. Some other reporters from the *Times* and the *World* who were also covering the dance were delighted to act gallantly, to take poor Louis by the shoulders and put him out of the hall, "protecting" me. I was neither a Christian nor a pacifist, and I certainly acted like neither. Had I been a Christian I would not have rebuffed the boy, and certainly would not have struck him had I been a true pacifist. Or, this little encounter having already happened, I would not have wanted others to come to my rescue, making a mountain out of a molehill.

I was not even acting like a good radical, lining myself up on the side of the "capitalist-imperialist" press, rather than on the side of my poor friend. Often, in looking back on my past life I can see that I was not a good radical, not worthy of respect like those great figures in the movement who were fighting the issues of the day.

I recall this tiny incident now because it illustrates a point that has since come up many times in our work with others. Our desire for justice for ourselves and for others often complicates the issue, builds up factions and quarrels. Worldly justice and unworldly justice are quite different things. The supernatural approach when understood is to turn the other cheek, to give up what one has, willingly, gladly, with no spirit of martyrdom, to rejoice in being the least, to be unrecognized, the slighted. I was making no pretensions to being a Christian at the time, but I was professing to be a radical. But I was not a good one. I was following the "devices and desires of my own heart." Sometimes it was perhaps the Baudelairian idea of "choosing the downward path that leads to salvation."

Mauriac, the great French novelist, talks a great deal of the subtler forms of hypocrisy: "There is a kind of hypocrisy which is worse than that of the Pharisees; it is to hide behind Christ's example in order to follow one's own lustful desires and to seek the company of the dissolute." Was this desire to be with the poor and the mean and the abandoned not mixed with a distorted desire to be with the dissipated? I write these things now because sometimes I am seized with fright at my presumption. I am afraid, too, of not telling the truth, or of distorting the truth. I cannot guarantee that I do not, for I am writing of the past.

I quoted those terrible lines from Mauriac in a book which I wrote about my conversion ten years ago, and Westbrook Pegler has delighted in them and quoted them completely out of context on two different occasions to make his point that I, as a former radical, speak of my former comrades as the subtlest of hypocrites, wishing to be with the poor to indulge their own vices. I was speaking of *myself*, of my own self-love, my own gropings for the love of others, my own desires for freedom and for pleasure.

Emma Goldman was the great exponent of free love in those days, and lectured on the subject, as well as on birth control, literature, anarchism, war, revolution. She had many lovers, and later when she wrote her story *Living my Life*, she spoke most frankly of her affairs. As I remember it, I was revolted by such promiscuity and even when her book came out would not read it because I was offended in my sex. Men who are revolutionaries, I thought, do not dally on the side as women do, complicating the issue by an emphasis on the personal.

I am quite ready to concede now that men are the single-minded, the pure of heart, in these movements. Women by their very nature are more materialistic, thinking of the home, the children, and of all things needful to them, especially love. And in their constant searching after it, they go against their own best interests. So, I say, I do not really know myself as I was then. I do not know how sincere I was in my love of the poor and my desire to serve them. I know that I was in favor of the works of mercy as we know them, regarding the drives for food and clothing for strikers in the light of justice, and an aid in furthering the revolution. But I was bent on following the journalist's side of the work. I wanted the privileges of the woman and the work of the man, without following the work of the woman. I wanted to go on picket lines, to go to jail, to write, to influence others and so make my mark on the world. How much ambition and how much self-seeking there was in all this!

In April, 1917, I was given an assignment by the city editor to go to Washington with a group of Columbia students to protest the passage of the conscription act. These young radicals who made up the Anti-Conscription League chartered a bus to make the trip. I had met some of them at meetings so I welcomed the opportunity as though for a holiday excursion. I had never traveled on an interstate bus before and it was a thrilling experience. I was nineteen and it was an early spring. We stopped at Philadelphia, Chester, Wilmington, and Baltimore to hold meetings in the afternoon or evening at other colleges. I can remember the names of some of the students, Milton Wein-handler, Charles Phillips, Eleanor Carroll, Owen Cattell, Jay Greenberg. Charlie and Eleanor were engaged. I fell briefly in love with Milton because it was spring and we were all young, and a war was in the air and they were fighting a losing battle.

In Baltimore there was a sudden riot. A group of hostile students broke up the meeting and tried to beat up the Columbia students, whom they called Jew radicals. I was there in the role of reporter and stood as close to the patrol wagon as I could to get the names of those whom the police were arresting. So I found myself in the very midst of a struggling group and had my first glimpse of mob spirit. It was not too serious, this first riot, and the police took the skirmishings good-naturedly. It was a different affair in labor struggles when I saw police ride down strikers and beat up demonstrators. This deliberate brutality on the part of the police aroused hatred and violence in return, so that labor leaders had a hard time holding their followers in check. It is a mysterious thing, this feeling of violence in a mob. Eugene Debs said that even a friendly mob has the smell of the beast. There were protests going on all that winter in New York against the high cost of living—bread riots, they were called. There was much unemployment, and daily demonstrations in front of the City Hall and in front of the Waldorf-Astoria, which was then on Fifth Avenue.

There were other kinds of protests for me to cover: street-corner meetings, marches to City Hall as well as appeals for playgrounds, recreation centers, babies' clinics, and better schools. Usually the protests grew out of some case of human misery—death in a family from a fire or from starvation, or eviction. The family actually suffering sat at home and mourned while all the neighbors took up the case and made their voices heard. There were always leaders to rush in trying to sway the people to their cause, either I.W.W.'s, anarchists or Socialist leaders, all of them combating each other vigorously the while.

In spite of the conflicts in the radical movement much was gained by this constant agitation. Evictions were halted, relief came, playgrounds were built, slum houses were torn down, and conditions have somewhat improved. We can say this in spite of the fact that still the Municipal Lodging Houses in New York are filled with men, women and children, thousands of families are doubled up with others. There are nowhere sufficient housing facilities right now. And I am writing of 1917! When I think of the human suffering, the terrible amount of energy needed to move even infinitesimally toward a more decent life I am amazed at human patience. Each of the radical groups had its own vision, and each was terrified that immediate gains would make the masses content and not willing to go further toward the new earth they were envisioning. They had faith in the people, but they knew too how prone they were to settle down with their gains.

I wavered between my allegiance to socialism, syndicalism (the I.W.W.'s) and anarchism. When I read Tolstoi, I was an anarchist. Ferrer with his schools, Kropotkin with his farming communes, the I.W.W.'s with their solidarity, their unions, these all appealed to me. But not the American anarchism that I had come in touch with. Not long after this I met Hypolite Havel, editor of an American anarchist paper, a Greenwich Village habitué. It was rumored that he had been in every jail in Europe. So I tried to see in him the revolutionist and admire him. The very fact that the anarchists were a minority made me incline to the mass movements. Socialism was too doctrinaire; I could not understand Marx. The I.W.W. had an immediate program for America so I signed up with them.

I do not remember any antireligious articles in the *Call*. As a matter of fact there was a long article by Dante Barton, vice-chairman of the Committee on Industrial Relations, which was an interview with Father O'Rourke, a Jesuit preacher. Reading it over in the public library I was surprised to find many quotations from *Rerum Novarum* of Pope Leo XIII and a very fair exposition of the Church's social teachings. I paid no attention to it at the time. Catholics were a world apart, a people within a people, making little impression on the tremendous non-Catholic population of the country.

There was no attack on religion because people were generally indifferent to religion. They were neither hot nor cold. They were the tepid, the materialistic, who hoped that by Sunday churchgoing they would be taking care of the afterlife, if there were an afterlife. Meanwhile they would get everything they could in this.

On the other hand, the Marxists, the I.W.W.'s who looked upon religion as the opiate of the people, who thought they had only this one life to live and then oblivion—they were the ones who were eager to sacrifice themselves here and now, thus doing without now and for all eternity the good things of the world which they were fighting to obtain for their brothers. It was then, and still is, a paradox that confounds me. God love them! And God pity the lukewarm of whom St. John said harshly (though he was the disciple of love) that God would spew them out of His mouth.

As that year passed and the war kept on, employment increased all over the country. Although there were high wages, the cost of living went up steadily, so there continued to be strikes in industry—streetcar strikes, strikes in garment factories, smelting plants, sugar refineries—and week after week that winter, food riots continued.

Out on the West Coast the year before there had been a Preparedness Day parade on Market Street. Suddenly there was an explosion of a dynamite bomb which left nine dead and forty injured. Labor leaders Thomas J. Mooney, Rena Mooney, his wife, Warren Billings, Edward D. Nolan and Israel Weinberg were arrested. Mooney had organized the streetcar employees and all of the others had opposed preparedness and had participated in work for peace. The fight centered around Mooney and Billings after the release of the others.

What with the confessed dynamiting of the Times Building in Los Angeles by the McNamara brothers, American Federation of Labor men, and the history of the Molly Maguires, every charge of violence brought against labor leaders was believed.

Yet again and again witnesses against them were shown to be perjurers, and in the Lawrence textile strike it was proved that the guards and detectives hired by the employers were the ones who planted evidence to frame a case against Giovannitti and Ettor, the strike leaders.

I met Mooney years afterward in San Quentin and was impressed with his cheerful simplicity. He was working in the prison hospital and explained his tardiness in receiving my visit in the prison office by telling me of the work he was doing trying to keep a patient alive.

Robert Minor, for whom I afterward worked in Chicago, played a big part in the defense campaign. He was a cartoonist and had given up a position on a St. Louis daily paper to join the radical movement. After the Russian Revolution, he became a Communist and was secretary to the party when Earl Browder was in the penitentiary. Charles Ashleigh, in Everett, Washington, was doing the defense work for the seventy I.W.W.'s being tried for murder after five of their own comrades had been shot down in a free-speech riot.

I got to know Ashleigh well in Chicago, after he had served a term in Leavenworth for being a member of the I.W.W. After the formation of the Communist party in this country, Ashleigh went to Russia and became editor of the Moscow *Daily News*. Still later, in 1941 when England became the ally of Russia in World War II, he had a propaganda job in London, selling Russia to the English, who were still thinking of Russia as an ally of Hitler and their enemy. There in London, Ashleigh ran into one of our nonpacifist Catholic Worker leaders, Jack English, who had been in charge of one of our hospices; he was a gunner on a bomber and stationed in England. The two of them sent me frequent postals from an English pub.

I met Trotsky in New York, before he returned to Russia. Exiled from Germany, France, and Spain successively, he had come to New York to write for the Russian Socialist daily, *Novy Mir*. The offices of that paper were then at 77 St. Mark's Place, and I went with another *Call* reporter to interview him. He refused to be lured into talking about his exile in Siberia or his various escapes in disguise, but instead talked of the failure of socialism to halt the war.

Perhaps it was his bitter criticism of the parliamentarianism of the Socialists of New York which kept the *Call* from printing more than one interview with him. His name appeared only twice in the paper.

The *Call* had been emphasizing constantly the work of the Socialists who had been elected to the legislature, and who were prominent in politics at that time. Trotsky said that where parliamentarianism was weakest the Socialist movement was the strongest. Where they sought to win the state, he said, they were won by the state. Trotsky predicted the ruin of the capitalist class, enormous increase in taxation, and concentration of power in the middle class.

"The social unrest after the war," he said, "will eclipse anything the world has ever seen. The workers will take a heavy accounting of masters and the future alone can tell what form the protest will take."

A few weeks later, he spoke at Cooper Union. "Revolution is brewing in the trenches," he said, little dreaming himself that on March 21, less than two months later, the New York masses would be celebrating at Madison Square Garden the downfall of the Czar. Ludwig Lore, formerly a writer for the *Post*, and at that time editor of *Volkzeitung*, introduced Trotsky.

Life on a newspaper, whether radical or conservative, makes one lose all sense of perspective at the time. You are carried along in a world of events, writing, reporting, with no time at all for thought or reflection—one day listening to Trotsky, and the next day interviewing Mrs. Vincent Astor's butler; writing articles about the Navy Department's charges against Charles Schwab and other munitions makers, then stories about child labor in rural regions and in the laundries (one fourteen-year-old boy working ninety hours weekly).

Nothing stood out in my mind. We reporters worked from twelve noon until twelve at night, covering meetings and strikes. We walked on picket lines; we investigated starvation and death in the slums. Our function as journalists seemed to be to build up a tremendous indictment against the present system, a daily tale of horror which would have a cumulative effect of forcing the workers to rise in revolution. Our editorial heads trusted in legislation and education, but we younger ones believed that nothing could be done except by the use of force.

On March 21, 1917, at Madison Square Garden, I joined with those thousands in reliving the first days of the revolt in Russia. I felt the exultation, the joyous sense of victory of the masses as they sang "Ei Euchnjem," the workers' hymn of Russia. It seemed to signify that "like the flowing of the river, is the progress of human events," as the *Call* said next day in a story which went on to describe the song as a "mystic gripping melody of struggle, a cry for world peace and human brotherhood."

Revolutionary striving, with all its human aspirations, longing for liberty, human love, and justice, had culminated in a tremendous fact. The Russian masses, living on one-sixth of the world's surface, had overthrown the Czar. Reading the diary of Krupskaya, Lenin's widow, years later, I came across the story of a Sunday afternoon in Paris where they were living in exile and in poverty. It told of a discussion group, of a workers' school, and of forty young people studying and planning. "It was a wonderful meeting," Krupskaya said. Forty people! And now, not many years later, these little bands were taking over the destiny of one-sixth of the world.

Jörgensen, the Danish poet and biographer, writes of the enthusiasm of the students at the news of the Russian Revolution. And Ignazio Silone, in an article in *Harper's Magazine*, spoke of the nostalgia of a young Russian who wished that he had lived in those times of revolution.

During these years I do not remember hearing any of the leaders of the time speaking. If I heard them, they did not stand out, except Elizabeth Gurley Flynn, who was campaigning for the striking miners of the Mesabi Iron Range. Ideas dominated, rather than personalities. It was after the heyday of Bill Haywood, Arturo Giovannitti, Ettor and Tresca.

The big strikes in lumber and textiles had already occurred. It was a time of constant agitation throughout the world. Perhaps people were looking for leaders; during the years ahead there would be Lenin and Trotsky, Stalin, Hitler, Mussolini, Churchill, Roosevelt, men so dominated by ideas that they sacrificed to them countless millions of human beings.

This has been no brief period of revolution. Unlike 1776, 1793, 1848, and 1864, we are now in a world revolution which began in 1917, has continued, and is continuing.

THE MASSES

IT WAS in April that the group of college students drove to Washington in the chartered bus and I went with them as a reporter for the *Call*. For a while after that I spent my entire time working with them. Because of a dispute with the city editor over my rudeness to Kramer at the anarchist ball, I left my job with the *Call* and worked for the students, until I was offered a job on *The Masses* and began to work with an older group. It is a strange and wonderful thing, the numbers of radical groups, the various aspects of a movement, the lack of cohesion among them all. The movement as I saw it then was Socialist, I.W.W., anarchist and liberal. Probably my analysis is too simple but I can only report it as I knew it.

The Socialists were the old trade-union groups who had carried on the early fight for organization of workers. They were doctrinaire and foreign. They sat in cafés on the East Side and went in for dialectics over interminable glasses of tea. Many of the meetings I attended were addressed in Yiddish.

The I.W.W. was American, with the traditions of the West, and smacked of the open wheatfields, the vast lumber camps, the mines, and more recently the textile mills of New England. But its great days were behind me. I felt that I was just too late for the strikes, the tremendous dramas that were played out in the early years before 1917. Now the leaders were suffering for their beliefs—many of them being arrested. The anarchist group was so small that I rejected it, without knowing anything about its traditions, its background, the history of its work in Italy, Spain or France. It was not yet the day of Sacco and Vanzetti and their long trial and eventual martyrdom.

The students I worked with were against the war and they had no particular political affiliations. In fact, I did not know what they believed. Afterward, some of them, having served a three-day jail sentence, went to Mexico to escape the draft. There they lived as best they could, teaching English, selling lemonade on street corners, starving and studying in true revolutionary tradition.

My association with them, so swift and intimate on that trip to Washington, was a short one, and then I found myself with the liberals—Max Eastman, Floyd Dell, Merrill Rogers, all of them editors of *The Masses* and friends of the artists and writers who made up its board of editors.

My association with them was during the last six months of the magazine's existence. The offices then were on the top of an old building facing Union Square, *The Masses* occupying the front half of the building and *Pearson's*, edited by Frank Harris, the back half. It was the last days of *Pearson's* also. Looking over an old number of *The Masses* recently, I found in it articles by Jack Reed, whose *Ten Days That Shook the World* has become a classic. He was a big, hearty Harvard graduate, a typical newspaperman, and very much the Richard Harding Davis reporter hero. Wherever there was excitement, wherever life was lived at high tension, there he was, writing, speaking, recording the moment, and heightening its intensity for everyone else. Arturo Giovannitti's poems stirred the blood; there was one on the murder of Frank Little, an I.W.W. organizer in the Northwest, that I can remember to this day. He was taken out by an armed mob and hanged from a railroad trestle, after a series of skirmishes between police and workers during which a policeman was killed.

There were cartoons and drawings by Art Young, Hugo Gellert, Boardman Robinson, Maurice Becker, Henry Glintencamp, and many others. Max Eastman was carrying on a scholarly controversy with President Wilson; the letters they exchanged

were printed monthly in the magazine which I helped to dummy
up at the printer's on Park Row with Floyd Dell, who patiently
taught me how to be an editor along these mechanical lines. He
himself was supposed to be doing the office job, opening the
mail, reading manuscripts, seeing visitors, but he was beginning
his first novel that summer and wanted time off. So after a few
months of teaching me make-up, he happily left for a little cabin
in New Jersey and I was editor! Max Eastman was away on a
speaking trip. Merrill Rogers was business manager and there
was a delightful summer in New York when I had their apartment on MacDougal Street to myself, and the job of editor to
play with. It was during that time that Rayna visited me and we
walked the streets of New York with Mike Gold and Maurice
Becker, sat on the ends of piers singing revolutionary songs into
the starlit night, dallied on park benches, never wanting to go
home to sleep but only to continue to savor our youth and its
struggles and joys. What work I did took not more than a few
hours every morning—everyone knew that with the outbreak of
war the days of the magazine were numbered—and in the afternoon we had picnics along the Palisades or took the ferry to
Staten Island and lay on the sands and talked.

The apartment on MacDougal Street belonged to Edna Kenton
and her sister, and they loaned it to Floyd, Merrill and David
Karb, who in turn shared it with me. It was while the boys were
away that Rayna came to visit me. The rooms were large and
well furnished and there was a good kitchen so that we could
have supper parties, and even breakfast parties, everyone chip-
ping in for the stew and for the breakfast brioche from a little
French bakery on Sheridan Square. In our radical ardor we made
friends with the world; many a time, coming home late at night,
we picked up men from the park benches and gave them whatever bed was empty in the place, ourselves sitting up all night,
continuing to talk.

Rayna wrote back such glowing accounts of our adventures
that Raph took the next train from Chicago and arrived to find
us having a dinner party at which the main guests were Donn
Byrne and Hi Moderwell, writer and journalist. Raph shipped

Rayna back home and stayed to work for Donn Byrne as his secretary, and to make himself a New York success in advertising and later in writing.

Nothing turned out as we intended in our personal relationships. Later on when Raph and Rayna married the following year, they found their interests were opposed, and Rayna continued to study at the University of Chicago. She thought my interest in radicalism purely emotional and I thought her approach to life too intellectual. She devoted herself to study and we saw little of each other even when I went back to work in Chicago some years later.

Afterward she met William Prohme, a Communist, whom she married and with whom she went to China. I read of her last years in Vincent Sheean's book *Personal History*, and was profoundly moved by his account of her. Her husband was agitating in the Philippines and Rayna was in Hankow with Borodin and Madam Sun Yat-sen. She escaped with them to Moscow after the fall of Hankow to Chiang Kai-shek and started to study at the Lenin Institute; then at the peak of her glowing, radiant life she died with tragic suddenness. Sheean, Anna Louise Strong, Louis Fischer and other American writers who were there at the time have told the story.

No one who knew Rayna would ever forget her warm enthusiasm, her vitality of spirit which transformed her frail flesh. She was always delicate, thin, a frail creature even in those college days, but she never spoke of her health, never complained of fatigue or weakness. Perhaps she was loved because she was so unself-conscious, so interested in others, so ready to hear and discuss all that interested them.

Sheean spoke of her fearlessness, her love of truth, her search for it, her profound interest in philosophy. She had not yet begun to question means and ends when she was taken by death.

She was given a "red" funeral; her beauty was consumed in flames; her ashes lie in Moscow.

She never met a Christian. This I am sure is literally true. When we were at the university together, we never met anyone who had a vital faith, or, if he had one, was articulate or apostolic.

There were no doubt those whose souls glowed with belief, whose hearts were warmed by the love of God, on all sides of us. But mingling as we did, in our life together, and in our life apart, with radical groups, we never met any whose personal morality was matched by a social morality or who tried to make life here for others a foretaste of the life to come.

When I think of Rayna, I think of Mauriac's statement in his life of Christ that those who serve the cause of the masses, the poor, working for truth and justice, have worked for Christ even while denying Him.

Mike Gold and I were reading Tolstoi at the time Rayna stayed with me in New York. He used to make fun of my religious spirit, but he himself was in sympathy with the Christianity expressed by Tolstoi, a religion without churches or a priesthood. Mike had had a religious upbringing in his home on the East Side and liked to sing Yiddish folk songs and Hebrew hymns.

During later months there were meetings in the MacDougal Street apartment. I remember one especially, the night before registration day, when a group of men argued all night as to whether or not they should register for the draft, and then when morning came, registered. Their opposition to the draft seemed not so much opposition to war as to the compulsion of conscription, the denial of liberty.

After the draft law went into effect, Hugo Gellert's younger brother was inducted and put in the guardhouse in a camp on Long Island because he refused to don a uniform in the capitalist war. Hugo was the artist whose work I admired most on *The Masses*. He was a young Hungarian, and when he was not drawing pictures of marching workers in overalls grasping their tools like weapons, he was making lovely pictures of goats and frolicking kids. Hugo painted posters and murals for the radical movement in addition to his work for *The Masses* for which he was not paid. It was considered an honor to have one's work published by *The Masses*. Hugo and Mike Gold and I went to see Hugo's brother in the guardhouse and he seemed cheerful enough then, considering his tragic situation. We were shocked to hear some weeks later that he was dead. The report was that he had taken his own life, but we could not believe it. He was a happy youth, friendly with the guards who smuggled his violin to him so that he could play to them. Hugo insisted that he had been murdered. He came from a revolutionary family in Hungary and he told us gruesome tales of prisoners being tortured, their nails torn out, their bodies beaten so that forever after they were crippled, mentally and physically.

It was hard for me to believe these things, that it was possible for people to be so inhuman, so brutal, cruel in so calculated a way. I could see that blind greed of the industrialist, the stupid lack of understanding "concerning the needy and the poor," the atrocity committed in the mad conflict of class war—but the cold, calculated torture and killing of prisoners was a mystery which left me shuddering.

JAIL

IT WAS after the suppression of *The Masses* that I again went to Washington, this time with a group to picket the White House with the suffragists. It was mainly because my friend Peggy Baird was going that I decided one evening to accompany her. The women's party who had been picketing and serving jail sentences had been given very brutal treatment, and a committee to uphold the rights of political prisoners had been formed.

Hypolite Havel, who had been in so many jails in Europe, described to us the rights of political prisoners which he insisted had been upheld by the Czar himself in despotic Russia: the right to receive mail, books and visitors, to wear one's own clothes, to purchase extra food if needed, to see one's lawyer. The suffragists in Washington had been treated as ordinary prisoners, deprived of their own clothing, put in shops to work, and starved on the meager food of the prison. The group who left New York that night were prepared to go on a hunger strike to protest the treatment of the score or more women still in prison.

In Washington it was known by the press and police that the picket line that day would be unusually large so when we left the headquarters of the women's party the park across from the White House was crowded with spectators. Many police held back the crowd and kept the road clear for the women picketers.

They started out, two by two, with colored ribbons of purple and gold across the bosoms of their dresses and banners in their hands. There was a religious flavor about the silent proceedings. To get to the White House gates one had to walk halfway around the park. There were some cheers from women and indignation from men, who wanted to know if the President did not have enough to bother him, and in wartime too! By the time the third contingent of six women reached the gates—I was of this group —small boys were beginning to throw stones, and groups of soldiers and sailors appearing from the crowd were trying to wrest the banners from the hands of the women. The police arrived at once with a number of patrol wagons. I had to struggle for my banner too, with a red-faced young sailor, before a policeman took me by the arm and escorted me to the waiting police van. Our banners were carried, protruding from the back of the car, and we made a gay procession through the streets.

Bail had been provided for us and after our names and addresses were taken at the police station we were released. The trial was set for ten o'clock the next morning. When the thirty-five of us appeared, the judge pronounced us guilty and postponed the sentence.

Again that afternoon we picketed and again there was arrest, release on bail, trial and postponement. The tactics were then changed, and when we were arrested once more and taken to the Central Station, we refused to give bail and were put in the House of Detention for the night.

The facilities there were inadequate for so many prisoners. We had to sleep fifteen in a room meant for two, with cots cheek by jowl so that it was impossible to stir. The next morning we were all sentenced. Many of the women on receiving their sentences took the occasion to make speeches to the judge, who sat patiently though somewhat uncomfortably facing the righteous wrath of the thirty-five women.

The leader of the picketers received a sentence of six months, the older women were sentenced to fifteen days, and the rest of us to thirty days. We started our hunger strike right after receiving our sentences. The scant meal of weak coffee, oatmeal and bread was the last one we expected to have until our demands (for the rights of political prisoners) were granted or we were released. I was too excited to worry much about food. I was to find that one of the uglinesses of jail life was its undertone of suppressed excitement and suspense. It was an ugly and a fearful suspense, not one of normal hope and expectation.

For many hours the women had to wait in a little room back of the court. This waiting, too, was part of the burden put upon us. Years later when I read Arthur Koestler's *Scum of the Earth*, he too spoke of the interminable hours of waiting experienced by prisoners who were being sent to a concentration camp.

Finally, at four o'clock, things began to happen to us. Prison wagons were brought, wagons that had only ventilators along the top and were otherwise closed. Two of them sufficed to carry the prisoners to the jail. When they reached that barren institution on the outskirts of the city, backed by a cemetery and surrounded by dreary bare fields, there was another long halt in the proceedings. After a low argument at the entrance (we never heard what people were saying and that too was part of the torture), the police vans were turned away and started off in another direction.

Those women who had served sentence before knew that we were being taken to the workhouse, and many stories had been told of what the prisoners had suffered at the hands of the violent keeper there, a man named Whittaker. We were all afraid.

It had been completely black in the prison vans but when we were ushered by a number of policewomen into a waiting train which rolled out of station immediately, the lamps along the road had not yet been lit. It was the beginning of November, and I sat with my face pressed against the glass watching the blue twilight, pierced with the black shapes of many scrawny trees. Here and there lamps glowed in farmhouse windows. In the west the sky still held the radiance of the sun which faded gradually and left one with a terrible sense of desolation and loneliness. It was sadly beautiful at that time of night. I was glad for the company of my friend Peggy, and we tried to stay near each other so that we would not be separated later.

There was more waiting after we had been driven from the railroad station to the administration building of the workhouse. A matron tried to take our names and case histories, which all of us refused to give.

We waited there in the administration building, while the matron sat behind her desk and knitted. The spokeswoman for our group was an elderly woman from a socially prominent family in Philadelphia and she had asked to see Mr. Whittaker, the superintendent, before we were assigned to our cells. The matron paid no attention to her request but left us all standing, until of our own accord we took benches and chairs about the room. Some of the younger ones sat on the floor and leaned against the wall. We were beginning to be very tired.

It was not until ten o'clock that Mr. Whittaker, a large stout man with white hair and a red face, came storming into the room, leaving the door open on the porch, from which came the sound of the shuffling feet of many men.

Our spokeswoman got up and began to announce that we were all going on hunger strike unless our demands were met, but before she could get the first words out of her mouth, Whittaker had turned to the door and beckoned. Immediately the room was filled with men. There were two guards to every woman, and each of us was seized roughly by the arms and dragged out of the room. It seems impossible to believe, but we were not allowed to walk, were all but lifted from the floor, in the effort the men made to drag, rather than lead us to our place of confinement for the night.

The leaders were taken first. In my effort to get near Peggy I started to cross the room to join her, and was immediately seized by two guards. My instinctive impulse was to pull myself loose, to resist such handling, which only caused the men to tighten their hold on me, even to twist my arms painfully. I have no doubt but that I struggled every step of the way from the administration building to the cell block where we were being taken. It was a struggle to walk by myself, to wrest myself loose from the torture of those rough hands. We were then hurled onto some benches and when I tried to pick myself up and again join Peggy in my blind desire to be near a friend, I was thrown to the floor. When another prisoner tried to come to my rescue, we found ourselves in the midst of a milling crowd of guards being pummeled and pushed and kicked and dragged, so that we were scarcely conscious, in the shock of what was taking place.

The account of what they termed a riot was printed in the *New York Times* later, and the story made the event much worse than it was, though it was bad enough. I found myself flung into a cell with one of the leaders, Lucy Byrnes, a tall red-haired schoolteacher from Brooklyn, with a calm, beautiful face. She was handcuffed to the bars of the cell, and left that way for hours. Every time she called out to the other women who had been placed up and down a corridor in a block of what we found out afterward were punishment cells, Whittaker came cursing outside the bars, threatening her with a straitjacket, a gag, everything but the whipping post and bloodhounds which we had heard were part of the setup at Occoquan.

An hour or so later, when things had quieted down, an old guard shuffled down the corridor and unlocked the handcuffs from the bars of the cell but left them on her wrists so that she had to sleep with them on. Each cell was made for one prisoner, so there was only a single bunk, a slab of wood in the corner. There were two blankets on it, and when I had unfastened her shoes and arranged the blankets, Lucy and I tried to make ourselves comfortable on the single slab. In spite of our exhaustion, we could not sleep, but lay there talking of Conrad's novels for some time. Early the next morning Lucy was taken away to what we afterward heard was a padded cell for delirium tremens patients and I was left alone to try to sleeep a good part of that first sad day.

There were no meals to break the monotony, and if the women tried to call out to one another, there were always guards on hand to silence them harshly. In the morning we were taken one by one to a washroom at the end of the hall. There was a toilet in each cell, open, and paper and flushing were supplied by the guard. It was as though one were in a zoo with the open bars leading into the corridor. There were only narrow ventilators at the top of the rear wall of the cell, which was a square stone room. The sun shone dimly through these slits for a time and then disappeared for the rest of the day. There was no way to tell what time it was. In the darkness of the night before we had not noticed a straw mattress in another corner of the cell. I put this on the built-in bunk. The place was inadequately heated by one pipe which ran along a wall. Suspense and fear kept one cold.

It was not until the next day that we were offered food. Then milk and toast were brought and left in the cells for an hour, but none of our group ate. Food was again brought that night. It was not stale toast and cold milk, but hot milk and fragrant toast that came to tantalize us for the next ten days.

Every now and then the women called out to each other. We had neither pencil nor paper so we could not write; no books, so we could not read. I found a nail file which I began automatically to use on my nails, and as though I had been spied on, a guard immediately came in and took it from me.

We had no idea how many were in the punishment block but estimated there could be no more than twelve since there were only so many single cells. The older women had been taken elsewhere. "Keep the strike," one of the girls called out once. "Remember, if it's broken we go back to worms in the oatmeal, and the workshop."

Personally I would have preferred the workshop and prison clothes to the hunger strike. Those first six days of inactivity were as six thousand years. To lie there through the long day, to feel the nausea and emptiness of hunger, the dazedness at the beginning and the feverish mental activity that came after.

I lost all consciousness of any cause. I had no sense of being a radical, making protest against a government, carrying on a nonviolent revolution. I could only feel darkness and desolation all around me. The bar of gold which the sun left on the ceiling every morning for a short hour taunted me; and late in the afternoon when the cells were dim and the lights in the corridor were not yet lit, a heartbreaking conviction of the ugliness, the futility of life came over me so that I could not weep but only lie there in blank misery.

I lost all feeling of my own identity. I reflected on the desolation of poverty, of destitution, of sickness and sin. That I would be free after thirty days meant nothing to me. I would never be free again, never free when I knew that behind bars all over the world there were women and men, young girls and boys, suffering constraint, punishment, isolation and hardship for crimes of which all of us were guilty. The mother who had murdered her child, the drug addict—who were the mad and who the sane? Why were prostitutes prosecuted in some cases and in others respected and fawned on? People sold themselves for jobs, for the pay check, and if they only received a high enough price, they were honored. If their cheating, their theft, their lie, were of colossal proportions, if it were successful, they met with praise, not blame. Why were some caught, not others? Why were some termed criminals and others good businessmen? What was right and wrong? What was good and evil? I lay there in utter confusion and misery.

When I first wrote of these experiences I wrote even more strongly of my identification with those around me. I was that mother whose child had been raped and slain. I was the mother who had borne the monster who had done it. I was even that monster, feeling in my own breast every abomination. Is this exaggeration? There are not so many of us who have lain for six days and nights in darkness, cold and hunger, pondering in our heart the world and our part in it. If you live in great cities, if you are in constant contact with sin and suffering, if the daily papers print nothing but Greek tragedies, if you see on all sides people trying to find relief from the drab boredom of their job and family life, in sex and alcohol, then you become inured to the evil of the day, and it is rarely that such a realization of the horror of sin and human hate can come to you.

This workhouse we were in was one of the most modern prisons. It was built on the cottage plan and men and women worked in the fields or sat at machines in the factory and sewed. Yet here were also solitary confinement cells, more bleak and barbarous than I could have imagined such cells to be. There were stories told of prisoners being left in these cells for six months. Six months! The thirty days stretched out before me interminably. I would be utterly crushed by misery before I was released. Never would I recover from this wound, this ugly knowledge I had gained of what men were capable in their treatment of each other. It was one thing to be writing about these things, to have the theoretical knowledge of sweatshops and injustice and hunger, but it was quite another to experience it in one's own flesh. There were those stories too of a whipping post and of bloodhounds wandering through the grounds to terrorize the prisoners. These things had been sworn to by a former matron of the workhouse, and the superintendent did not deny them.

I had no sense as I lay there of the efficacy of what I was doing. I had instead a bitter awareness of the need of self-preservation, the need to escape, the need to endure somehow through the days of my imprisonment. I had an ugly sense of the futility of human effort, man's helpless misery, the triumph of might. Man's dignity was but a word and a lie. Evil triumphed. I was a petty creature, filled with self-deception, self-importance, unreal, false, and so, rightly scorned and punished. I was willing not only to say two and two were five, but to think it.

The incomplete and sullen silence of the place was broken by the far-off squealing of pigs at their evening meal, by the twitter of a sparrow just outside the ventilator, by an occasional shuffle from a cell along the corridor as someone turned on her straw mattress.

These suppressed sounds were a torture. But worst of all were the hurrying footsteps. They were never moderate or leisurely or happy or complacent. If I could only control the rush of expectancy, the frantic feeling, that they aroused in me. I always expected something to happen and then nothing ever did.

At night heavy dreams came to me. A few I could remember, and one of them made me tear myself from sleep, trembling and perspiring. I had been in a theater where a benefit performance was being given to a crowd of little children from a house of correction. The chattering and gleeful children filled the main floor and the balcony. No one tried to keep them quiet and it was an ominous leniency.

When the play began, a dread silence came on the young audience and there were whimperings of fear. The players wore frightful death masks and were crippled and gruesome in body. One little child gave a shriek as he leaned over the railing and then toppled over, falling to the main floor. His limp body hurtled down on the children below and my horror awakened me.

The cry seemed to ring out still and I could not bear to go back to sleep. Sometimes when I was about to fall asleep I felt my body swelling and swelling and nothing would dispel the feeling until I sat up in bed and pinched myself to keep awake. Sometimes I just lay through the long night and wept.

For five days the toast and warm milk were brought to the cell three times a day and three times a day it was taken away. If you drank all the hot water you could when you were let go to the washroom at the end of the corridor and then clamored all the rest of the day for hot water, you could get rid of the empty feeling. The hunger was not so bad—it was the dark and the cold.

I began asking for a Bible the second day I was imprisoned, and by the fourth day it was brought me. I read it with the sense of coming back to something of my childhood that I had lost. My heart swelled with joy and thankfulness for the Psalms. The man who sang these songs knew sorrow and expected joy.

When the Lord brought back the captivity of Sion we became like men comforted. Then was our mouth filled with gladness: and our tongue with joy. Then shall they say among the Gentiles: The Lord hath done great things for them. The Lord hath done great things for us: we are become joyful. Turn again our captivity, O Lord, as a stream in the south. They that sow in tears shall reap in joy. Going, they went and wept, casting their seeds. But coming, they shall come with joyfulness, carrying their sheaves.

If we had faith in what we were doing, making our protest against brutality and injustice, then we were indeed casting our seeds, and there was the promise of the harvest to come.

I clung to the words of comfort in the Bible and as long as the light held out, I read and pondered. Yet all the while I read, my pride was fighting on. I did not want to go to God in defeat and sorrow. I did not want to depend on Him. I was like the child that wants to walk by itself, I kept brushing away the hand that held me up. I tried to persuade myself that I was reading for literary enjoyment. But the words kept echoing in my heart. I prayed and did not know that I prayed.

The hunger strike lasted for ten days. After six days we were placed in hospital cells where there was light and warmth. My small room then was next to Peggy's, and the radiator which warmed my room ran through the wooden partition so that we could pass notes, written on toilet paper with a stub of pencil which Peggy somehow managed to keep when everything else was taken from us. On the other side one of the older women lay in silence all through the day. Twice a day orderlies came to the room. Holding her down on the bed, they forced tubes down her throat or nose and gave her egg and milk. It was unutterably horrible to hear her struggles, and the rest of us lay there in our cubicles tense with fear.

Peggy weakened on the eighth day, and took the milk toast which was brought in to us still. She urged me to keep her company, and I refused. "Don't be a fool," she whispered through the aperture by the radiator. "Take this crust then and suck on it. It's better than nothing."

I accepted this compromise, and she carefully tore off the crust of the bread and stretched it out to me. I was just able, thanks to her long fingers and my own, to reach it and draw it in. With what intense sensual enjoyment I lay there in my cot, taking that crust crumb by crumb. I did not feel guilty for breaking the strike in this way after eight days. All but two or three of the suffragists were holding fast and worrying the State Department, the President, the great newspaper public, besides the jail authorities. I upheld Peggy, my friend, by sharing her crust, for which I was deeply grateful, and I continued the protest we had undertaken. Cheating the prison authorities was quite in order, I reasoned.

On the tenth day the strike was broken by the announcement that all our demands would be granted, and that we would be transferred to the City Jail to which we had been sentenced. Our clothes were returned to us, our mail was given us and we were allowed the liberty of the corridors. Delicious meals were served, milk toast at first and then chicken, and the white-clad internes tried to provide us with books and magazines.

Within a few days we were taken in limousines into Washington. The air was invigorating, with the smell of snow; the woods still glowed in spots and the sun was warm.

In the Washington jail we chose our own cells and Peggy and I chose one on the top tier furthest from the matron's prying eyes. There was more air there, too. The high windows that stretched from the first to the third tier were kept open at the top by the request of the women, a request granted after previous skirmishes and window breaking. The first prisoners had been kept locked in their cells, but we were allowed freedom during the day to roam around the corridors from eight in the morning until eight at night. On the other side of the female quarters were the cells for colored prisoners, most of whom seemed to be doing some sort of work around the jail. There were three girls awaiting trial for murder and many who had been arrested in stabbings and general disorderly conduct while drinking. These prisoners kept up their chatter after eight o'clock and the matron kept puffing around the place trying to quell the giggling, singing and quarreling.

Before the doors were closed for the night, and after the work of the day was done, there were card games and dances in the corridors, some of the girls dancing and the others beating time and singing.

Saturday nights the six tubs at the end of the corridor—the authorities would not allow the suffragists to bathe because the tubs were used by the colored girls—were filled again and again and there was a steady tumult while the girls scrubbed and primped and arranged their hair for the next day. Sunday was the one day in the week when they caught a glimpse of man. There were two church services during the day and for both the two balconies on either side of the auditorium were filled. Hundreds joined in the hymns. The men and women were separated, but I saw sex and felt it at its crudest and was ashamed that I should be stirred by it.

I had no thought of religion these last days. I was very much in the world again, talking with others, reading and writing letters, and I no longer thought of the depths I had been in. To be so degraded was to be shamed and humbled, but I rejected the humiliation. I had seen myself too weak to stand alone, too weak to face the darkness of that punishment cell without crying out, and I was ashamed and again rejected religion that had helped me when I had been brought to my knees by my suffering.

FREELANCE

When I came back from Washington I worked wherever I could, living in one furnished room after another, moving from the lower East Side to the upper East Side and then down again to the lower West Side. It was a bitterly cold winter and the rooms I lived in were never adequately heated. We were still at war, and it was the time of heatless Mondays and meatless Tuesdays. There were times when it was pleasanter to spend the night with friends rather than face an ugly sordid room. The poverty of the East Side had been a cozy poverty, living as I had in the midst of a struggling family, compared to the poverty of the ordinary rooming house.

For a time I worked on the *Liberator*, the magazine which succeeded *The Masses* and was edited by Crystal Eastman, but the charm of my summer job on the older paper was gone. It was not the same, and I soon gave it up. It was more fun to hang around the Provincetown Playhouse where Eugene O'Neill and others of my friends had plays in rehearsal. After rehearsals, or after performances, the usual meeting place was the back room of a saloon on the corner of Fourth Street and Sixth Avenue, nicknamed Hell Hole by its customers. Here Eugene O'Neill, Terry Karlin, an old Irish anarchist who had known the Haymarket martyrs, and whom Gene afterward supported till his death, Hypolite Havel, who died a few months ago in the former anarchist colony at Stelton, New Jersey, Michael Gold, and others, were my constant companions. No one ever wanted to go to bed, and no one ever wished to be alone. It was on these cold bitter evenings that I first heard "The Hound of Heaven," in an atmosphere of drink and smoke. Gene could recite all of Francis Thompson's poem, and would sit there, black and dour, his head sunk as he intoned, "And now my heart is as a broken fount, wherein tear drippings stagnate." The idea of this pursuit by the Hound of Heaven fascinated me. The recurrence of it, the inevitableness of the outcome made me feel that sooner or later I would have to pause in the mad rush of living and remember my first beginning and my last end.

Many a morning after sitting all night in taverns or coming from balls at Webster Hall, I went to an early morning Mass at St. Joseph's Church on Sixth Avenue and knelt in the back of the church, not knowing what was going on at the altar, but warmed and comforted by the lights and silence, the kneeling people and the atmosphere of worship. People have so great a need to reverence, to worship, to adore; it is a psychological necessity of human nature that must be taken into account. We do not like to admit how people fail us. Even those most loved show their frailty and their weaknesses and no matter how we may *will* to see only the best in others, their strength rather than their weakness, we are all too conscious of our own failings and recognize them in others.

A friend who has no formal religion or belief said once to me that surely some such great cataclysm as the Fall must have taken place to explain the evil in the world. Original sin and the gravitational pull toward the animal in man were easy to understand, accepting this fundamental teaching. Certainly I felt again and again the need to go to church to kneel, to bow my head in prayer. It was a blind instinct, one might say, and I was not conscious of praying. But I went. I put myself there in the atmosphere of prayer—it was an act of the will.

It seems to me a long time that I led this wavering life, in my ignorance not knowing that we are of body, mind and soul, and that all our faculties can be brought into harmony. I felt strongly that the life of nature warred against the life of grace.

Then again the life of the flesh called to me as a good and wholesome life, regardless of man's laws, which I felt rebelliously were made for the repression of others. The strong could make their own law, live their own lives; in fact, they were beyond good and evil. What was good and what was evil? It is easy enough to stifle conscience for a time. The satisfied flesh has its own law.

How much time I wasted during those years—the long walks, the afternoons and evenings of talk and banter; and how much of the talk was about ideas, about the theory of revolution in which we were all interested! We took the revolution for granted. We watched its progress; we were thrilled by its victories. We read the accounts in the newspapers about Russia as we had read the accounts of strikes and labor conflicts before the war. We read Anderson-Nexo's *Pelle, the Conqueror*, the great proletarian novel. We became internationally minded. We lived in one world, and it was a world where dreams came true, where there was a possibility of the workers beginning to take over the means of production and starting to build that kind of society where each received according to his need and worked according to his ability. We never examined the fundamental principles of that revolution. We were not students of Marxism. There was the Rand School, a workers' school set up for adult education to popularize the works of Marx, Engels and Lenin. But we belonged to that school of youth which lived in the present, lived the life of the senses. Lenin was to excoriate that school in his famous letters to Rosa Luxemburg when he talked of bourgeois youth and its bourgeois morality. He spoke rightly. But it was not to be expected that all had his genius. His life followed the pattern of all great men—a single-mindedness, a purity of heart, a search for the new society for man.

Lenin left Samara, a farm which he attempted to work with hired labor and where he spent some two years of study after receiving his law degree from the university. After going to St. Petersburg, he met Krupskaya, a daughter of the lesser nobility who was giving her life to the poor. She lived in slums; she taught the proletariat at night and on Sundays, and helped establish workers' libraries and bookshops. Just as Tolstoi had used the royalties from his writings to get out penny editions of the classics, and so make contact with the peasants, so radical students used libraries to get into contact with the workers of Russia. Lenin was a student, the son of a school inspector, and had never had contact with the peasants and workers. What he learned about them on his farm at Samara had led him to turn to industrial workers as the leaders of the coming revolution. Krupskaya was his link with the workers, whom he studied with the view of "raising up leaders of workers who themselves were workers."

We young people did not know these things then. We probably would have scorned Krupskaya and her cultural activities. We were arrogant and impatient of study and felt we were carried along on a wave of success.

Of course the time came when Lenin modified his ideas about the dictatorship of the proletariat, the great mass of dispossessed industrial workers. It was to be a dictatorship of the proletariat in name only; it was to become a dictatorship by the elite few, by the members of the party.

"The people," according to Romano Guardini, "is the primary association of those human beings who by race, country, and historical antecedents share the same life and destiny. . . . The people is mankind in its radical comprehensiveness. And a man is of the people if he embraces, so to speak, the whole within himself."

On the one hand, as young people we were attracted to the

people, to the poor, and we lived in slums and suffered in order to do the work we chose. Ours was the natural virtue of voluntary poverty. We helped others, it is true, but we did not deprive ourselves in order to help others. We had no philosophy of poverty.

And what was this love of our fellows? Certainly we loved them in the mass; we were moved by the account of their sufferings, and by what we saw of their sufferings, and our hearts burned with the desire for justice and were revolted at the idea of a doled-out charity. The word charity had become something to gag over, something to shudder at. The true meaning of the word we did not know.

Ivan, in *The Brothers Karamazov*, protested that it was quite impossible to love man as he was, with his cruel instincts, his lust for power, his greed, his instincts of self-preservation. It was not a natural thing to think in terms of laying down one's life for one's fellows. In the same book however, Father Zossima spoke glowingly of that love for God which resulted in a love for one's brother. The story of his conversion to love is moving, and that book, with its picture of religion, had a lot to do with my later life.

The trial of the editors of *The Masses* was held that winter and I was subpoenaed as a witness for the state. Morris Hillquit, the Socialist attorney whom I admired as a great and generous man, defended them and we worked together over the testimony. I was a bad witness for the state and a good one for the defense.

Then suddenly a succession of incidents and the tragic aspect of life in general began to overwhelm me and I could no longer endure the life I was leading. Some friends of my family were nurses; it was wartime, and although I was pacifist in my views— pacifist in what I considered an imperialist war though not pacifist as a revolutionist—I decided that nursing the sick was not contrary to my principles. So many nurses had joined the Red Cross and had gone abroad with the armed forces that there was a great need at home. So I signed on as a probationer in King's County Hospital, in Brooklyn.

KING'S COUNTY

I hate being Utopian and trying to escape from reality [I wrote to a friend at that time]. Now that we are in the thick of war and there is so much work to be done, I might as well try to do some of it instead of sitting around playing at writing. And what is my writing now but book reviews, editing, toying with a novel of social significance? What good am I doing my fellow men? They are sick and there are not enough nurses to care for them. I refuse to admit that I am helping the war effort in going into training. My friends are saying that I am releasing nurses to go to the front, but they are all trying to enlist anyway, the glamor of war has gotten them. It's the poor that are suffering. I've got to do something.

From the beginning I enjoyed the work. In 1918 nursing was a simpler thing than it is today. We went on the ward at seven in the morning and our work day lasted twelve hours. For two hours in the afternoon we were off duty, not to rest, but to attend lectures on materia medica, physiology or anatomy. For the first three months we were probationers and wore pink uniforms with big white aprons. At the end of three months we passed to blue and white striped dresses with stiff white collars and a white starched cap, of which we were most proud. For three years until graduation this was the uniform, and then we wore white.

There was strict etiquette. You stood when a head nurse entered the ward. You stood aside for your seniors to pass through a door first. You were taught an almost military deference and respect for the superior officer, or for the doctor. From the first, in addition to bed-making and care of the ward, we were given nursing to do, straight nursing, which delights every woman's heart. We had to keep charts, but there was a minimum of paper work. We took temperatures and pulses, gave medicine, baths, alcohol rubs, distributed trays, gave hypodermics, enemas and douches. We tried to make the patients comfortable, and changed sheets daily. Never have I seen such a profligate use of bed linens, eggnogs and medicines as during that year at King's County

Hospital. My experience there reassured me as to the care one received from the city. It was a care given to citizens, not to paupers. And it was all free. Of course, we had nothing to do with the social service department so saw nothing of the interviewing of the poor.

My first patient was an old Canadian woman, ninety-four years old. Granny objected to being bathed, saying that she had bathed the day before and at her time of life she did not see why she had to be pestered with soap and water the way she was. Argument was useless, so she began to fight with the nurses, clawing at them and screaming and sitting in the middle of her bed like a whimpering monkey.

"Let us help you," one of the other nurses said soothingly. "Can't you see that we want to take care of you because we love you?"

"Love be damned," the little old lady cried, "I want my wig." And she began to cry and whimper again. She sat there perched on the end of her thin spine, her eyes blazing black and clear. Her arms were clasped about her bare and scrawny knees. Around a large bare spot on her head she had a thin fringe of hair which stood up like a field of ferns.

"She has been crying for her wig since she came in," the other nurse said. "We let her have her teeth, but she wants her wig. I don't see why they don't let her have it."

It was Miss Adams who was my companion in the work. She was Catholic and stood out at once in my mind. She made me think of Mrs. Barrett and Mary Harrington. She had sympathy and understanding and realized that the little old lady needed more than soap and water and clean bed linen. She needed more than to be loved. She wanted to be respected as a person, and for that she needed to have her wishes respected. She needed such appurtenances as her wig. I remember we compromised with a cap and so pleased her.

There were two women dying in the ward, a woman of fifty and a girl of twenty-two. Mary Windsor was slowly fading from the whiteness of the ward around her into a gray shadow on the long slim bed. She had a grown son who came to visit her every evening when the wards were twilit and the evening toilets were completed. He brought bunches of flowers which were fragrant and colorful, and every time I passed the bed, a thrill shook me, life and death were so close there. Mrs. Windsor never spoke but lay motionless, looking out of wide gray eyes, looking at the death she saw so plainly, with a dull wonder.

Irma was pathetically young. Her finely shaped mouth was always contorted with pain and there was a fierce protesting light in her eyes. The lines that agony had drawn in the ivory skin were like those of passion. She might have been clutching a lover in a last embrace, knowing that when he rose from the bed he would go out and close the door forever. There was the smell of death around her, I kept thinking, and there was no one to bring her flowers to deaden it.

For a while I worked on the fracture ward where there were old ladies with fractures of the hip and leg. The most youthful of them were over sixty years. They approached the elderly stage when they were eighty and when they had passed ninety-five it was admitted they were old. It seemed strange at first to call them by their Christian names, but it was the custom of the hospital and I soon became used to it.

This ward broke me, the work was so hard. There was one bearded woman with no breasts and the nurses spoke of her furtively as being a freak. She was ugly in temper, threw things at the nurses, and was filthy in her habits so that she constantly needed to be cleaned. She tried to spit at the nurses and to dirty their clean uniforms. It was an ugly trial to care for her. I had to grit my teeth and hold my breath while I washed her, to control my aversion.

Working on this ward was the hardest part of my hospital career. One afternoon when I had been cleaning up filth all day, and the perverse patient had again thrown her bedpan out on the floor dirtying my shoes and stockings, I left the ward in tears and sat in the washroom weeping uncontrollably at the ugliness and misery of life. I could not stop crying long enough to tell Miss Adams, so that my patients would not be left alone, but did the unforgivable thing and ran away, going to my room where I continued to cry. I shall always remember with what gentleness the assistant superintendent of nurses came and talked to me about the responsibilities of the nurse and the dignity of her profession and the "sacrament of duty." She might not have used those words, but that was the tenor of her talk and I have never forgotten it. She took me off the difficult ward for the time, transferring me to medical where there were fifty patients with influenza. This was the time of the "flu" epidemic and the wards were filled and the halls too. Many of the nurses became ill and we were very short-handed. Every night before going off duty there were bodies to be wrapped in sheets and wheeled away to the morgue. When we came on duty in the morning, the night nurse was performing the same grim task.

For a time I was on the men's medical ward and Miss Adams and I were alone all day from seven until seven, excepting time for meals. We were so short-handed that the head nurse had to take the ward on the floor above and could only occasionally run down to advise us.

There was one head nurse, a Swede, who was a martinet. She used to come and look over our wards with a grimly critical eye, watching for carelessness, for unevenness in the lining up of the beds, for a spread awry, for a cluttered bedside table. It was hard not to be careless at this time when every day ten or twelve new patients were carried in or walked staggeringly only to fall unconscious as soon as their clothes were taken from them.

According to this nurse, each ward in the hospital should be in order by ten o'clock every morning. In order to get the work under way Miss Adams and I went without our breakfasts in the nurses' dining room and came on the ward at sixy-thirty. There we could take a hasty cup of coffee and count on a mid-morning snack after the dreaded visit of the head nurse was over. There were a few up-patients who helped us and without them we would have had a harder time. I remember Red Reynolds, who had been a bartender in Coney Island, and who now was in charge of the diet kitchen. He used to give us scrambled eggs, toast and coffee every morning and helped us make eggnogs for the patients on the ward.

When we went on duty in the morning, the up-patients were already at work, sweeping, polishing, getting the linen in order and helping other weaker patients into their wheel chairs. These were trundled out into the solarium, where they sat all day, chewing tobacco and gossiping of wine, women and war and occasionally of God. Sometimes you could hear the cracked voice of a sailor singing a chanty or the booming voice of an old German whose bones were turning to stone singing a hymn.

My first task was to pour out the medicine for a hundred patients, a task demanding concentration and a steady hand. When I first started pouring, I continued it in my dreams every night until I was able to associate every patient with the medicine which he took. For instance whenever I saw Smith, my brain immediately flashed

> Arom. Spt. Am. Dr. 1
> Donov. Sol. M. 10
> Pot. Iod. Gr. 15
> Stokes M. Dr. 1

There were almost as many mixtures for each patient, and it was a job which took two hours.

Nursing was like newspaper work. It was impossible to suffer long over the tragedies which took place every day. One was too close to them to have perspective. They happened too continuously. They weighed on you, gave you a still and subdued feeling, but the very fact that you were continually busy left you no time to brood.

There was a brightness of the sun pouring in on the ward and over the white spreads and the feeling of spring in the air. Out in the grounds on warm days the patients from the old people's homes sat together, men and women, and it was tragic to think that some of them were married and could not spend their last days together. They smoked, many of the women, and had their pipes and tobacco just like the men, but in that year it was still a rare thing for a woman to be seen smoking a cigarette and the nurses were not permitted to smoke. I used to snatch a surreptitious smoke by taking a roundabout walk behind the powerhouse and laundries going to and from the nurses' home. What discipline I submitted to because I loved the work!

It was very restful there in the grounds around the hospital buildings, and sometimes I just sat for a brief rest and watched the sparrows and starlings looking for crumbs from the apron pockets of the old women. An occasional pigeon strutted up and down and a large brindle cat slunk under the benches with her eye on the birds. The trees were flecked with the dapple of autumn leaves.

There was another beauty which came into my life at that time. Every Sunday morning Miss Adams went to early Mass and I dragged myself out of my heavy sleep and went with her. The chapel was on the grounds and it was packed even at that early hour. One day, I told myself as I knelt there, I would have to stop to think, to question my own position: "What is man, that Thou art mindful of him, O Lord?" What were we here for, what were we doing, what was the meaning of our lives?

One thing I was sure of, and that was that these fellow workers and I were performing an act of worship. I felt that it was necessary for man to worship, that he was most truly himself when engaged in that act.

A TIME OF SEARCHING

I worked at the hospital for a year, or until after the influenza epidemic was over. Then a longing to write, to be pursuing the career of journalist which I had chosen for myself, swept over me so that even though I loved the work in the hospital, I felt that it was a second choice, and not my vocation. My work was to write and there was no time for that where I was. I was rebelling too against the discipline, long hours, and steady hard work. The war was over, and we had been working so hard that we scarcely knew it. We read about Armistice Day; we did not experience it. We only knew that the whistles blowing on the false Armistice Day frightened some of the patients into hysterics so that on the true Armistice Day there was not the clamor in that peaceful section of Brooklyn as on the first. We were far from Times Square, where the crowds of New York and the countries around are wont to celebrate. We were too utterly exhausted with the care of the sick and dying to dissipate our energies in rejoicing.

But by January my rebellion began to set in. I went to the superintendent's office and announced to her that I was leaving. I can remember her cold scorn. She felt that I could not take it. I did not know whether her idea of a supervisor's duties meant going through the papers of the student nurses, but I did know that she was very conscious of the fact that I was aspiring to be a writer. Probably I left manuscripts around. Perhaps I had shown printed copies of my reviews. At any rate she flung in my teeth my ambitions and told me sneeringly that I had always felt myself too good for the work, that it was too much for me. She hurt me cruelly and it took the comforting of the assistant, who had been so kind to me before, to help me over the difficult task of leaving. I was convinced that I must go and I felt too that I had been a good and sympathetic nurse. I knew that I loved the work, and that if I had not had the irresistible urge to write, I would have clung to the profession of nursing as the most noble work women could aspire to.

In trying to write about the next few years of my life I find that there is little to say. I have never intended to write an autobiography. I have always wanted instead to tell of things that brought me to God and that reminded me of God. I cannot write too intimately of the next few years, because I do not want to write about other people with whom I was intimately associated. I do not want to write in detail about a trip to Europe. In London I walked and took bus rides and explored and thought of De Quincey and Dickens. In Paris it was the same, but there Balzac and De Maupassant and Victor Hugo were my companions. Italy I loved; the six months I spent in Capri meant that forever after, the smell of Italian cooking, the sound of buzzing flies, the loud strong voices of my Italian neighbors, the taste of spaghetti and polenta and the sour red wine brought me back to the months I spent beside the Mediterranean, or wandering around the streets of Naples, or driving on sightseeing trips behind the shabby horses with their voluble drivers. They were always considerate of their horses (even to the point of fanning them and wiping their faces, and getting out to walk as we climbed the hills) and so inconsiderate of their wives, who carried heavy burdens and worked long hours and were always gracious, with a dignity and beauty far surpassing that of any other women I have ever seen.

The time I spent there made me love later on the writings of Ignazio Silone and when I read Levi's *Christ Stopped at Eboli*, I felt that I too had seen some of what he wrote about. I could understand a little of that poverty I had seen, but I could see also the beauty of it too, a beauty which was lacking in the destitution of our own southern rural slums.

I spent a year writing and I cared little about the political situation, though it was a time when fascism was rising in Italy. But I was living through a time of my own personal joy and heartbreak and what happened in the world had little effect on me.

When I returned to the United States I went to Chicago and threw myself back into the life I had known there. I lived in a slum on Ontario Street in a huge room which I shared with a young student and for which I paid twenty-five dollars a month. Some artist friends lived downstairs and I had made other friends in the city on a previous short visit. It was easy to find work at that time. I worked at Montgomery Ward's in a clerical capacity; another time I took work as a copyholder to a proofreader; there was a job in the public library as a helper at fifteen dollars a week and another as a cashier in a restaurant. For a time I earned extra money posing for art classes. I worked for the City News Bureau and became acquainted with the courts of the city: the children's court, the court of domestic relations, the morals court. I met other reporters, among them Ben Hecht and Charlie Mac-Arthur, all of whom were aspiring to write the great play, the great novel.

One evening I was sitting with some radical friends in a Chinese restaurant on the South Side. In the midst of our dinner, I noticed a black-bearded man on the other side of the room who kept looking at me persistently. His gaze was so often on me that I became conscious of him and began in my turn to look at him fixedly, whereupon he put his finger to his lips and got up with what seemed exaggerated caution and left the restaurant.

I thought little of this seemingly ridiculous incident but a few days later a knock came at my door and on opening it there was the black-bearded man whom I had encountered in the restaurant. Only this time, instead of being furtive, he was radiant, his eyes beaming, his wide mouth open in a grin which made him seem very young in spite of his heavy beard.

"Don't you recognize me," he shouted exuberantly, and when I confessed that I did not he revealed himself as one of the Columbia College students with whom I had gone to Washington, for whom I had worked as secretary of the Anti-Conscription League.

He was using, he said, the name of Gomez, since he had fled to Mexico to avoid being conscripted. There the lovely young student who had become his wife had left him with an artist for a walking trip through Spain and he had gone to Russia to attend the Third International. He had returned to Mexico with a young Russian woman and now had made his way to Chicago, there to be engaged in underground Party business.

It made me happy to see him, and from then on we spent many Sundays together at workers' picnics on the outskirts of Chicago and at meetings. I did not know what was going on but I was happy to be with friends again who were active in the work of changing the world. In New York the work had all been that of the journalist, making public opinion, bringing things out into the light of day. Now it was another story. Everything was under cover. A newspaper was being founded, *The Liberator* was being started again as a Communist monthly, a continuation of the old *Masses*, with Robert Minor as its editor.

Whenever I think of Minor, the cartoonist, I think of the story of the desert fathers and the cook who insisted on leaving his job to make baskets like the rest of the brethren. He left a great talent buried and unused in order to be an editor and a journalist.

For a short while I worked as his secretary but I knew nothing of what was going on in the Party at that time. I only knew that when I took dictation from Bob, he kept telling his friends that he was being followed. Pacing up and down the room, glancing out of the window he would say, "At this moment of writing there is a man standing in the doorway across the street who has been shadowing me for the past week." This was repeated in each letter.

What I liked best of all were the workers' meetings, and those Sunday afternoon picnics which were like those I saw in Lincoln Park when I used to take my baby brother there. It was good to get out of the city to the outlying parks, to listen to the playing and singing of the foreign-language groups and to see their national costumes and watch their dancing. There were all nationalities in Chicago and there were Socialist groups in every nationality. They had come to the United States to better their condition, and they became the exploited in sweatshops, in the stockyards. They lived in dilapidated frame houses; they were unorganized, with little chance of becoming owners and escaping from their proletarian position. I could understand no other language than my own and there were Slovaks, Poles, Bohemians, Croatians, Ukrainians and Germans, Lithuanians and Esthonians. The thing I felt strongly was that there were changes taking place in the world. This was not just a social gathering, people of one nationality and background coming together for recreation. They were coming to listen to long and tiresome speeches. They were part of a movement, a slow upheaval. Among them was a stirring and a groping and they were beginning to feel within themselves a power and a possibility.

"There can be no revolution without a theory of revolution," Lenin said. They were listening to the theory of revolution. They were pondering their dignity as men, their responsibilities, their hunger for freedom as well as for bread.

But I was to see another side of Chicago, not a pleasant side, before I left it again. I had a strange and unforgettable experience, a shocking experience, but one which I would not have done without. I was arrested again, and this time under quite different circumstances from those in Washington some years before. Then I had been part of an organized body of women of all ages and stations in life. There had been the wife of the president of the board of trustees of Bellevue Hospital. There had been society women of Philadelphia, Baltimore and Boston. There had been schoolteachers, writers, ardent champions of feminism, women who had worked in the cause in England as well as in the United States. There had been the solidarity of the group. Now I was to have a solitary taste of the injustice, or the ugliness of men's justice, which set me more squarely on the side of the revolution.

The Industrial Workers of the World had headquarters on the West Side, on Madison Street, the Skid Row of Chicago. There were a printing press and offices and among many cheap rooming houses, also a "flop house" where visiting Wobblies stayed. I had been there a few times.

During the past year I had come to know intimately a rough young woman who had been a shoplifter and a drug addict but had cured herself after many years of addiction. She had spent years in reformatories and was probably about thirty at the time. She had fallen in love with a newspaperman who had introduced her to our group and she had been our constant companion on evening parties for some months. In a fit of depression she swallowed some bichloride of mercury tablets and was taken to the county hospital. Within a few days she recovered enough to sign herself out of the hospital. The tie between us was that we were in love with the same man, and when she telephoned me and asked me to come over to the Wobbly headquarters to see her and to bring her something to eat and to wear, I went at once. The doctors had not been willing for her to leave the hospital but she had insisted. When I saw how sick she still was I decided to spend the night there in the room which the I.W.W.'s had given her. It was not a place for women though it was clean and well cared for. They let her stay because they did not know what else to do with her. She knew some of the printers and they realized that she was sick and needed help. I do not believe they knew I was there, since I came during the evening.

It was the time of the "Palmer Red Raids" and that night detectives raided the I.W.W. hotel as a disorderly house and arrested all they found there. Many of the men who were old radicals and had gone through persecution on the West Coast made their escape out of fire escapes and over roofs, but Mae and I, not knowing what was happening, were awakened by a pounding on the door and the voice of the police.

Perhaps it was not a new thing to Mae, but it was an unutterably horrifying experience for me. I had opened the door in fear and trembling and had been forced to dress practically in the presence of two detectives, leering. With Mae snarling and cursing, we were then escorted down to the street corner together with several men and forced to stand there waiting for a police wagon which had been summoned. We were being arrested as inmates of a disorderly house. Fortunately I did not realize this until later, so I was able to endure the shame and humiliation of standing there at midnight on the street corner under the gaze of whatever idlers were around at that time of night.

Not many years ago there was a theater advertisement which appeared on billboards on elevated and subway platforms all through New York. It showed a girl of the streets standing under a lamp post in a revealing dress, the subdued light of the street lamp and the posture as well as the dress making her look peculiarly naked. We have all had dreams of not being properly clothed, and here was this experience which contained in it all the horror of that dream. And when I saw these billboard pictures, they reminded me forcefully of that horrible night when I stood with Mae, who had been a prostitute, under those too glaring street lights and waited for the patrol wagon.

I do not like even to write about this now, but I must tell of the experience, and I am glad indeed that I had it. It was part of the experience of thousands who had worked for labor—hotel workers, miners, the textile workers—throughout the country. I had walked on picket lines in cities with restaurant workers, with garment workers; I had felt that peculiar vulnerability that the picketer feels, who is set apart by his protest from the rest of mankind. I had felt what it was to be a fool for the cause of justice, tilting at windmills like any Don Quixote. Every strike was an unjust strike according to the newspapers, and every strike ended in failure to achieve the demands of the workers according to these same papers. The reader never took into account the slow and steady gains, wrung reluctantly from the employer by virtue of every one of these strikes, the slow advance through countless failure. One always felt that sense of being made to appear in the wrong when on a picket line. This is the most I had suffered in the cause of labor.

In Washington I had felt that suffering for all who had been in prison, but there had also been the glow at the beginning of working with others, at being part of a noble cause. I may have lost that when I was actually confined to a cell, but it was regained after our hunger strike; there was never any sense of shame attached to the experience, to deepen it and embitter it.

But this arrest in Chicago was different. I was a victim, yes, of the red hysteria at the time, but I was also a victim of my own imprudence, of my own carelessness of convention. On the one hand there were the loose moral standards of the radicals, those same standards condemned by Lenin. And on the other there was the world's judgment of those same moral standards. It was the I.W.W. house which was being raided, but we as women had no right to be in that house. Our presence there meant only one thing to the men who arrested us, and when we were booked for the morals court, they had the law on their side, and we had by our very presence there given that place the reputation of being a disorderly house.

It was as ugly an experience as I ever wish to pass through, and a useful one. I do not think that ever again, no matter of what I am accused, can I suffer more than I did then of shame and regret, and self-contempt. Not only because I had been caught, found out, branded, publicly humiliated, but because of my own consciousness that I deserved it.

When Eugene Debs wrote, as he did in his innocence, that as long as there were men in prison he was one with them, they were noble words and went down in history. But I have always felt that he could never have suffered, noble and gentle man that he was, that same shame and self-contempt that I felt, and that I felt in common with the prisoners with whom I was confined.

We were driven first of all through the dark and silent streets of the city to the West Chicago Avenue police station. The cell into which we were thrown had bars in front through which we could look out into the common room and toward the desk of the matron, whose name was Day. We were questioned, listed, and booked to appear two days later. We were searched and deprived of everything we had in our pockets and purses, for fear that we might have drugs. But later we were permitted to buy cigarettes and food. I gave a false name and always had to be spoken to twice before I recognized it. The next day we were photographed and fingerprinted and brought back to the cell again. That cell was large and contained six beds, one of which was turned upside down on the floor, the herculean feat of some previous inmate suffering from lack of drugs or liquor. The room was foul. The beds had mattresses, but no sheets or pillow slips. It was summer so there was no need for blankets. Fortunately, open windows gave enough light and air. On one side was a niche in which there was a toilet, unscreened by any door. There was one wash basin.

Somehow I slept soundly that first night and escaped from my misery. Mae slept too—it was no new experience for her. She joked with the matron and the police officers and was solicitous for me. "Keep your chin up," she kept comforting me. "Don't take it too hard." I had thought I was hiding my feelings, was maintaining my composure, but she saw through me. I was twenty-two, a child to her thirty-two years.

All the next day groups of girls were brought in, because in addition to the red raids there was a series of vice raids going on around Twenty-second Street. There were three groups of five or six each who were put in our cell, which was supposed to be for six. These girls, all under thirty years old, I judged, carefully took off their dresses and asked for hangers so that they would not be mussed when they had to appear in court. They went around for the rest of the day in their slips. Some of them wore only shorts and bras and cavorted gaily around the cells like a group of chorus girls. They did not hesitate to dance to the front of the cell whenever there was another arrested person brought in and to call out to the police in uniform as well as to the detectives. They were gay and jaunty to the authorities, jeering at them contemptuously, but they were kindly and sympathetic to me. They judged my silence to be despair, and tried to tell me that there was always a first time, not to worry, that everything passed, that life had far worse things to offer than an occasional arrest and fine. They neither realized nor would they have believed in our innocence and there was little use in talking about it.

We were given nothing to eat all that day that we did not pay for. For a cup of coffee and a bun that morning we had to pay a dollar. For a package of cigarettes we had to pay another dollar. To get a sandwich at noon the charge was another dollar. I had nothing left in my purse to pay for supper, and the girls who were our companions insisted on treating us to sandwiches and coffee again. They also called for a few decks of cards and whiled away the day and the long night in playing. They were used to these emergencies. They seemed not at all shocked at the charges made for food, nor for the condition of the cell.

"You don't know the worst of it," they scoffed at my naïveté. "One of the matrons here runs a house of her own and asks us to come over and help her on Saturday nights."

During the day two other girls were brought in, one of them a quiet blonde who looked like Greta Garbo in *Anna Christie*. The other was an elderly woman, an alcoholic who had been caught with a man in the park. The girls all jeered at her cruelly, taunting her with "giving it away," knowing that she sold herself for a drink. "All cats are gray in the dark," they sneered. "Men don't care what they get." "Just a little human warmth," Mae murmured.

Some lost children were brought in and the girls modified their language and put on their clothes. One little girl had been sent to the store to buy groceries and had spent the money on a red purse. She had been afraid to go home and had lost herself. A policeman brought her to the station house to wait until her relatives could be fetched. She cried at the thought of the penalty for her theft until the girls comforted her and put some money in her purse. One of them held her in her arms and sang to her and told her stories. Later in the day, when a hard-faced aunt had come for the child, she told of her own two children, whom she was supporting with relatives.

All the evening before we were taken to court, the girls prepared me for what would happen. We would be taken to a doctor's office where we would be examined for venereal diseases. Then, if we did not give bond in the court, we would be sent for thirty days to Lawndale Hospital as a period of quarantine until we were brought to trial again. So far we had been offered no opportunity to call a lawyer or a friend, and we were certainly judged as guilty before we were tried.

Late at night the lights were put out and the talking ceased but how anyone was expected to sleep I do not know. Some of the girls took the beds—Mae and I were allotted one as having prior right, having been there first. The others doubled up as best they could, three in a bed, some on the floor. All during the rest of the night, they got up quietly one by one, made their toilets, and by the time the long early morning hours were passed, we were ready to be taken to the court at nine.

All of us were bundled into the patrol wagon again, together with some bloody prisoners chained together by handcuffs, with whom we shared our last cigarettes. Out in front of the county building, I was amazed and happy beyond measure to see Manny Gomez passing. When he recognized me he rushed over, half laughing as though to say, "Where will I see you next?" and promised he would get in touch with my friends and with a lawyer.

I was so happy, so reassured, that from then on the ordeal did not seem so dreadful. I went through the routine examination with the other prisoners. I was held in the room in back of the court for what seemed hours; then after the rest had all been taken care of by bail and had made their way gaily from the court, Mae and I, having neither lawyer nor as yet bondsman, were sent not to Lawndale as we dreaded, but to the city jail near where I had been living. I do not remember the name of the street, but I had passed it often, and had often seen people standing on the curb on the opposite side of the street, gesturing up at the barred windows, through a second row of bars to the tiers which contained the cells of friends. One could almost visit in this way.

But the women's section did not open on the street. Here were new indignities awaiting us. I did not want to be spared one of them. It was a valid experience, I felt, and I was sharing, as I never had before, the life of the poorest of the poor, the guilty, the dispossessed.

We were searched for drugs. We were stripped naked. We were given prison clothes and put in cells. The routine was to keep us locked in the cells, then leave us free to roam the corridors in alternate periods of several hours each. In the next cell to me there was a drug addict who beat her head against the bars or against the metal walls of her cell and howled like a wild animal. I have never heard such anguish, such unspeakable suffering. No woman in childbirth, no cancer patient, no one in the long year I had spent in King's County Hospital had revealed suffering like this. I pressed my hands to my ears, and covered my head with my pillow to try to muffle the sounds. It was most harrowing to think that this pain, this torture, was in a way self-inflicted, with full knowledge of the torture involved. The madness, the perverseness of this seeking for pleasure that was bound to be accompanied by such mortal agony was hard to understand. To see human beings racked, by their own will, made one feel the depth of the disorder of the world.

I felt the sadness of sin, the unspeakable dreariness of sin from the first petty little self-indulgence to this colossal desire which howled through the metal walls! And yet I do not think I thought of these things as I thought of God while in the solitary confinement cell at Occoquan. I just suffered desperately and desired to be freed from my suffering, with a most urgent and selfish passion. The instinct for self-preservation made me forget everything but a frantic desire for freedom, to get away from these depths into which I had fallen.

I could get away, but what of the others? I could get away, paying no penalty, because of my friends, my background, my education, my privilege. I suffered but was not part of it. I put it from me. It was too much for me.

I think that for a long time one is stunned by such experiences. They seem to be quickly forgotten, but they leave a scar that is never removed.

This particular experience lasted only a few days. Manny Gomez arranged our release by getting a lawyer, and the case was afterward dismissed.

What else is there that I must remember about Chicago? There is the winter I spent in a little apartment on the North Side where there was a furnished room which I shared with a French Canadian milliner who used to do most of her work at home. I was ill that winter, and unhappily in love. I had a job on the City News Bureau and tried to work, but twice I had to leave my work to go home and spend a few days in bed. I had much time to brood and ponder over my life, and in spite of an almost desperate unhappiness at the time, I now look back on that period as one of strange happiness too. Our apartment was in a Catholic household, a most ordinary one. There was an Irish mother and a German father, who was a butcher. They did not get on well with each other and there were long periods when they did not speak. On these occasions when I was home, they let me eat with them in the kitchen. They had one daughter, Bee, still at home. She worked for the streetcar company and spent some of her wages each Saturday night for her hope chest. She had a young man who came to see her Wednesdays and Saturdays and they spent long quiet hours in the stiff cold front room. They went to Mass together every Sunday and when there was a mission at the parish church, or novena, they made that together. I became acquainted with Catholic terminology, which at first seemed strange and even illiterate. "To make a mission, to pray for someone's intention—" what kind of jargon was this?

After her young man had gone home, Bee used to come in and sit with Blanche and me and they talked of their moral problems. Bee worried about premarital intimacy and the depths of her feelings. Blanche suffered because she was in love with a Mason and was forbidden by the Church law to marry him. She too resolutely prepared her hope chest just the same, but she prayed long and fervently on her knees, every night and morning and wept sometimes very quietly when she thought I was asleep.

I too had difficulties, heartaches, questionings, as I lay there, feeling very much alone in the world, lost, set apart, without help from the living or the dead. Bee and Blanche had their God whom they worshiped, they had their saints to pray to, I thought resentfully. I had nothing.

I wondered why they never made any attempts to interest me in their faith. I felt that Catholicism was something rich and real and fascinating, but I felt outside, and though I went with them to the mission, it never occurred to them that I might want to talk to a priest. Of course they knew that my standards were not theirs, that I belonged to radical groups who had a different code of morals, who did not believe in God or if they did, felt no necessity for worship in an organized Church. Yet, knowing all this, they accepted me, on the grounds I suppose of our common humanity. We were three girls together, with our problems of life and love, of men and children and a home, of what we wanted and what we were afraid we would never have. Bee was the nearest to what she wanted and she was radiantly happy, working and saving to furnish her nest. Of course she would not work after marriage, but begin to prepare for her children. The sight of her mother and father and their unhappiness with each other did not bother her at all, as far as I could see. The love of each generation as it came was something new and it was impossible to believe that it could ever end.

Could it be true, all that kindness and delicacy with which they treated me that winter? Or was it that I did not see their distrust, their animosity to an outsider, their judgment of a woman who did wrong and broke the moral code they accepted? Perhaps they did gossip about me behind my back, but their behavior to me was ever kind and good to my face. I have long since come to believe that people never mean half of what they say, and that it is best to disregard their talk and judge only their actions.

They were kind to me. I saw them wrestling with moral problems, with the principles by which they lived, and this made them noble in my eyes. I saw them pray, and the public prayer in the church and Blanche's kneeling down by the table on which was spread out her hats and trimmings did something to me which I could not forget. As with the sight of Mrs. Barrett kneeling beside her bed, this posture, this gesture, convinced me that worship, adoration, thanksgiving, supplication—these were the noblest acts of which men were capable in this life.

Then there were the books I read. That winter I came upon Huysmans in the home of my friend Sam Putnam, who was working on a newspaper then. I read *En Route, The Oblate, The Cathedral,* and it was these books which made me feel that I too could be at home in the Catholic Church, without becoming a Catholic. They acquainted me with what went on there. A friend of mine once said that it was the style to be a Catholic in France, nowadays, but it was not the style to be one in America. It was the Irish of New England, the Italians, the Hungarians, the Lithuanians, the Poles, it was the great mass of the poor, the workers, who were the Catholics in this country, and this fact in itself drew me to the Church.

I felt the age, the antiquity of the Mass, and here to find in Huysmans detailed instructions in regard to rubrics, all the complicated ritual, was a great joy to me, so that I went more often to the Cathedral.

A man with whom I had been deeply in love for several years was a lover of Pascal, so I became acquainted with his *Pensées,* which I did not understand but which stirred me. This same friend was a reader of Dostoevski, and, whereas I had read him as a matter of routine, because I loved the Russians, now I read him with an understanding of men and suffering. This same man hated James Joyce, the flavor of whose books fascinated me; once when we were riding on a North Avenue elevated, and I was speaking of Joyce to him, he wrested the book which happened to be *Portrait of the Artist as a Young Man* from my hands and threw it out the window of the train.

And always there was the New Testament. I could not hear of Sonya's reading the gospel to Raskolnikov in *Crime and Punishment* without turning to it myself with love. I could not read Ippolyte's rejection of his ebbing life and defiance of God in *The Idiot* without being filled with an immense sense of gratitude to God for life and a desire to make some return.

The first rosary I ever had was given me by a friend of my disorderly life, who afterward became a Communist and was active in work for Loyalist Spain. Tired of my life in Chicago, I went with her to New Orleans to have a change and to work there for a time. I had a book finished and accepted by a publisher and I was at loose ends, waiting to see what would happen to it, whether I would get enough to live on from it so as not to have to think of a job for a while. I wanted to go on writing.

It was easy for me to find work in New Orleans. I wrote a few feature articles and then was given a steady job on the *New Orleans Item*. I got it, of course, only at the usual price of the capitalist paper, of writing sensational articles. My first assignment was to work as a taxi dancer in a cheap dance hall on Canal Street and write a series about the lives of the girls.

I was glad I had my friend Mary with me. She was a big golden-haired, pink-cheeked girl with an irresistible sense of humor and a huge appetite for a "good time." We had taken a large room with a balcony in the French Quarter, on St. Peter Street, near the Cathedral which faced Jackson Square. There was a kitchenette and a gas meter into which we put quarters. The gas was apt to run out just when we had spent our last cent on a rabbit stew which took hours to boil. Rabbit stew, rice and shrimp seemed to be our staple dishes that winter.

It was in borrowing quarters that we became acquainted with our neighbors, two other girls like ourselves, both of whom were out of work and were only too anxious to go taxi-dancing with us. There were occasional young men, one a wounded cameraman from Hollywood who had gone through the war and come back with many scars and minus a leg, and another silent, mysterious young man on his way to South America who told me he carried a revolver in a holster under his arm and slept with it under his pillow.

After I had written my series of articles, the two young girls continued to dance in the cheap halls and Mary went back to Chicago. My work kept me busy during the day and took me out on occasional evening assignments.

Since I had to be at the office before seven (it was an afternoon paper), I often finished early in the afternoon and could go home to rest before some evening work. I had time to do my housework, wash clothes, go to the Cathedral for a visit and often to Benediction.

It was because I was always dropping into the Cathedral that Mary had given me the rosary. I did not go to Mass because of the early hour I had to get to work.

There were a few serious assignments that winter, one of which was to interview the outgoing governor of the state and the incoming governor. But the job in general was a stopgap. In the spring my book was published and I received news by long-distance telephone that the moving-picture rights in my novel had sold for $5,000. I was happy to go back to New York.

It was my friend Peggy who persuaded me then to buy a little house on the beach of Staten Island where I could settle down to study and "to write."

Part Two

NATURAL HAPPINESS

MAN IS MEANT FOR HAPPINESS

THE man I loved, with whom I entered into a common-law marriage, was an anarchist, an Englishman by descent, and a biologist. His mother and father had both come from England and he and his seven sisters were born in Asheville, North Carolina. He had attended school at the University of Georgia and of Virginia, and spent most of his time during World War I hospitalized with influenza, from which he did not recover until the war was over. When I met him he was out of uniform and had begun to get back some of the seventy-five pounds he had lost during his hospital year. His friends were mostly liberals and his sympathies were decentralist and anti-industrialist, though he loved the machine and the illusion of progress. When the World's Fair came to Flushing Meadow many years later, he spent half his time there like any child at Coney Island. He was never active in any of the groups in which we mingled. His position probably approximated that of those who came later to be called the Southern agrarians. Peggy, my former cell-mate at Occoquan, had married Malcolm Cowley (it was his first marriage and her second) and it was at their apartment in the village that I met Forster. One of his sisters was married to Kenneth Burke at that time and she became my very good friend.

Peggy and Malcolm, Kenneth and Lily—these were the friends I visited when I was in New York. Later, when Forster and I shared an apartment in winter with my sister, Allen Tate and his wife Caroline Gordon lived across the street, and Hart Crane used to drop into all our homes for coffee and conversation. Allen was poet as well as biographer and historian. Caroline was writing her first novel. Hart Crane had just become famous for his poem *The Bridge*. I knew nothing about poetry and had little knowledge of the techniques of writing. I was a journalist, a reporter. At that time Kenneth was translating, editing *The Dial* and writing the first of his strange books.

This again was another "set," liberal, radical, Bohemian, engaging in literary controversies. They reminded me of Samuel Johnson and his crowd. Malcolm felt more akin to the writing group of Paris—he had just returned from driving an ambulance in France; Allen was always a southern traditionalist; and Kenneth was a philosopher.

I can remember one conversation among Malcolm, Kenneth and John Dos Passos which stood out especially in my memory because I could not understand a word of it.

All of this group loved the country and lived there when their work permitted. Some of them had jobs in the city to which they commuted; others worked at home and tried to make a living by free-lance writing. Later on, some of them bought farms in New York, New Jersey or Connecticut. Forster and I shared the house on the beach in Staten Island.

Small country places could be had at that time for a few thousand dollars. Members of the group did not live in one community, one section, probably because they wanted to get away from too close association with each other. They had enough of that in the city. There was always a great deal of partying and drinking.

Forster's work took him into the city during the week, and I looked forward to his homecomings on Friday. Sometimes work was slack—he made gauges—and he spent all his time on the beach. We fished together, we walked every day for miles, we collected and studied together, and an entire new world opened up to me little by little. We did not talk much but "lived together" in the fullest sense of the phrase. I was an indefatigable novel reader and spent those first few winters on the beach with Tolstoi, Dostoevski and Dickens. I did little real studying but I began to read the Bible again and the *Imitation of Christ*. Forster read perhaps one novel a year, and his favorite authors were D. H. Lawrence and Aldous Huxley. When he came home he would rush out to the garden with his flashlight to see how things were growing. Winter nights he had charts and studied the stars. His enthusiasms were such that I could not help but be fascinated by the new world of nature he opened up to me, and I shared in his joys, except that of fishing. Sitting in an open boat out in the bay for long hours was too much for me, and when the water was choppy I got seasick. But these absorptions of his gave me time for my own work. I wrote a few serial stories, articles on gardens for the Staten Island paper, a few features for the *New Masses*. My radicalism at that time was confined to conversations and week-end beach parties with Communist friends. I was not a party member in the card-holding sense, but I admired the dedicated lives of party members. One girl who was too flirtatious with the husbands of several other party women was disciplined by suspension from the party. At that time Bill Dunne, one of the party leaders, was always being suspended too for drinking. "Bourgeois morality" could mean not only insistence on wedding ceremonies before intercourse but also irregularities in drink and sex which interfered with one's party work.

My Communist friends at that time were Wally and Rose Carmen, whom I had known in Chicago and who were just on their way to Russia, and Mike Gold and his brothers, one of whom was married and had two children. My liberal friends were Freda and Sasha Maruchess with their son Dick, and their Russian friends, Saletan, Salama, Dzarjevsky and the Bulgakoff family. The latter were refugees and actors. Freda and I helped teach English to Varya Bulgakoff, correcting her pronunciation as she read aloud from Voltaire's *Candide*, which happened to be the book nearest at hand those evenings. Her son Shura stayed with Freda often and played with Dick and my brother John, who was now thirteen and spent much time with me.

When I was a child, my sister and I kept notebooks; recording happiness made it last longer, we felt, and recording sorrow dramatized it and took away its bitterness; and often we settled some problem which beset us, even while we wrote about it.

Most of those early diaries kept irregularly have been lost, others destroyed. But when I moved down to the country, my peace and happiness were such that I once again took to keeping a notebook.

It was a peace, curiously enough, divided against itself. I was happy but my very happiness made me know that there was a greater happiness to be obtained from life than any I had ever known. I began to think, to weigh things, and it was at this time that I began consciously to pray more.

Because I feel that this period of my life was so joyous and lovely, I want to write at length about it, giving the flavor, the atmosphere, the mood of those days.

The little house was furnished very simply with a driftwood stove in one corner, plenty of books, comfortable chairs and couches. My writing table faced the window where I could look out at the water all day. On the walls hung the fruits of our collecting—horseshoe crabs, spider crabs, the shell of a huge sea turtle, whelks' cocoons, hanging like false curls, several mounted fish heads, boards covered with starfish, sea horses, pipe and file fish, all picked up in little pools at low tide.

Down the beach were a Belgian couple; next door in an old hotel was an Italian woman from Bleeker Street who took boarders during the summer. The grocer and the hardware storekeeper a mile away in the village were Irish. There were five other bungalows in our small colony, three occupied by Catholic families, and the other two by my own friends who moved there after I did. They were Russian and Rumanian Jews.

On the sands in a tiny shack lived a beachcomber fisherman who was a friend to the entire neighborhood. "Everybody says to me, 'Lefty, why don't you get to work this winter and do some painting for me?' But what happens when I do get work? Last spring I painted Mr. Cleary's house for him and I kept drinking liquor that he sells. By the time I got through I didn't have a cent of money coming to me, but he handed me a bill for ten dollars. Money is bad for me, I know it. I can trade my fish and clams for fuel and food and what else do I need?" And he waved his arms expansively around and indicated the beauties of his life.

He kept his shack in good order, with crab traps, clam forks and fishing paraphernalia suspended from the ceiling.

I often sat down on the sand in front of his cabin in a steamer chair which he kept especially for me, and watched him cook.

Lefty had had lobster pots out and when he pulled them in he found lobsters and a few crabs. In addition to all these delicacies he had a huge frying pan full of potatoes, and another of whiting, which were coming in so thick that fall that we had to carry them in bushel baskets. I was going to salt them down for winter eating.

Late in the afternoon the wind dropped, the door of Lefty's shack stood open and he sat there contemplating the sunset. The waves lapped the shore, tinkling among the shells and pebbles, and there was an acrid odor of smoke in the air. Down the beach, the Belgians were working, loading rock into a small cart which looked like a tumbril, drawn by a bony white horse. They stopped as though in prayer, outlined against the brilliant sky, and as I watched, the chapel bell at St. Joseph's rang the Angelus. I found myself praying, praying with thanksgiving, praying with open eyes while I watched the workers on the beach and the sunset, and listened to the sound of the waves and the scream of snowy gulls.

"Coffee?" Lefty asked me, and I accepted the big cup from his hand and bit into a thick slice of buttered toast with fried mushrooms on top.

Later in the evening the wind rose again and whistled around the house, and the noise of the sea was loud. Those evenings I read until late in the night, and in my preoccupation the fire went out, so that I had to get into bed to keep warm, clutching my books with ice-cold hands.

We enjoyed our neighbors and liked to talk with them and about them.

Sasha and Freda, their relatives and children, were a Gerhardi story which I read from day to day with a great deal of interest; Malcolm and Peggy were Huxley or Waugh, smart and rather consciously sophisticated. Pierre, the bootlegger, and his wife were out of Knut Hamsun. But Mrs. Hubert was a story told by herself which was harder to classify. She was a mixture of Marie Corelli, Mrs. L. T. Meade and Florence Barclay, with a good dash of Balzac. Some Catholic neighbors down the road were a mixture of Kathleen Norris and James Farrell.

This neighborhood we lived in was most tolerant. Human failings which were common to us all were excused on the grounds of our nationality. Pierre and his wife were Belgians whose sole aim in life seemed to be to wrest from the beach and the waters of the bay a fortune to enjoy in their old age. They sold whiskey and wines too, but bootlegging was a failing common to the neighborhood. The Catholic grocer sold liquor, calling it olive oil when he took orders for it over the telephone. Mrs. Mario, in the old hotel next door, occasionally sold a bottle of very good wine, but under protest, for she was a cautious soul. The hotelkeeper in the village both sold and drank his own stuff, but one Christmas he fell down the stairs and broke his neck. Even the policeman who rode around in a little Ford car, and fished in the evening from the end of the pier, had set up his own bootlegging establishment in a deserted shack on the beach. He enraged his rivals because he undersold them.

Pierre and his family were thrifty and hardworking, but they regarded Lefty and his idleness leniently, calling it a shiftless Yankee trait in him. Mrs. Hubert talked about the stinginess of the foreigners, citing both Mrs. Mario and Mrs. Pierre as most grasping. Sasha and Freda often had riotous guests who sang and played the balalaikas all night, stimulated by *zakuska* (if it's spelled as it's pronounced) and vodka, and they were excused on the grounds that they were Russians. And Mr. Schmidt, who once was a lion tamer and was accused of throwing knives at his son and daughter, was excused because he was a German. There were several French and Spanish families, all with their failings, but everybody was on affable visiting terms.

One afternoon as I sat on the beach, I read a book of essays by William James and came on these lines:

Poverty is indeed the strenuous life,—without brass bands or uniforms or hysteric popular applause or lies or circumlocutions; and when one sees the way in which wealth-getting enters as an ideal into the very bone and marrow of our generation, one wonders whether the revival of

the belief that poverty is a worthy religious vocation ma
transformation of military courage, and the spiritual refo
time stands most in need of.

Among us English-speaking peoples especially do the p
erty need once more to be boldly sung. We have grown literally
to be poor. We despise anyone who elects to be poor in order to simplify
and save his inner life. If he does not join the general scramble, we
deem him spiritless and lacking in ambition. We have lost the power
even of imagining what the ancient realization of poverty could have
meant; the liberation from material attachments, the unbribed soul, the
manlier indifference, the paying our way by what we are and not by
what we have, the right to fling away our life at any moment irrespon-
sibly,—the more athletic trim, in short, the fighting shape.

I always felt that these lines applied to Forster, who refused
to do other than live from day to day and insisted on his freedom
of body and soul. And it applied, too, to Lefty, who agreed
heartily when I read them to him.

Freda, my next-door neighbor, had to go into town for the
day to do her weekly shopping, and Sasha strummed lazily on
his guitar, picking at his lunch and directing the children's feeding. Mrs. Hubert hung out her wash, and further down the
beach, in front of his huge white house, Mr. Harding exercised,
bending and swaying, twisting and turning, very gracefully.
He looked like a big polar bear with his white head. Mrs. Harding, her crutches beside her, read in her little screened-in pavilion.
All those neighbors were within shouting distance, but only
Freda and I cared enough about each other to shout back and
forth.

Down on the beach there was a new sound. Lefty, whistling
happily, purged and purified of all earthly desires because he
was drunk over the week end. He sold dozens of sand worms,
and as fast as the money came in he staggered down to Pierre's
to buy half pints. He slept lying in the sand, and as he was a
neat and tidy man, he probably washed and shaved before he
went to dig more sand worms and enough clams to make himself
clam broth, which he said was the best "pick-me-up" in the
world.

It was a pleasure to watch the daintiness with which he cooked.

He prepared his small fire on the sand, banked up with bricks; carefully scrubbed the clams in the pools among the rocks; steamed them with just a little water, opened them to take out the clams and juice and put them back on the fire to warm with a dash of butter, salt and pepper. Then he sipped the broth with a slice of buttered toast.

It had been a difficult week end for me though there were no guests, and I was happy and peaceful that it was over.

Forster, the inarticulate, became garrulous only in wrath. And his wrath, he said, was caused by my absorption in the supernatural rather than the natural, the unseen rather than the seen.

He had always rebelled against the institution of the family and the tyranny of love. It was hard for me to see at such times why we were together, since he lived with me as though he were living alone and he never allowed me to forget that this was a comradeship rather than a marriage.

He worked as little as possible, he shared in all the expenses of the house, but he never spent any money if he could help it. He hated social life and fled from it, and seemed afraid of any actual contact with the world, but he was much engrossed in its concerns. He read the *Times* faithfully, and all I knew of the political and foreign situation I knew from his reading aloud at the breakfast table. Usually if anyone reads aloud to you, you can listen or not, at will, but the vehemence and passion of Forster's interest and his rebellion at all injustice forced me to realize the situation with him. So I continued to go around in a stew and foment over our intervention in Nicaragua and the political situation in New York. I had listened to Forster's bitter comments on all man-made institutions, and the blundering of our fellow creatures. He loved nature with a sensuous passion and he loved birds and beasts and children because they were not men.

The very fact that his suffering and rebellion against life as man had made it was an abstract thing and had little to do with what he had suffered personally, made me respect his ideas, as ideas honestly held, so our quarrels were not acrimonious. For instance he loved his family tenderly, but he saw and suffered keenly at what havoc a possessive family feeling sometimes wrought. He personally had not suffered want, but economic inequality was a terrible thing to him. He personally had not been in jail, but his rage at the system which confined political agitators to jail ate into him. And yet he did nothing but enclose himself into a shell, escape out on the bay with his fishing, find comfort in digging for clams or bait, or seek refuge in tending a garden.

Sasha was a Jew with a Portuguese name who was born in Russia and whose parents lived in Russia most of their lives. Freda was a German Jew born in Russia. Sasha's mother, a temperamental woman, lived with them. Whenever she became upset by anything, she bowed her head to the table and wept, beating her forehead against the boards. She was always sitting at the table, chewing on bits of sugar and sipping tea. Sasha sat by with an aloof and haughty expression and played on his guitar.

> There are gooseberries and raspberries in the garden. . . .
> I am so happy because I have my five fingers.

Occasionally he said to *babushka,* as they called the grandmother, "You bore me. Do keep still. You have an insensitive and crude disposition."

She sat and looked at him for a few minutes. Then, "You cannot repress me. . . . If you repress me I would go insane." But she ceased her complaining for a while. Not for very long however. If it was a sunny day, "Ach, how the sun hurts my eyes. The glare on the sand and the water is terrible." And if it was cloudy, "I am very melancholy today. My soul is dead." The wind made her nervous and when it was calm there was always a roaring in her ears. The doctor forbade her to eat meat or to drink tea with sugar. "But what is life if I cannot have my tea? And I am so weak—so near to my grave anyway—I must have meat. What difference does it make?" And she sighed and shrugged her shoulders and took another lump of sugar.

Freda felt repressed. All day she went around with a broom in her hands, sweeping out the sand which Dickie and Shura and Sasha carted in. "They want us to be slaves," she said thoughtfully, speaking of husbands in general. "Once I was slim and young and now I go around the house with a broom in my hands. I am always making meals and serving them and I never sit down to the table, but nibble and so I become fat. Sasha is assured that I am his, his alone, and rejoices in it. It is strange."

She stretched her lovely throat, lifted her arms, and dropped the broom to the floor and sighed.

She loved Sasha devotedly and with all the years they had been together her love did not abate. They were fifteen when she tried to hold him first and for years he eluded her. He rushed away, but always he returned.

He rebelled against Freda's scatterbrained housekeeping, but he would not have a woman come in even for the day and clean. Occasionally he himself took a broom and purposefully set to work but by the time he finished one half of their living room, he was tired and sat down to his books and his guitar, leaving the clutter piled in the middle of the room. Freda left it there, thinking of the soup she was making for lunch, unheeding that the beds on the sleeping porch were not yet made.

And, "We need more windows in this corner of the house, Sasha. We have not enough view. The Jersey shore looks like the coast of Italy on a morning like this."

"Let us go to the Isle of Cyprus. I'd like to be there in a little villa. Here I am living like a vagabond, but a vagabond without adventures."

"You talked this way eight years ago—always wanting to be moving about. Do not suggest rushing away again. My heart aches."

Unheeding, he played on his guitar.

Sasha had jet-black hair and wide gray eyes which were so dark as to appear brown very often. There was a warm, kind look in them usually; even when he was harsh and impatient, or cruelly satirical, his eyes never became cold but seemed sadly morose, as though he were indulging himself merely to escape an unutterable melancholy. When he was sad, he held his head on one side, and pulled his shoulders up to his ears as though he were cold; when he was happy, he threw his head back and tossed his hair and sang. He usually kept a cigarette tucked behind his ear and wore bright red blouses around the house.

We quarreled very often because I did not have the same riotous enthusiasms he had for people. The half-dozen people whom he liked very well he was always describing in the most extravagant way, and if I were calm in my judgment he was greatly disappointed in me and my capability for appreciation of the unique.

"But he is marvelous—an extraordinary man. Really! you do not know—you have no conception of how superb he is." And Sasha sighed as though the man's qualities were beyond his power of describing. "But you don't like him."

"I tell you, I do like him. I like him very much. But why do I have to go into raptures about him? Do you want me to fall in love with him? But that is just it—the only thing I do not like about him is that he always is raving about women—kissing his hand to them, going down on his knees to them and saying 'Ah, how I love them, and how they have wrecked my life!'

"Women don't like such a man. He is too easy to get. They prefer a more aloof type so that if he does make love to them they can flatter themselves that there is some rare quality in them which made him succumb."

But Sasha refused to understand. "You just do not like him," he sighed, as though he had found me lacking. And what he insinuated was that I was irritated because this friend had not fallen in love with me exclusively but paid amorous attention to other women he came in contact with.

But Sasha and I did not always quarrel. "I want to go to Paris," he said discontentedly. "I am too happy down here. It is not good to be happy and stodgy as I am getting. I must get away from here. I have not been to Paris since I was a youth. My father—he was a doctor—came to America and we lived in Brooklyn. He wished to be alone with my mother—he loved her so much—so he rented another apartment across the street and we children lived there. There were four of us. We were very independent and would not go to school—my sister was giving music lessons, my two brothers were working in offices, and I was so proud I refused to be a white-collar slave but went to work as a dental mechanic. We were none of us eighteen yet.

"One day we got very angry at my father and went away to another neighborhood. And then he died soon afterward, calling us to him and reconciling himself to us. But we were already used to our independence and none of us would live at home again.

"I had saved two hundred dollars. I don't know why I was so careful. I never save anything now. So I decided to go back to Russia, visiting Paris first. There I lived in the cafés with the students and spent all my money, and an elderly woman became interested in me and gave me a ticket to Odessa. I arrived there with a cheap American straw suitcase with nothing in it but a huge sausage and a couple of rolls.

"A friend in Brooklyn had given me a letter of introduction to his family, saying that they would take me in until I found work. I would accept from him, but I would not write home to get help from my family. But when I went to his home, I found his mother a huge angry peasant woman who was on bad terms with her son and refused to have anything to do with me. I think he gave the letter of introduction to me as a joke. She asked me to sit down to a cup of tea, but she glared at me all the while I drank it, so I went away.

"On the street I met a student and hailed him. We started talking and he liked me—told me to come with him and stay in his room. He was a revolutionist and I went with him to meetings and tried to organize unions and start strikes. All the while working and earning enough to live on.

"I remember one time the Cossacks chased us and we took refuge in empty freight trains and hid there. They did not find us, but they shot my hat off my head before we reached the freight trains. We had revolvers, of course, but they were not much good. Many times I escaped being killed.

"I did not like Odessa. It was exciting there. I had a great many friends and a love affair, but I did not like the city itself. I got away in a year and went to Tula. That was where my people had always lived, and Tolstoi was there. He had known me when I was a little child and we had many talks together.

"When I came back to America he urged me to go on studying and gave me letters to some college professors but I was proud and tore them up. I wanted to work with my hands, not with my head. At least if I worked with my hands I was free to think. So now I am a mechanic. But I earn enough money to loaf a good deal too," he added proudly.

"Tolstoi did a lot for us and for our children," he went on. "No one who lived in Tula could be an ordinary parent. We may have our faults, but they are not the faults of the parents of the last generation or so. His idea was, not especially that the children should rule the household, but that they should rule themselves. I remember one nobleman's family. There were six children, and even the littlest one, a child of four, had a vote in the republic they created for themselves. Once they boycotted one of the brothers for some breach of the peace—would have nothing to do with him for two weeks. The parents lived their own lives and the children lived theirs.

"All the families in Tula were influenced by Tolstoi's ideas. They influenced my mother too. That is why she permitted my father to establish us in separate quarters. I knew we were the scandal of the neighborhood in Brooklyn, living alone as we were and having crowds of young people at the house till all hours of the night. Those were the days we could sit up all night discussing some abstraction. Everybody talked against my mother because she appeared to have no control over us, but we went to her in every trouble and received her help."

Freda came in while he was talking, carrying a kettle of boiling water for tea. It was always tea with them—every hour of the afternoon and evening.

And what tea it was! A pot of strong tea was made and left standing on the leaves, and whenever anyone wanted a glass, a bit of this "essence" as they called it was poured out and then the glass was filled with hot water. Sasha and Freda and the *babushka* drank it clear and seemed to judge it by its color rather than its taste. If there was jam on hand they put a big spoonful in and did without sugar. Forster came to drink it as carelessly as they did, but since he poured the hot water first and added milk and sugar before he added the tea, he often absent-mindedly forgot to put any tea in at all.

Freda had noble eyes with long lashes and straight tragic brows. There was a little down on her upper lip which made the line of her mouth soft but firm. In obedience to Sasha's request she let her hair grow, and it was always escaping from its combs and falling to her shoulders. She insisted on wearing out old evening gowns which she could no longer wear in town, so generally even in the coldest weather she exposed a large expanse of splendid back and bosom. If it became too cold, she pulled on a sweater—one too ragged for Sasha or Dickie to wear.

She never came into my house without husband or children following after, both with some demands. So she never sat down but stood poised by the window or fireplace with a cup of tea, talking hastily before she was dragged back to find skates or shovels or marbles or a piece of bread and butter.

Peggy and Malcolm moved to the Island. They were the most respectable members of our community in that they had steam heat and hot water. Freda and I had bathtubs but we heated our houses with driftwood fires and it was a chore heating water for bathing. Every now and then I went to spend the evening with Peggy and bask in the warmth of her tub.

One night I luxuriated in the hot water with a cigarette and a copy of *Cousin Pons* in my hands. It was after nine, the time Peggy usually selected for such jobs as washing her kitchen floor or cleaning closet shelves, tasks which are conventionally performed in the early morning hours.

"What are you opening the back door for?" I hollered, feeling a frightful draft and sinking down until the water was up to my ears and about to submerge *Cousin Pons*. Peggy's bathroom was just opposite the outside kitchen door and the door fitted loosely with no catch or lock to make it stay closed.

"I must get out to pick my cosmos and marigolds," she called. "It's going to be a bitter night."

I chuckled over the picture I knew she made. Bundled in a fur coat so that only her high-bred nose and chin showed, wearing a pair of gaily colored Bavarian mittens with *Aus Muenchen* woven into them, carrying shears and a garden basket.

"Are you crazy," I grumbled at her, as she fussed around the kitchen looking for things, leaving the door wide open.

In all probability Peggy had spent the day over solitaire or crossword puzzles, in both of which amusements she took extreme delight while her dishes were unwashed and her house disordered.

Peggy's flowers were her greatest passion. During the coldest winter months when she and Malcolm lived in town, her little apartment overlooking the East River bloomed with narcissus, geraniums and boxes of herbs. She always had a cat or two which she carried between city and country in a bright-colored basket. Her neighbors were used to her peculiarities. They accepted her gaudy dresses and flaming stockings and did not question anything she did.

I remember once coming home from a late party with Peggy. She wore a black evening gown, the only one she possessed. It was rather disreputable, with frayed edges where a goat had started to eat it at a fete in Dijon, she said, and spotted with wine. But she wore it with an easy assurance of splendor. On this occasion she didn't help the dress any by breaking up boxes on the curbstones and carrying home the pieces for firewood.

"Yes, Peggy does do the strangest things," Malcolm said in his slow and ponderous way, at least fifteen minutes later when she had come in and I had joined them by the fire. He had been reading and conversation stole most gradually into his mind. It was one of those interminably gray evenings when thoughts go a long way.

"Yes, we do queer things," she agreed. Evidently she too had been reflecting on her oddities. "Do you remember that party at Montpelier, Malcolm, when we went to the workingmen's fair and I danced with the grocer and you danced with his wife?"

That was just like Peggy, thinking it was eccentric to dance with the grocer. Of course if I had seen the grocer, I might have agreed with her.

I had been alone most of the week, since Forster was in town. I had been trying to work on the serial I was writing for the Bell syndicate. But work progressed slowly and I could not seem to do a thing. The syndicate had just started to promote the story and I had thirty installments ahead, but the editor wanted more all the time and was clamoring for love interest. I was trying to write two thousand words of hectic love scenes while I sat with Peggy.

Influenced by my industry, she threw down Blake's *Songs of Innocence* which she had been reading, with the determination, she announced, of illustrating them.

"I'm tired of this," I groaned. "I've been ranting about how the fragrance of her hair made him reel, and how she shielded her flushed face with one slender arm, and I've had him talking at a great rate—'I'm mad about you' (repeated hoarsely several times with lots of dots in between). And she stammers, 'Oh, please,' six dots, and 'You mustn't kiss me!' a few dots more—until I'm sick. I'm stealing Robert W. Chambers' stuff, I'm sure. I'd like to cut loose and say 'They went on in this asinine way for half an hour or so' and let it go at that!"

I could talk in this flippant way of my work, but if others regarded it too lightly I defended it, though not as Freda was always defending it for me. Her whole-souled enthusiasm for creative effort led her to assure me that I was following in the footsteps of Balzac and Dostoevski in writing serials for the newspapers.

"As a piece of work which presents difficulties," I answered her tartly, "it is worth doing well. When you're writing an article or short story which you hope will be accepted by *Harper's Magazine*, for instance, you are confronted by an entirely different problem. But every now and then I realize overwhelmingly the people I am trying to reach."

Tired of his quiet life, Sasha went into town and was offered a job in a play with Eva Le Gallienne's company. All he had to do was stand in the background dressed in a bright Mexican costume and play on his guitar while the heroine, a barmaid, sang. He came on the stage for only fifteen minutes, and the work suiting his languid mood, he accepted it. So Freda and I were alone with much time to sit around and gossip. We took our meals together, Freda cooking them and I cleaning up after them.

Happy at his absence during the week, Freda was as expectant as a young lover on Saturday and spent the day cooking and making salads and cakes for him, and Saturday night we sat up late and listened to his adventures of the week in the city.

He was rather disgruntled when he came in this particular Saturday. He was one of those childish people who like to look out of the window in the train. Even the little journey from the city down to the beach was filled with sights which he enjoyed as I did.

The trip took an hour and I knew every house along the countryside. I noticed new roofs going up, a lean-to being built here, a basement being put in there. I noticed what neat stacks of wood one old farmer piled up conveniently by the kitchen porch. I enjoyed especially the Italian homes, because no matter how inclement the weather there was always some activity or improvement going on around their houses: grape arbors being repaired, cold frames constructed, or perhaps there was some old lady sitting out in the winter sun, peeling vegetables for dinner.

I took especial note of the houses I would have liked to live in myself, and contemplated improvements on my own beach bungalow. I peered out of the window to catch a glimpse of goats in one bleak meadow. One spring when my sister Della was visiting me and we went walking every afternoon, we came on one farmyard where there were half a dozen baby goats. They were so sweet that Della insisted on going back there every visit to hang about their necks garlands of flowers, which they promptly ate. Freda and I were always contemplating buying one to crop the grass in our gardens and play with the children and perhaps give milk with which we could make pastoral cheese, but the Italian woman who owned them refused to sell.

Sasha usually brought home news of these families by the railroad tracks but that day he announced glumly that all his time had been taken on the train.

"I hate to have people talk to me, and tonight, a gray-bearded old man sat down by my side. 'I think I have seen you down on the beach, haven't I?' he asked me. 'Fine day, isn't it?' I just grunted at him, 'A lousy day!' 'Ah, but all days are God's days, so this is a good day.'

"I snorted at him. 'And are you a Christian?' he asked me.

" 'I am an agnostic.'

" 'Is that a Protestant sect?'

"I tried to read, but he pursued me with conversation. 'Because I am a Christian, I am not afraid to die,' he told me. 'Every day I am ready for death.'

"I told him he was crazy—that everybody was afraid to die. Even Jesus Christ in the garden of Gethsemane prayed God that His cup of sorrow be taken from Him. And Tolstoi spent his last twenty years preparing for death and when he felt its near approach, he fled like a craven. No one can reconcile himself to death.

"Do you remember, Freda, how for years I was absorbed by the thoughts of death and studied and struggled to overcome them? I studied the dissolution of all the old men I saw and fought against this degrading cowardice in me. I took your old grandfather to live with us—he was over ninety—so that I could see his last days and watch how he would meet the end. At the last he turned to God. 'If there is a God, I must be friends with Him!' he told me.

"Now I have put the thoughts of death aside, but every time I hear of the death of a friend or an acquaintance, I think, 'Soon you too will have your turn,' and I am still very much afraid.

"The old man on the train told me he was a vegetarian, and by that time I was so irritated with him that with great glee I spoke of the nice fresh fish which we threw in the frying pan squirming, and of the eels which tried to hop out, skinned and headless as they were. And I told about the turtle which John had killed and I did not tell him how we were all conscience-stricken and revolted at ourselves and did not eat any of it."

"How could you, Sasha!" Freda exclaimed at him. "The poor

old man probably thought you a sadist. You probably made him very unhappy."

"No—just the opposite. He will think me an evil creature and pray for me and then he will have a great sense of his own goodness and magnanimity."

"It is just because he followed you into the train and would not let you have your childish amusement of looking out the window. If you had met him on the end of the pier you would have been charmed by him and invited him over for tea and philosophic conversation."

"I invited him for tea anyway," Sasha confessed sheepishly. "He can talk to Dickie about God."

"Dickie is religious already," Freda said. "He comes to me and asks me who God is. So I ask Dorothy and she tells him from the catechism. He is always asking her what she prays for and he prays himself. He asks me why I don't go to church and pray to God, so I tell him that somehow the world was made, and we do not know who made it, but some people think it was God, and that I just don't know. So then he goes to Dorothy and she gives him a crucifix to hang over his bed and he calls it 'his friend, Jesus Christ.'"

Whenever Freda was at a loss as to how to correct Dickie and had scolded and berated him, she finally said, "Really, Dickie, I'll just have to talk religion to you, if you don't mend your ways. I really don't see how to make you understand that you must have consideration for other people and not be mean and cruel. Ethics are too abstract and I can't make you see the ethical side of things."

And although this talk of religion was held over the boy in the form of a threat it did not intimidate him or frighten him. He came to me with wide, brilliant eyes and listened as though I were telling him a beautiful fairy story.

I know several other mothers who felt the need of religious instruction for their children, but because they had no faith themselves, they did not know how to go about instilling faith in their children. They surreptitiously had them baptized when they were born and then nothing further was done about it.

Sasha disposed of the subject by saying, "Religious faith is a talent, a gift which I do not possess. I cannot believe."

One night I listened to the radio for the first time in months. The tempests of winter had blown down the aerial, there was something wrong with the cords which attached the earphones to the box, and I had not the patience to mend the thing. My young brother John suddenly became interested in radio again, having received a present of an old set from a friend of his, and he magnanimously repaired mine so that he could share with me his pleasure in listening.

We heard a symphony orchestra and were both delighted with Liszt's *St. Francis Preaching to the Birds*. I told John about St. Francis, gave him *The Little Flowers of St. Francis* to read, and felt inspired by the beautiful music.

HAVING A BABY

I WAS surprised that I found myself beginning to pray daily. I could not get down on my knees, but I could pray while I was walking. If I got down on my knees I thought, "Do I really believe? Whom am I praying to?" A terrible doubt came over me, and a sense of shame, and I wondered if I was praying because I was lonely, because I was unhappy.

But when I walked to the village for the mail, I found myself praying again, holding in my pocket the rosary that Mary Gordon gave me in New Orleans some years before. Maybe I did not say it correctly but I kept on saying it because it made me happy.

Then I thought suddenly, scornfully, "Here you are in a stupor of content. You are biological. Like a cow. Prayer with you is like the opiate of the people." And over and over again in my mind that phrase was repeated jeeringly, "Religion is the opiate of the people."

"But," I reasoned with myself, "I am praying because I am happy, not because I am unhappy. I did not turn to God in unhappiness, in grief, in despair—to get consolation, to get something from Him."

And encouraged that I was praying because I wanted to thank Him, I went on praying. No matter how dull the day, how long the walk seemed, if I felt sluggish at the beginning of the walk, the words I had been saying insinuated themselves into my heart before I had finished, so that on the trip back I neither prayed nor thought but was filled with exultation.

Along the beach I found it appropriate to say the *Te Deum*. When I worked about the house, I found myself addressing the Blessed Virgin and turning toward her statue.

It is so hard to say how this delight in prayer grew on me. The year before, I was saying as I planted seeds in the garden, "I *must* believe in these seeds, that they fall into the earth and grow into flowers and radishes and beans. It is a miracle to me because I do not understand it. Neither do naturalists understand it. The very fact that they use glib technical phrases does not make it any less of a miracle, and a miracle we all accept. Then why not accept God's mysteries?"

I began to go to Mass regularly on Sunday mornings.

When Freda went into town, I was alone. Forster was in the city all week, only coming out week ends. I finished the writing I was doing and felt at loose ends, thinking enviously of my friends going gaily about the city, about their work, with plenty of companionship.

The fact that I felt restless was a very good reason to stay on the beach and content myself with my life as a sybaritic anchorite. For how could I be a true anchorite with such luxuries as the morning paper, groceries delivered to the door, a beach to walk on, and the water to feast my eyes on? And then the fresh fish and clams, mushrooms, Jerusalem artichokes, such delicacies right at hand. I invited Lefty to supper and discussed with him the painting of the house. I read Dickens every evening.

In spite of my desire for a sociable week in town, in spite of a desire to pick up and flee from my solitude, I took joy in thinking of the idiocy of the pleasures I would indulge in if I were there. Cocktail parties, with prohibition drinks, dinners, the conversation or lack of it, dancing in a smoky crowded room when one might be walking on the beach, the dull, restless cogitations which come after dissipating one's energies—things which struck me with renewed force every time I spent days in the city. My virtuous resolutions to indulge in such pleasure no more were succeeded by a hideous depression when neither my new-found sense of religion, my family life, my work nor my surroundings were sufficient to console me. I thought of death and was overwhelmed by the terror and the blackness of both life and death. And I longed for a church near at hand where I could go and lift up my soul.

It was pleasant rowing about in the calm bay with Forster. The oyster boats were all out, and far on the horizon, off Sandy Hook, there was a four-masted vessel. I had the curious delusion that several huge holes had been stove in her side, through which you could see the blue sky. The other vessels seemed sailing in the air, quite indifferent to the horizon on which they should properly have been resting. Forster tried to explain to me scientific facts about mirages and atmospheric conditions, and, on the other hand, I pointed out to him how our senses lie to us.

But it was impossible to talk about religion or faith to him. A wall immediately separated us. The very love of nature, and the study of her secrets which was bringing me to faith, cut Forster off from religion.

I had known Forster a long time before we contracted our common-law relationship, and I have always felt that it was life with him that brought me natural happiness, that brought me to God.

His ardent love of creation brought me to the Creator of all things. But when I cried out to him, "How can there be no God, when there are all these beautiful things," he turned from me uneasily and complained that I was never satisfied. We loved each other so strongly that he wanted to remain in the love of the moment; he wanted me to rest in that love. He cried out against my attitude that there would be nothing left of that love without a faith.

I remembered the love story in Romain Rolland's *Jean*

Christophe, the story of his friend and his engrossing marriage, and how those young people exhausted themselves in the intensity of their emotions.

I could not see that love between man and woman was incompatible with love of God. God is the Creator, and the very fact that we were begetting a child made me have a sense that we were made in the image and likeness of God, co-creators with him. I could not protest with Sasha about "that initial agony of having to live." Because I was grateful for love, I was grateful for life, and living with Forster made me appreciate it and even reverence it still more. He had introduced me to so much that was beautiful and good that I felt I owed to him too this renewed interest in the things of the spirit.

He had all the love of the English for the outdoors in all weather. He used to insist on walks no matter how cold or rainy the day, and this dragging me away from my books, from my lethargy, into the open, into the country, made me begin to breathe. If breath is life, then I was beginning to be full of it because of him. I was filling my lungs with it, walking on the beach, resting on the pier beside him while he fished, rowing with him in the calm bay, walking through fields and woods—a new experience entirely for me, one which brought me to life, and filled me with joy.

I had been passing through some years of fret and strife, beauty and ugliness—even some weeks of sadness and despair. There had been periods of intense joy but seldom had there been the quiet beauty and happiness I had now. I had thought all those years that I had freedom, but now I felt that I had never known real freedom nor even had knowledge of what freedom meant.

Now, just as in my childhood, I was enchained, tied to one spot, unable to pick up and travel from one part of the country to another, from one job to another. I was tied down because I was going to have a baby. No matter how much I might sometimes wish to flee from my quiet existence, I could not, nor would I be able to for several years. I had to accept my quiet and stillness, and accepting it, I rejoiced in it.

For a long time I had thought I could not bear a child, and

the longing in my heart for a baby had been growing. My home, I felt, was not a home without one. The simple joys of the kitchen and garden and beach brought sadness with them because I felt myself unfruitful, barren. No matter how much one was loved or one loved, that love was lonely without a child. It was incomplete.

I will never forget my blissful joy when I was first sure that I was pregnant—I had wanted a baby all the first year we were together. When I was finally sure, it was a beautiful June day and we were going on a picnic to Tottenville to see a circus, Malcolm and Peggy, Forster and I. It was a circus in a tent, and it was Peggy who insisted on going. We brought dandelion wine and pickled eels and good home-made bread and butter. A fantastic lunch, but I remember enjoying the root beer and popcorn later, and feeling so much in love, so settled, so secure that now I had found what I was looking for.

It did not last all through my pregnancy, that happiness. There were conflicts because Forster did not believe in bringing children into such a world as we lived in. He still was obsessed by the war. His fear of responsibility, his dislike of having the control of others, his extreme individualism made him feel that he of all men should not be a father.

Our child was born in March at the end of a harsh winter. In December I had come in from the country and taken an apartment in town. My sister came to stay with me, to help me over the last hard months. It was good to be there, close to friends, close to a church where I could pray. I read the *Imitation of Christ* a great deal during those months. I knew that I was going to have my child baptized, cost what it may. I knew that I was not going to have her floundering through many years as I had done, doubting and hesitating, undisciplined and amoral. I felt it was the greatest thing I could do for my child. For myself, I prayed for the gift of faith. I was sure, yet not sure. I postponed the day of decision.

A woman does not want to be alone at such a time. Even the most hardened, the most irreverent, is awed by the stupendous fact of creation. Becoming a Catholic would mean facing life alone and I clung to family life. It was hard to contemplate giving up a mate in order that my child and I could become members of the Church. Forster would have nothing to do with religion or with me if I embraced it. So I waited.

Those last months of waiting I was too happy to know the unrest of indecision. The days were slow in passing, but week by week the time came nearer. I spent some time in writing, but for the most part I felt a great stillness. I was incapable of going to meetings, of seeing many people, of taking up the threads of my past life.

When the little one was born, my joy was so great that I sat up in bed in the hospital and wrote an article for the *New Masses* about my child, wanting to share my joy with the world. I was glad to write this joy for a workers' magazine because it was a joy all women knew, no matter what their grief at poverty, unemployment and class war. The article so appealed to my Marxist friends that the account was reprinted all over the world in workers' papers. Diego Rivera, when I met him some four years afterward in Mexico, greeted me as the author of it. And Mike Gold, who was at that time editor of the *New Masses*, said it had been printed in many Soviet newspapers and that I had rubles awaiting me in Moscow.

When Tamar Teresa—for that is what I named her—was six weeks old, we went back to the beach. It was April and, though it was still cold, it was definitely spring.

Every morning while she napped on the sunny porch, well swathed in soft woolen blankets, I went down to the beach and with the help of Lefty brought up driftwood, enough to last until next morning. Forster was home only week ends and then he chopped enough wood to last a few days. But when the wind was high and piercing it penetrated the house so that much wood was needed, and it was a pleasure to tramp up and down the beach in the bright sun and collect wood which smelled of seaweed, brine and tar. It was warmer outside than it was in the house, and on the porch Teresa was nicely sheltered. Sometimes in the afternoon I put her in her carriage and went out along the woods, watching, almost feeling the buds bursting through their warm coats. Song sparrows, woodpeckers, hawks, crows, robins, nuthatches and of course laughing gulls made the air gay with their clamor. Starlings chattered in the branches of the old pine in front of the porch. We collected azalea buds, dogwood, sassafras and apple-tree branches to decorate the room. Best of all there were skunk cabbages, gleaming mottled-green, dark red, and yellow, small enough to make a most decorative centerpiece, propped up with stones. They were never so colorful as they were that year, and spring after spring since I have watched for them thrusting up vigorously in marshy places. Skunk cabbages and the spring peepers—these tiny frogs—mean that the winter is over and gone.

There was arbutus still buried under the leaves so that one had to look carefully for it like buried treasure. There were spring beauties and adder's-tongue and dandelion greens. The year before I had been planting radishes on March first but this year gardening gave way to more delightful tasks.

Supper always was early and the baby comfortably tucked away before it was dark. Then, tired with all the activities that so rejoiced and filled my days, I sat in the dusk in a stupor of contentment.

Yet always those deep moments of happiness gave way to a feeling of struggle, of a long silent fight still to be gone through. There had been the physical struggle, the mortal combat almost, of giving birth to a child, and now there was coming the struggle for my own soul. Tamar would be baptized, and I knew the rending it would cause in human relations around me. I was to be torn and agonized again, and I was all for putting off the hard day.

LOVE OVERFLOWS

"THOU shalt love the Lord thy God with thy whole heart and with thy whole soul and with thy whole mind." This is the first Commandment.

The problem is, how to love God? We are only too conscious

of the hardness of our hearts, and in spite of all that religious writers tell us about *feeling* not being necessary, we do want to feel and so know that we love God.

"Thou wouldst not seek Him if thou hadst not already found Him," Pascal says, and it is true too that you love God if you want to love Him. One of the disconcerting facts about the spiritual life is that God takes you at your word. Sooner or later one is given a chance to prove his love. The very word "diligo," the Latin word used for "love," means "I prefer." It was all very well to love God in His works, in the beauty of His creation which was crowned for me by the birth of my child. Forster had made the physical world come alive for me and had awakened in my heart a flood of gratitude. The final object of this love and gratitude was God. No human creature could receive or contain so vast a flood of love and joy as I often felt after the birth of my child. With this came the need to worship, to adore. I had heard many say that they wanted to worship God in their own way and did not need a Church in which to praise Him, nor a body of people with whom to associate themselves. But I did not agree to this. My very experience as a radical, my whole make-up, led me to want to associate myself with others, with the masses, in loving and praising God. Without even looking into the claims of the Catholic Church, I was willing to admit that for me she was the one true Church. She had come down through the centuries since the time of Peter, and far from being dead, she claimed and held the allegiance of the masses of people in all the cities where I had lived. They poured in and out of her doors on Sundays and holy days, for novenas and missions. What if they were compelled to come in by the law of the Church, which said they were guilty of mortal sin if they did not go to Mass every Sunday? They obeyed that law. They were given a chance to show their preference. They accepted the Church. It may have been an unthinking, unquestioning faith, and yet the chance certainly came, again and again, "Do I prefer the Church to my own will," even if it was only the small matter of sitting at home on a Sunday morning with the papers? And the choice was the Church.

There was the legislation of the Church in regard to marriage, a stumbling block to many. That was where I began to be troubled, to be afraid. To become a Catholic meant for me to give up a mate with whom I was much in love. It got to the point where it was the simple question of whether I chose God or man. I had known enough of love to know that a good healthy family life was as near to heaven as one could get in this life. There was another sample of heaven, of the enjoyment of God. The very sexual act itself was used again and again in Scripture as a figure of the beatific vision. It was not because I was tired of sex, satiated, disillusioned, that I turned to God. Radical friends used to insinuate this. It was because through a whole love, both physical and spiritual, I came to know God.

From the time Tamar Teresa was born I was intent on having her baptized. There had been that young Catholic girl in the bed next to me at the hospital who gave me a medal of St. Thérèse of Lisieux.

"I don't believe in these things," I told her, and it was another example of people saying what they do not mean.

"If you love someone you like to have something around which reminds you of them," she told me.

It was so obvious a truth that I was shamed. Reading William James' *Varieties of Religious Experience* had acquainted me with the saints, and I had read the life of St. Teresa of Avila and fallen in love with her. She was a mystic and a practical woman, a recluse and a traveler, a cloistered nun and yet most active. She liked to read novels when she was a young girl, and she wore a bright red dress when she entered the convent. Once when she was traveling from one part of Spain to another with some other nuns and a priest to start a convent, and their way took them over a stream, she was thrown from her donkey. The story goes that our Lord said to her, "That is how I treat my friends." And she replied, "And that is why You have so few of them." She called life a "night spent at an uncomfortable inn." Once when she was trying to avoid that recreation hour which is set aside in convents for nuns to be together, the others insisted on her joining them, and she took castanets and danced. When some older nuns professed themselves shocked, she retorted, "One must do things sometimes to make life more bearable." After she was a superior she gave directions when the nuns became melancholy, "to feed them steak," and there were other delightful little touches to the story of her life which made me love her and feel close to her. I have since heard a priest friend of ours remark gloomily that one could go to hell imitating the imperfections of the saints, but these little incidents brought out in her biography made her delightfully near to me. So I decided to name my daughter after her. That is why my neighbor offered me a medal of St. Thérèse of Lisieux, who is called the little Teresa.

Her other name came from Sasha's sister Liza. She had named her daughter Tamar, which in Hebrew means "little palm tree," and knowing nothing of the unhappy story of the two Tamars in the Old Testament, I named my child Tamar also. Tamar is one of the forebears of our Lord, listed in the first chapter of Matthew, and not only Jews and Russians, but also New Englanders used the name.

What a driving power joy is! When I was unhappy and repentant in the past I turned to God, but it was my joy at having given birth to a child that made me do something definite. I wanted Tamar to have a way of life and instruction. We all crave order, and in the Book of Job, hell is described as a place where no order is. I felt that "belonging" to a Church would bring that order into her life which I felt my own had lacked. If I could have felt that communism was the answer to my desire for a cause, a motive, a way to walk in, I would have remained as I was. But I felt that only faith in Christ could give the answer. The Sermon on the Mount answered all the questions as to how to love God and one's brother. I knew little about the Sacraments, and yet here I was believing, knowing that without them Tamar would not be a Catholic.

I did not know any Catholics to speak to. The grocer, the hardware storekeeper, my neighbors down the road were Catholics, yet I could not bring myself to speak to them about religion. I was full of the reserves I noted in my own family. But I could speak to a nun. So when I saw a nun walking down the

road near St. Joseph's-by-the-Sea, I went up to her breathlessly
and asked her how I could have my child baptized. She was not
at all reticent about asking questions and not at all surprised at
my desires. She was a simple old sister who had taught grade
school all her life. She was now taking care of babies in a huge
home on the bay which had belonged to Charles Schwab, who
had given it to the Sisters of Charity. They used it for summer
retreats for the Sisters and to take care of orphans and unmarried
mothers and their babies.

Sister Aloysia had had none of the university summer courses
that most Sisters must take nowadays. She never talked to me
about the social encyclicals of the Popes. She gave me a catechism
and brought me old copies of the *Messenger of the Sacred Heart*,
a magazine which, along with the Kathleen Norris type of success story, had some good solid articles about the teachings of the
Church. I read them all; I studied my catechism; I learned to
say the Rosary; I went to Mass in the chapel by the sea; I walked
the beach and I prayed; I read the *Imitation of Christ,* and St.
Augustine, and the New Testament. Dostoevski, Huysmans
(what different men!) had given me desire and background.
Huysmans had made me at home in the Church.

"How can your daughter be brought up a Catholic unless you
become one yourself?" Sister Aloysia kept saying to me. But she
went resolutely ahead in making arrangements for the baptism
of Tamar Teresa.

"You must be a Catholic yourself," she kept telling me. She
had no reticence. She speculated rather volubly at times on the
various reasons why she thought I was holding back. She brought
me pious literature to read, saccharine stories of virtue, emascu-
lated lives of saints young and old, back numbers of pious magazines. William James, agnostic as he was, was more help. He had
introduced me to St. Teresa of Avila and St. John of the Cross.

Isolated as I was in the country, knowing no Catholics except
my neighbors, who seldom read anything except newspapers and
secular magazines, there was not much chance of being introduced to the good Catholic literature of the present day. I was

in a state of dull content—not in a state to be mentally stimulated. I was too happy with my child. What faith I had I held on to stubbornly. The need for patience emphasized in the writings of the saints consoled me on the slow road I was traveling. I would put all my affairs in the hands of God and wait.

Three times a week Sister Aloysia came to give me a catechism lesson, which I dutifully tried to learn. But she insisted that I recite word for word, with the repetition of the question that was in the book. If I had not learned my lesson, she rebuked me, "And you think you are intelligent!" she would say witheringly. "What is the definition of grace—actual grace and sanctifying grace? My fourth-grade pupils know more than you do!"

I hadn't a doubt but that they did. I struggled on day by day, learning without question. I was in an agreeable and lethargic, almost bovine state of mind, filled with an animal content, not wishing to inquire into or question the dogmas I was learning. I made up my mind to accept what I did not understand, trusting light to come, as it sometimes did, in a blinding flash of exultation and realization.

She criticized my housekeeping. "Here you sit at your typewriter at ten o'clock and none of your dishes done yet. Supper and breakfast dishes besides. . . . And why don't you calcimine your ceiling? It's all dirty from wood smoke."

She brought me vegetables from the garden of the home, and I gave her fish and clams. Once I gave her stamps and a dollar to send a present to a little niece and she was touchingly grateful. It made me suddenly realize that, in spite of Charlie Schwab and his estate, the Sisters lived in complete poverty, owning nothing, holding all things in common.

I had to have godparents for Tamar, and I thought of Aunt Jenny, my mother's sister, the only member of our family I knew who had become a Catholic. She had married a Catholic and had one living child, Grace. I did not see them very often but I looked them up now and asked Grace and her husband if they would be godparents to my baby. Tamar was baptized in July. We went down to Tottenville, the little town at the south end of the island; there in the Church of Our Lady, Help of Christians, the seed of life was implanted in her and she was made a child of God.

We came back to the beach house to a delightful lunch of boiled lobsters and salad. Forster had caught the lobsters in his traps for the feast and then did not remain to partake of it. He left, not returning for several days. It was his protest against my yearnings toward the life of the spirit, which he considered a morbid escapism. He exulted in his materialism. He well knew the dignity of man. Heathen philosophers, says Matthias Scheeben, a great modern theologian, have called man a miracle, the marrow and the heart of the world, the most beautiful being, the king of all creatures. Forster saw man in the light of reason and not in the light of faith. He had thought of the baptism only as a mumbo jumbo, the fuss and flurry peculiar to woman. At first he had been indulgent and had brought in the lobsters for the feast. And then he had become angry with some sense of the end to which all this portended. Jealousy set in and he left me.

As a matter of fact, he left me quite a number of times that coming winter and following summer, as he felt my increasing absorption in religion. The tension between us was terrible. Teresa had become a member of the Mystical Body of Christ. I didn't know anything of the Mystical Body or I might have felt disturbed at being separated from her.

But I clutched her close to me and all the time I nursed her and bent over that tiny round face at my breast, I was filled with a deep happiness that nothing could spoil. But the obstacles to my becoming a Catholic were there, shadows in the background of my life.

I had become convinced that I would become a Catholic; yet I felt I was betraying the class to which I belonged, the workers, the poor of the world, with whom Christ spent His life. I wrote a few articles for the *New Masses* but did no other work at that time. My life was crowded in summer because friends came and stayed with me, and some of them left their children. Two little boys, four and eight years old, joined the family for a few months and my days were full, caring for three children and cooking meals for a half-dozen persons three times a day.

Sometimes when I could leave the baby in trusted hands I could get to the village for Mass on Sunday. But usually the gloom that descended on the household, the scarcely voiced opposition, kept me from Mass. There were some feast days when I could slip off during the week and go to the little chapel on the Sisters' grounds. There were "visits" I could make, unknown to others. I was committed, by the advice of a priest I consulted, to the plan of waiting, and trying to hold together the family. But I felt all along that when I took the irrevocable step it would mean that Tamar and I would be alone, and I did not want to be alone. I did not want to give up human love when it was dearest and tenderest.

During the month of August many of my friends, including my sister, went to Boston to picket in protest against the execution of Sacco and Vanzetti, which was drawing near. They were all arrested again and again.

Throughout the nation and the world the papers featured the struggle for the lives of these two men. Radicals from all over the country gathered in Boston, and articles describing those last days were published, poems were written. It was an epic struggle, a tragedy. One felt a sense of impending doom. These men were Catholics, inasmuch as they were Italians. Catholics by tradition, but they had rejected the Church.

Nicola Sacco and Bartolomeo Vanzetti were two anarchists, a shoemaker and a fish peddler who were arrested in 1920 in connection with a payroll robbery at East Braintree, Massachusetts, in which two guards were killed. Nobody paid much attention to the case at first, but as the I.W.W. and the Communists took up the case it became a *cause célèbre*. In August, 1927, they were executed. Many books have been written about the case, and Vanzetti's prison letters are collected in one volume. He learned to write English in prison, and his prose, bare and simple, is noble in its earnestness.

While I enjoyed the fresh breeze, the feel of salt water against the flesh, the keen delight of living, the knowledge that these men were soon to pass from this physical earth, were soon to become dust, without consciousness, struck me like a physical blow. They were here now; in a few days they would be no more. They had become figures beloved by the workers. Their letters, the warm moving story of their lives, had been told. Everyone knew Dante, Sacco's young son. Everyone suffered with the young wife who clung with bitter passion to her husband. And Vanzetti with his large view, his sense of peace at his fate, was even closer to us all.

He wrote a last letter to a friend which has moved many hearts as great poetry does:

I have talked a great deal of myself [he wrote]. But I even forget to name Sacco. Sacco too is a worker, from his boyhood a skilled worker, lover of work, with a good job and pay, a bank account, a good and lovely wife, two beautiful children and a neat little home, at the verge of a wood near a brook.

Sacco is a heart of faith, a lover of nature and man.

A man who gave all, who sacrificed all for mankind, his own wife, his children, himself and his own life.

Sacco has never dreamed to steal, never to assassinate.

He and I never brought a morsel of bread to our mouths, from our childhood to today which has not been gained by the sweat of our brows. Never.

O yes, I may be more witful, as some have put it, I am a better blabber than he is, but many many times in hearing his heartful voice ringing a faith sublime, in considering his supreme sacrifice, remembering his heroism, I felt small at the presence of his greatness and found myself compelled to fight back from my eyes the tears, and quanch my heart, trobling to my throat to not weep before him,—this man called thief, assassin and doomed. . . .

If it had not been for these things I might have lived out my life talking at street corners to scorning men. I might have died, unmarked, un-known, a failure. This is our career and our triumph.

Never in our full life could we hope to do such work
for tolerance, for justice,

for man's understanding of man,
as we now do by accident.
Our words, our lives, our pains—nothing!
The taking of our lives,—lives of a good shoe maker
and a poor fish peddler—all!
That last moment belongs to us
—that agony is our triumph.

The day they died, the papers had headlines as large as those which proclaimed the outbreak of war. All the nation mourned. All the nation, I mean, that is made up of the poor, the worker, the trade unionist—those who felt most keenly the sense of solidarity—that very sense of solidarity which made me gradually understand the doctrine of the Mystical Body of Christ whereby we are the members one of another.

Forster was stricken over the tragedy. He had always been more an anarchist than anything else in his philosophy, and so was closer to these two men than to Communist friends. He did not eat for days. He sat around the house in a stupor of misery, sickened by the cruelty of life and men. He had always taken refuge in nature as being more kindly, more beautiful and peaceful than the world of men. Now he could not even escape through nature, as he tried to escape so many problems in life.

During the time he was home he spent days and even nights out in his boat fishing, so that for weeks I saw little of him. He stupefied himself in his passion for the water, sitting out on the bay in his boat. When he began to recover he submerged himself in maritime biology, collecting, reading only scientific books, and paying no attention to what went on around him. Only the baby interested him. She was his delight. Which made it, of course, the harder to contemplate the cruel blow I was going to strike him when I became a Catholic. We both suffered in body as well as in soul and mind. He would not talk about the faith and relapsed into a complete silence if I tried to bring up the subject. The point of my bringing it up was that I could not become a Catholic and continue living with him, because he was averse to any ceremony before officials of either Church or state. He was an anarchist and an atheist, and he did not intend to be a liar or a hypocrite. He was a creature of utter sincerity, and however illogical and bad-tempered about it all, I loved him. It was killing me to think of leaving him.

Fall nights we read a great deal. Sometimes he went out to dig bait if there were a low tide and the moon was up. He stayed out late on the pier fishing, and came in smelling of seaweed and salt air; getting into bed, cold with the chill November air, he held me close to him in silence. I loved him in every way, as a wife, as a mother even. I loved him for all he knew and pitied him for all he didn't know. I loved him for the odds and ends I had to fish out of his sweater pockets and for the sand and shells he brought in with his fishing. I loved his lean cold body as he got into bed smelling of the sea, and I loved his integrity and stubborn pride.

It ended by my being ill the next summer. I became so oppressed I could not breathe and I awoke in the night choking. I was weak and listless and one doctor told me my trouble was probably thyroid. I went to the Cornell clinic for a metabolism test and they said my condition was a nervous one. By winter the tension had become so great that an explosion occurred and we separated again. When he returned, as he always had, I would not let him in the house; my heart was breaking with my own determination to make an end, once and for all, to the torture we were undergoing.

The next day I went to Tottenville alone, leaving Tamar with my sister, and there with Sister Aloysia as my godparent, I too was baptized conditionally, since I had already been baptized in the Episcopal Church. I made my first confession right afterward, and looked forward the next morning to receiving communion.

I had no particular joy in partaking of these three sacraments, Baptism, Penance and Holy Eucharist. I proceeded about my own active participation in them grimly, coldly, making acts of faith, and certainly with no consolation whatever. One part of my mind stood at one side and kept saying, "What are you doing? Are you sure of yourself? What kind of an affectation is this? What act is this you are going through? Are you trying to induce emotion, induce faith, partake of an opiate, the opiate of the people?" I felt like a hypocrite if I got down on my knees, and shuddered at the thought of anyone seeing me.

At my first communion I went up to the communion rail at the *Sanctus* bell instead of at the *Domine, non sum dignus*, and had to kneel there all alone through the consecration, through the *Pater Noster,* through the *Agnus Dei*—and I had thought I knew the Mass so well! But I felt it fitting that I be humiliated by this ignorance, by this precipitance.

I speak of the misery of leaving one love. But there was another love too, the life I had led in the radical movement. That very winter I was writing a series of articles, interviews with the workers, with the unemployed. I was working with the Anti-Imperialist League, a Communist affiliate, that was bringing aid and comfort to the enemy, General Sandino's forces in Nicaragua. I was just as much against capitalism and imperialism as ever, and here I was going over to the opposition, because of course the Church was lined up with property, with the wealthy, with the state, with capitalism, with all the forces of reaction. This I had been taught to think and this I still think to a great extent. "Too often," Cardinal Mundelein said, "has the Church lined up on the wrong side." "Christianity," Bakunin said, "is precisely the religion par excellence, because it exhibits, and manifests, to the fullest extent, the very nature and essence of every religious system, which is the impoverishment, enslavement, and annihilation of humanity for the benefit of divinity."

I certainly believed this, but I wanted to be poor, chaste and obedient. I wanted to die in order to live, to put off the old man and put on Christ. I loved, in other words, and like all women in love, I wanted to be united to my love. Why should not Forster be jealous? Any man who did not participate in this love would, of course, realize my infidelity, my adultery. In the eyes of God, any turning toward creatures to the exclusion of Him is adultery and so it is termed over and over again in Scripture.

I loved the Church for Christ made visible. Not for itself,

because it was so often a scandal to me. Romano Guardini said the Church is the Cross on which Christ was crucified; one could not separate Christ from His Cross, and one must live in a state of permanent dissatisfaction with the Church.

The scandal of businesslike priests, of collective wealth, the lack of a sense of responsibility for the poor, the worker, the Negro, the Mexican, the Filipino, and even the oppression of these, and the consenting to the oppression of them by our industrialist-capitalist order—these made me feel often that priests were more like Cain than Abel. "Am I my brother's keeper?" they seemed to say in respect to the social order. There was plenty of charity but too little justice. And yet the priests were the dispensers of the Sacraments, bringing Christ to men, all enabling us to put on Christ and to achieve more nearly in the world a sense of peace and unity. "The worst enemies would be those of our own household," Christ had warned us.

We could not root out the tares without rooting out the wheat also. With all the knowledge I have gained these twenty-one years I have been a Catholic, I could write many a story of priests who were poor, chaste and obedient, who gave their lives daily for their fellows, but I am writing of how I felt at the time of my baptism.

Not long afterward a priest wanted me to write a story of my conversion, telling how the social teaching of the Church had led me to embrace Catholicism. But I knew nothing of the social teaching of the Church at that time. I had never heard of the encyclicals. I felt that the Church was the Church of the poor, that St. Patrick's had been built from the pennies of servant girls, that it cared for the emigrant, it established hospitals, orphanages, day nurseries, houses of the Good Shepherd, homes for the aged, but at the same time, I felt that it did not set its face against a social order which made so much charity in the present sense of the word necessary. I felt that charity was a word to choke over. Who wanted charity? And it was not just human pride but a strong sense of man's dignity and worth, and what was due to him in justice, that made me resent, rather than feel proud of so mighty a sum total of Catholic institutions. Besides, more and more they were taking help from the state, and in taking from the state, they had to render to the state. They came under the head of Community Chest and discriminatory charity, centralizing and departmentalizing, involving themselves with bureaus, building, red tape, legislation, at the expense of human values. By "they," I suppose one always means the bishops, but as Harry Bridges once pointed out to me, "they" also are victims of the system.

It was an age-old battle, the war of the classes, that stirred in me when I thought of the Sacco-Vanzetti case in Boston. Where were the Catholic voices crying out for these men? How I longed to make a synthesis reconciling body and soul, this world and the next, the teachings of Prince Peter Kropotkin and Prince Demetrius Gallitzin, who had become a missionary priest in rural Pennsylvania.

Where had been the priests to go out to such men as Francisco Ferrer in Spain, pursuing them as the Good Shepherd did His lost sheep, leaving the ninety and nine of their good parishioners, to seek out that which was lost, bind up that which was bruised. No wonder there was such a strong conflict going on in my mind and heart.

JOBS AND JOURNEYS

I NEVER regretted for one minute the step which I had taken in becoming a Catholic, but I repeat that for a year there was little joy for me as the struggle continued. I knew a good priest who helped me along the way. I was living in New York that winter and went to confession in a church on West Fourteenth Street, Our Lady of Guadaloupe. It was a narrow little church, served by the Augustinian Fathers of the Assumption, and there were Masses at seven, eight and nine o'clock each morning. Before every Mass priests came from the rectory next door to hear confessions. There were three confessionals on either side of the entrance door, and there were bells on the confessionals so that at any other time of the day one could ring a bell and a priest would appear. My priest's name was Father Zachary and his previous assignment had been in the Holy Land. He was a Spaniard, a gentle old man who was good and patient with me. He was so gentle that one welcomed his questions, and when he found that I was baptized but not confirmed he began preparing me for confirmation. He gave me Challoner's book of meditations to read and a St. Andrew's missal so that I could learn to follow the seasons of the Church, the saints of the day, and have the doctrinal instruction containing many quotations from the Fathers of the Church that the missal gave before each Sunday Mass.

One confessor years later told me he found little of Christ in my writing but much of self. I would have taken that criticism humbly except that he added, "I will tell you when to write." Since this priest was one who objected to all my social interests on the ground that it was too late to do anything except prepare for death, I left him and found another. Thank God one can change one's confessor. As a matter of fact I have been singularly fortunate in good parish priests, order priests and diocesan, to whom I could go. I was happy indeed with Father Zachary.

In turn Father Zachary read some of my articles and short stories, and confessed that he found them very dull and unadorned. "You have no style," he would complain. "You are too grim, too realistic."

Often when I had finished my confession and my act of contrition and he had given me absolution, he would lean over and whisper, "Have you sold any stories lately?"

Such an interest was not as mundane as one might think. I was still working for the Anti-imperialist League and Father Zachary told me to keep my Communist job until I found another one.

My confirmation was a joyous affair. I went one Sunday afternoon on the feast of Pentecost to the Convent of the Holy Souls on Eighty-fifth Street near Third Avenue. There, in company with a large group of adults, to the sweet singing of the nuns, I received the sacrament of confirmation. I took the name of Maria Teresa.

Back on Staten Island the following summer I did not suffer so much from being alone, because we had more children to take care of. Freda and Sasha had a friend who ran a school in Spuyten Duyvil called the Hoffman School of Individual Development. She wished to have a free summer that year, so she asked Freda to take a dozen of her children for the vacation months. Freda and I were both limited as to room, but between the two of us we could manage it. I took the littlest ones and Freda crowded in the big ones dormitory style; she cooked and I washed dishes. It was a happy summer. One cannot be miserable with a group of growing children around. There was little time to think.

When I went into town the following winter, I found housekeeping rooms on West Fourteenth Street in order to be near Our Lady of Guadaloupe Church. Freda and Sasha had long been toying with the idea of running a restaurant, so they took a very large ten-room apartment with three rooms which opened into each other and there they started their venture. I spent a good deal of time with them. Eva Le Gallienne's troupe were across the street playing stock in an old theater. The members of the company often ate dinner with us, and came over after the performance. Though it was prohibition time, Sasha served drinks, and I never could understand why my friends left their venture poorer than when they started. They were typically Russian, large-hearted, generous, so doubtless they fed many who could not afford to pay. It was when I was working with the Fellowship of Reconciliation, eating at Sasha's and leaving Tamar in the Nazareth Day Nursery on Fifteenth Street that I wrote the play which afterward brought me a contract with Pathe.

It was a hard winter. My work was not difficult—hours were from ten to three—but I became ill with intestinal influenza and was weak and ailing. During the worst part of my illness, it happened that my sister was sick also. She had married the year before and was expecting a baby shortly, otherwise she would have come to my rescue as she often had.

My friends were busy also and did not know how ill I was. I lay in bed for several days. Fortunately I had food in the house, and milk was delivered at the door, so we managed, the baby and

I, to get along. She played in the long gloomy dark room which faced north to a high apartment house on the next street. I was able to drag myself up every now and then to feed and bathe her and put her to bed. It was a grim few days because I had a high temperature. I lay there and thought of how horrible it would be if I should die and no one would know until the milkman found the bottles accumulating outside the door or the landlady came to collect the rent. It was not like the East Side tenement apartments that I had known where the neighbors ran in to see how you were getting on, with offers of a bowl of soup or a dish of fresh rolls. How I longed for my Jewish neighbors during that time of illness! I had gone to the West Side and rented my two housekeeping rooms because I wanted to be near the Church of Our Lady of Guadaloupe, but I made up my mind then that I would live hereafter on my beloved East Side. Here I was surrounded by the ordinary American with his own desire for privacy, for going his own way. I shall never forget that siege of illness in a rooming house where each one was isolated from the other, each afraid another would ask something from him. However, little Tamar did not seem to suffer too much during that illness of mine. She was fretty at times, but since she got little attention, she reconciled herself to my silence and played with her toys. She was almost three then and could already hold a big needle and try to sew.

In the spring of that year a friend who had lost her son came to live with me. She had had two children, her husband was dead, the older son was married and had little to do with her, and her younger son had committed suicide the month before. Lallah's grief and my own depression following my attack of sickness made these days sad ones. I had not been able to earn enough to pay the taxes on the house on the beach and they had accumulated. So I decided to work for the summer in a children's camp where I could keep Tamar with me and rent my little house to pay my debts. My parish church on Staten Island was Our Lady Star of the Sea in Huguenot, and on Saturday nights Marist Fathers helped hear confessions. After confession one Saturday in

May when I was spending a week end on the island I spoke to the priest about getting work in a camp.

"Our novitiate in Prince's Bay is closed for the summer and there are only three priests and three brothers there, so why don't you come and cook for us? Brother Philip has been cooking, but he wants to work in the garden. We were to have a group of Mexican nuns to work in the kitchen, but we have not been able to get them, and we have a whole wing off the kitchen, chapel included, which you can have to yourself. You'll only have the three meals to get and no marketing. The brothers do the washing and scrubbing."

It was my first contact with Father McKenna, and we became good friends at once. He was easy to talk with, a gentle, understanding soul who helped me along little by little, never judging or condemning my former comrades. He brought me books to read and introduced me to such writers as Karl Adam and showed me how to say the Little Office of the Blessed Virgin. When my guests came, he brought candy and cigarettes for them, and drove them to the station as they came to and from the city. He had never seen any Communists and anarchists before, and they had never been so close to a priest. They were a little wary of each other and there was not much conversation between them.

He loved Tamar and took her around with him to the barns, to watch the brothers milk the cows and feed the chickens, and she was devoted to him. She found a nest of field mice when they were cutting hay and brought them in to make homes for them in muffin tins. She helped Brother Philip water the garden with a little sprinkler.

Between meals, sitting on a stool by a high kitchen table while the stew boiled on the stove and Tamar played with the pots and pans in the closet, I wrote stories and articles, one of which I sold to *The Commonweal*, a Catholic weekly.

On the feast of the Assumption, August fifteenth, while I was in the kitchen preparing supper, I received a telephone call from California, from Pathe, saying they had liked a play which I had submitted to Metro-Goldwyn some months before. They would like me to sign a contract with them for writing dialogue on the Coast. I did not know whether they were going to use the play I had submitted. They talked of it with great enthusiasm, comparing it to Chekhov. They were full of the great things I was capable of.

I was delighted of course. Change was always welcome and I was glad to leave New York. It was one of those small contracts, not the fabulous kind one reads about: a three-months affair, at one hundred and twenty-five dollars a week and transportation to and from the Coast.

Like all Hollywood-bound authors, I thought of the money that I would make that would free me for a simple life in the future and for work on the novel I was always writing.

The Marist novitiate was to reopen in September and my work was to have ended then anyway, but I parted from Father McKenna with sorrow.

It had been a wonderful summer. I had begun it with sadness, a heavy mood which was the result not only of my own weakness but Lallah's grief. As a matter of fact, I had begun my days there weeping. Father McKenna, catching me at it as I sat at the kitchen table, and not being able to get at the cause of my tears, had offered a Mass for me. The sorrow had gone at once, thanks, I firmly believed, to that good man's prayers, and the power of the Sacrament. I ended the summer with high hopes that were soon dispelled. In the first place I soon found I could save little money in California, in spite of a salary which I considered huge at that time. I had nothing to do, so what I received was like a retaining fee. But Lallah, who had come west with me, became ill and had to be hospitalized for a minor operation. Since there were no free hospitals that I could discover in our section of Los Angeles, I had to pay her bills. Another time, Lallah, Tamar and I were invited to a comrade's little ranch over the week end. Tamar was asked to stay a week and when I returned to work I was surprised to find a large bill for our hospitality.

My money evaporated week after week—it was only by rigid economy for the last month of my stay in Culver City where

Pathe was located that I was able to save enough money to go to Mexico.

I suppose I had hopes, when I went west, of living a stimulating creative life, with time to read and study and write. There was plenty of time to read. I was cooped up in my own office, with chaise longue, having nothing to do all day and every day, except to wait for mail from home and read. The atmosphere was not one conducive to study. It was hectic, crowded and yet I knew no one; stages were set up, productions were being put on piece-meal; no one knew what was going on or whether indeed anything were being put on at all. Occasionally a group of us, not one knowing the other, were summoned in to a most comfortable lounging room, where we sat in chairs with ash trays by our sides and viewed some stupid production (I can remember none of them now) and were invited to give our views on it. I remember one most inane office conference where we were supposed to discuss the plot of some such typical story as *The Grand Duchess and the Waiter*, and of course the waiter turns out to be a grand duke or prince. There was no thought. There was no discussion of ideas or attempt to portray ideas. The only serious films I had seen were probably *The Cabinet of Dr. Caligari, Crime and Punishment,* and a few other so-called morbid foreign films which no one there was interested in. There were none of the universal appeal of *Paisan,* or *The Baker's Wife,* or the *Bicycle Thief,* or *Monsieur Vincent.* There seemed to be no common ground on which any of us could meet, we who passed each other in the corridors of the Colonial-residence-type building which housed the offices and studios of Pathe.

I knew Dudley Nichols from his newspaper days in New York and there were occasional visits, but he, who also intended to save his money and return east to live on a farm and write novels, had become one of the foremost screen writers there and he was as busy as I was idle. He was the newspaperman of genius who could take any material and make it come alive.

I was lonely, deadly lonely. And I was to find out then, as I found out so many times, over and over again, that women especially are social beings, who are not content with just husband

and family, but must have a community, a group, an exchange with others. A child is not enough. A husband and children, no matter how busy one may be kept by them, are not enough. Young and old, even in the busiest years of our lives, we women especially are victims of the long loneliness. Men may go away and become desert Fathers, but there were no desert mothers. Even the anchoresses led rather sociable lives, with bookbinding and spiritual counseling, even if they did have to stay in one place.

I would have gone back to New York when my contract was not renewed, but to me at that time New York was an occasion of sin. I hungered too much to return to Forster. I had to stay away for a while longer. So I went to Mexico.

I lived in Mexico as I lived in New York, with the poor. I took rooms with a Mexican family—an old one-armed woman, her daughter, and their orphaned nephew and niece. The daughter, who helped earn the living for the family by selling stockings from a pushcart in the little park of St. Joseph around the corner from their home, cooked a delicious meal for us every day. Breakfast and supper I prepared for Tamar and myself on a little oil stove. I was able to earn enough to remain in Mexico for six months, and to have in addition to my rooms in Mexico City a little stone hut in Xochimilco where birds flew in and out of the one shuttered window. There were no glass panes. There were no plumbing facilities; one brought jars of water from the village well and washed clothing and dishes in the canals which surrounded the many islands that made up Xochimilco.

Living was so cheap in Mexico that I would have remained perhaps if Tamar had not become ill. She recovered as soon as we returned to New York, where we arrived just after the May Day riots in Union Square. The great depression, which began with a stock market crash the autumn before while I was in California, was well under way.

More and more people were losing their jobs, more families were being evicted, the Unemployed Councils were being formed by the Communist groups and the Workers Alliance sprang into existence. It was a time for pressure groups, for direct action, and radicalism was thriving among all groups except the Catholics. I felt out of it all. There was Catholic membership in all these groups of course, but no Catholic leadership. It was that very year that Pope Pius XI said sadly to Canon Cardijn, who was organizing the workers in Belgium, "The workers of the world are lost to the Church."

And yet for me personally that was an extraordinarily happy time for some reason or other. Maybe it was the deepening of my spiritual life. Maybe it was because I had sufficient interesting work to do to support Tamar and myself, and leave leisure for my own reading and writing. It was a beautiful clear summer in 1932, with sparkling weather, not too hot, so that after some of the research work I was doing at the library I was able to walk home and savor the beauty of the city and of the day. For there is a beauty of the city, of the wide avenues, of the clean houses on orderly streets, of trees and little porches, and there were streets I loved and walks I loved that were not in the slums where I was living.

One can conceive of a city with art and culture and music and architecture, and the flowering of all good things, as the image of the heavenly city. Heaven is pictured as a city, the heavenly Jerusalem. I was enjoying the city that summer.

There was the companionship of my brother John and his wife, a young Spanish girl whom he had met when he was living with me on the beach. Neither was yet twenty. For the first six months of his marriage he had worked on a newspaper. Then when the staff was cut, he was forced to accept the hospitality of Tessa's parents, who had two other daughters at home. They had a great sense of hospitality. "There is always enough for one more," the mother of the household said. "Everyone just takes a little less."

When the young couple found they were to become parents, there was that other Spanish saying to reassure them, "A baby is always born with a loaf of bread under its arm."

Now they were living with me, I was taking my turn at hospitality, and I enjoyed their company very much. My sister with her husband and two small babies had taken my five-year-old Tamar with them to their country home and I went down to them every fortnight for a long week end.

I was living in a "railroad flat," or a "dumb-bell apartment" as they are called, with a large room in front, a kitchen in the back and the two dark airless bedrooms in between. It was on the first floor and narrower than those upstairs and noisier, what with tenants going in and out and the milkman starting the long parade early in the day. But the house was spotlessly clean. The Riedel family lived on the third floor rent free and received a salary to keep the place clean, to dispose of the garbage and refuse from the other seven families who lived there. It was an Italian and German neighborhood in a section of the East Side where the houses have been torn down since, to make way for an immense housing project. I was attracted to the house on Fifteenth Street because of the beautiful back yards, separated by wooden fences. Each house had its flower garden, divided by a home-built wire fence from a cement-paved yard where the children could play without trampling flowers. There were tall untrimmed privet hedges against the back fences. When these were in bloom there was a pleasant acrid odor in the air. Beds of perennials grew in profusion, and kept increasing every year. Between borders of ice plant and widows' tears there were brick walks, and in the center of each plot there was, wonder of wonders, a fig tree which had to be well corseted in winter with straw and bound up to keep warm. There were many of these in New York, in the back yards of the Italians. Tamar needed a yard to play in and the additional rooms gave me space to invite my brother and sister-in-law to live with me in the fall.

There was no heat in the house, so we used the gas stove in the kitchen for both heating and cooking. In the coldest months, this meant that the bill would come to twenty dollars a month. The rent of the apartment was also twenty. I felt that the four rooms with their cross ventilation from street to back garden gave me air and breathing space, and I settled down to work and writing with great peace and joy.

I was writing a novel. I have always been a journalist and a diarist pure and simple, but as long as I could remember, I dreamed in terms of novels. This one was to be about the depression, a social novel with the pursuit of a job as the motive and the social revolution as its crisis. There was to be the struggle between religion and otherworldliness, and communism and this-worldliness, replete with a heroine and hero and scores of fascinating characters. I put my own struggle and dreams of love into the book and was very happy writing it.

But my life was too full. I progressed slowly. I had to work for a living. I walked to and from my work. I arose early for Mass, and I began to go to daily communion for the first time in the four years I had been a Catholic. This was at the urging of a priest whom I never happened to see, to whom I spoke in the confessional, to whom I confided my struggles from week to week.

Father Zamien was Salesian and was not long afterward sent back to Jugoslavia. He was the kind of priest who gave you spiritual counsel, who recommended spiritual books to read, who advised daily Mass and daily communion and made you know your importance as a child of God.

In that little church there were two priests who heard confessions every morning before and after Mass, one on either side of the rear of the church. When Father Zamien was no longer there I turned to Father Pelligrini, who even now is still hearing confessions in his stifling little box on the right-hand side of the church of Our Lady, Help of Christians, on East Twelfth Street. On the other side of the church, the windows were open all summer, and your eyes could wander if the sermon was too long (and in Italian), out to the window boxes of the tenements on Avenue A. There were the ever-present petunias, the boxed basil, the tomato plants, and the morning glories climbing up the fire escapes.

Yes, I was happy that summer. In the evening I went back to the church for Benediction of the Blessed Sacrament. Then in the quiet evening I went home to read the life of St. Teresa of Avila and her foundations. She charmed me completely.

After I had become a Catholic I began little by little to lose track of my friends. Being a Catholic, I discovered, put a barrier between me and others; however slight, it was always felt.

I still saw my Staten Island friends Freda and Sasha. There were also Mike Gold and his brothers George and Manuel and their wives who, the last year of my stay there, had bought a house in Staten Island down the road from me. We were still very close. In the fall when Tessa and John came to live with me Mike used to drop in often. It was before his marriage, and he longed for children. "All the world loves a pregnant woman," he would say wistfully, and he would lay his hand on Tessa's body.

His brother George was married to a glowing blonde girl from Greenpoint. They had two children and George did everything and anything to make a living for them. He made furniture; he and Gert took children to care for while their parents worked. That fall George was working with the Unemployed Councils which had been formed to combat unemployment, demand relief, protest evictions. Now there was a plan to rent trucks and bring groups to Washington, there to be met by other groups from all over the country. Those who could not go with a truck came by boxcar from as far west as Seattle, Portland and San Francisco and joined the trucks in some eastern city. A number of them gathered in Union Square to start the Hunger March, as they called it, to Washington.

George had told me of the projected trip. His job was to hire the trucks. There was an Unemployed Council in every neighborhood and the members garnered their small resources of money and men to go to Washington and present the case of the destitute. The councils were Communist dominated, of course, but the rank and file membership was made up of every political color and creed.

Since I could leave my daughter with John and Tessa, I decided I would go to Washington, not as a delegate, but as a reporter, for *The Commonweal*, the first Catholic publication for which I had written. At the same time as this demonstration of the unemployed, there was a Farmers' Convention in Washington, made up of rank and file small farmers and tenant farmers from around the country. This was also Communist inspired. *America,* the Jesuit weekly, offered to pay me for an article about that.

Getting an advance from *The Commonweal* to cover expenses, I took the bus with Mary Heaton Vorse, that valiant labor reporter, whom I had known in the days when I worked for the old *Masses* and the *Liberator.* She knew all the reporters in Washington and we went to the home of one of them when we arrived to get the latest news on the demonstrators. Mary was always helping support her children and her children's children, so she traveled and lived as cheaply as she could, in lodging houses all over the world. She had worked for the labor movement in America in addition to writing stories for *Collier's* and the women's journals, stories which she called lollipops; but her real love was "Labor."

She had covered every major strike in the country. She knew the aristocrat of New England as well as the radical and the Bohemian; in her family there had been a long tradition of high thinking for generations back. Her first two husbands had died, and she had married Robert Minor, who took Earl Browder's place when he was imprisoned during the early years of World War II, as general secretary of the Communist party. Bob had struggled through from a faith in the I.W.W., the anarcho-syndicalist, to that of the Communist, with much soul-searching and study, Mary said, and was a sincere though a rather dull revolutionist. Later they separated, he to marry a younger woman (one with no career of her own) and Mary to continue her work as a world reporter.

I had had such a peaceful summer and fall. Now at the beginning of December, I was in the thick of the struggle again, writing not the nice leisurely novel but the immediate flash story of revolt. That was how the newspapers interpreted it. It was an impressive demonstration. Leaving New York, the procession of old trucks and cars, such as the Joad family in *Grapes of Wrath* traveled in some years later in quest of land and work, paraded through various cities, and, where they could, stopped to hold meetings in Protestant churches and labor halls. In one such church in Wilmington, Delaware, the police broke up the meeting by throwing tear-gas bombs through the windows and when the marchers broke out from the church in disorderly fashion, clubbed and arrested those whom they suspected of being the leaders.

In spite of such incidents, and there were others, the hunger marchers persisted and went on to Washington. We had been late in starting, Mary and I, and when we arrived, they were there before us.

This was not long after the tear-gassing and routing of the veterans, who had encamped for a while in Washington to bring their plight before the legislators of the country. Now the papers were full of the Communist menace. There were scare headlines, and as a result of the hysteria built up by the press, police had stopped the procession of trucks as it entered Washington on Route One; there the men remained encamped for three days and nights. The road was closed and all other traffic was rerouted. On one side was a park of sorts and on the other railroad tracks; the police hemmed in the demonstrators, keeping them there with threats of tear gas and machinegunning. The demonstrators slept in trucks and on the roadside those first days of December when the weather was already bitter, while the respectable citizen slept in his warm bed and read comfortably of the "reds" who had come to take over Washington. I do not think the people themselves were frightened. Left to themselves they would reasonably have permitted the demonstration, have listened to the complaints, passed on the recommendations to the proper authorities, expecting in due course that something might be done.

But the newspapers had to have their story. With scare heads, yellow journalism, and staccato radio, the tense, nervous stories built up, of communism at home and Communist atrocities in the rest of the world.

If there was not a story, the newspapers would make a story. If there was not a war, the press would see to it that there was a class war, a war in which all the weapons were on the side of the authorities. The newspaper reporters were infected by their own journalism and began to beg city editors to give them tear-gas masks before they went out to interview the leaders of the unemployed marchers. They knew what they were building up to.

Mary Vorse and I stayed in a tourist house on Massachusetts Avenue, and ate cheaply in lunch wagons. We felt that when people were enduring the hardships these men and women were suffering, it was not the time for us to be comfortable. We ate frugally and we put up in dollar-a-night lodgings so there was something left over to contribute to the food fund of the strikers. Mary had always been that kind of a reporter. Her brand of journalism was different.

And then, after three days of mounting hysteria, suddenly permission was given to the marchers to proceed. On a bright sunny day the ragged horde triumphantly with banners flying, with lettered slogans mounted on sticks, paraded three thousand strong through the tree-flanked streets of Washington. I stood on the curb and watched them, joy and pride in the courage of this band of men and women mounting in my heart, and with it a bitterness too that since I was now a Catholic, with fundamental philosophical differences, I could not be out there with them. I could write, I could protest, to arouse the conscience, but where was the Catholic leadership in the gathering of bands of men and women together, for the actual works of mercy that the comrades had always made part of their technique in reaching the workers?

How little, how puny my work had been since becoming a Catholic, I thought. How self-centered, how ingrown, how lacking in sense of community! My summer of quiet reading and prayer, my self-absorption seemed sinful as I watched my brothers in their struggle, not for themselves but for others. How our dear Lord must love them, I kept thinking to myself. They were His friends, His comrades, and who knows how close to His heart in their attempt to work for justice. I remembered that the first public act of our Lord recorded in the New Testament was the overthrowing of the money-changers' tables in the temple. The miracle at Cana, when Christ was present at the wedding feast and turned water into wine, has been written of as the first public act of our Lord. It was the first miracle, it was the sanctifying of marriage, but it was not the social act of overturning the tables of the money changers, a divine courage on the part of this obscure Jew, going into the temple and with bold scorn for all the riches of this world, scattering the coins and the traffickers in gold.

The demands of the marchers were for social legislation, for unemployment insurance, for old-age pensions, for relief for mothers and children, for work. I remember seeing one banner on which was inscribed, "Work, not wages," a mysterious slogan having to do with man's dignity, his ownership of and responsibility for the means of production.

The years have passed, and most of the legislation called for by those workers is on the books now. I wonder how many realize just how much they owe the hunger marchers, who endured fast and cold, who were like the Son of Man, when He said, "The foxes have holes, and the birds of the air have nests but the Son of man hath not where to lay his head."

When the demonstration was over and I had finished writing my story, I went to the national shrine at the Catholic University on the feast of the Immaculate Conception. There I offered up a special prayer, a prayer which came with tears and with anguish, that some way would open up for me to use what talents I possessed for my fellow workers, for the poor.

As I knelt there, I realized that after three years of Catholicism my only contact with active Catholics had been through articles I had written for one of the Catholic magazines. Those contacts had been brief, casual. I still did not know personally one Catholic layman.

And when I returned to New York, I found Peter Maurin— Peter the French peasant, whose spirit and ideas will dominate the rest of this book as they will dominate the rest of my life.

Part Three

LOVE IS THE MEASURE

PEASANT OF THE PAVEMENTS

WHEN I walked into my apartment, I found waiting for me a short, stocky man in his mid-fifties, as ragged and rugged as any of the marchers I had left. I like people to look their part, and if they are workers, to look like workers, and if they are peasants to look like peasants. I like to see the shape of a man's hands, the strength of his neck and shoulders.

This man introduced himself briefly: "I am Peter Maurin." He pronounced it Maw-rin, with the accent on the first syllable, deliberately anglicizing the word. "George Shuster, editor of *The Commonweal*, told me to look you up. Also, a red-headed Irish Communist in Union Square told me to see you. He says we think alike."

How to describe Peter and the effect he had on me. Certainly I knew at once that he was French. It was difficult to become accustomed to his accent, which he kept although he had already been twenty years in America. He was intensely alive, on the alert, even when silent, engaged in reading or in thought. When he talked, the tilt of his head, his animated expression, the warm glow in his eyes, the gestures of his hands, his shoulders, his whole body, compelled your attention. I remember several things about that first meeting, characteristics of Peter that were to impress themselves more and more on me during the years that followed. He spoke in terms of ideas, rather than personalities, and he stressed the importance of theory. As people gathered around us in the movement which sprang up, this attribute stood out. While others were always analyzing, talking about one another, using one another's lives and attitudes to illustrate ideas, Peter was always impersonal, delicately scrupulous never to talk about others, never to make the derogatory remark.

169

"Lenin said, 'There can be no revolution without a theory of revolution,' so I am trying to give the theory of a green revolution," he said.

He delighted in the title of agitator. Though he spoke of ideas, and men of ideas, he made these ideas dynamic by coloring them in his own way—"I knew a man who—" or "Peguy's mother mended chairs in Notre Dame Cathedral—"

The nearest he came to being critical with me was to tell me that my education lacked Catholic background. He began to give it to me by talking about the history of the Church, by going even further back into time and speaking of the prophets of Israel as well as the Fathers of the Church. His friends were Jews, Protestants, agnostics, as well as Catholics, and he found a common ground with all in what he termed the Thomistic doctrine of the common good. He ignored differences to stress concordance. He did not use such terms as ecumenical, though he was not afraid of the unusual word (agronomic universities were part of his program), but he thought in terms of our common humanity, of our life here today. He stressed the need of building a new society within the shell of the old—that telling phrase from the preamble to the I.W.W. constitution, "a society in which it is easier for people to be good," he added with a touching simplicity, knowing that when people are good, they are happy.

He was a man of tremendous ambition, in spite of his simplicity, or perhaps because of it. He wanted to make a new synthesis, as St. Thomas had done in the Middle Ages, and he wanted to enlist the aid of a group of people in doing this. He was no more afraid of the non-Catholic approach to problems than St. Thomas was of the Aristotelian.

With all his knowledge, he was no isolated scholar. It was the state of the world which filled him with these vast desires. Man was placed here with talents, to play his part, and on every side he saw the children of this world wiser in their generation than the children of light. They built enormous industrial plants, bridges, pipe lines, skyscrapers, with imagination and vision they made their blue prints, and with reckless and daredevil financing made them actual in steel and concrete. Wheels turned and engines throbbed and the great pulse of the mechanical and physical world beat strong and steady while men's pulses sickened and grew weaker and died. Man fed himself into the machine.

Peter rejoiced to see men do great things and dream great dreams. He wanted them to stretch out their arms to their brothers, because he knew that the surest way to find God, to find the good, was through one's brothers. Peter wanted this striving to result in a better physical life in which all men would be able to fulfill themselves, develop their capacities for love and worship, expressed in all the arts. He wanted them to be able to produce what was needed in the way of homes, food, clothing, so that there was enough of these necessities for everyone. A synthesis of "cult, culture and cultivation," he called it, as he tried to give me the long view, the vision.

It was hard for me to understand what he meant, thinking as I always had in terms of cities and immediate need of men for their weekly pay check. Now I can see clearly what he was talking about, but I am faced with the problem of making others see it. I can well recognize the fact that people remaining as they are, Peter's program is impossible. But it would become actual, given a people changed in heart and mind, so that they would observe the new commandment of love, or desired to.

Peter made you feel a sense of his mission as soon as you met him. He did not begin by tearing down, or by painting so intense a picture of misery and injustice that you burned to change the world. Instead, he aroused in you a sense of your own capacities for work, for accomplishment. He made you feel that you and all men had great and generous hearts with which to love God. If you once recognized this fact in yourself you would expect and find it in others. "The art of human contacts," Peter called it happily. But it was seeing Christ in others, loving the Christ you saw in others. Greater than this, it was having faith in the Christ in others without being able to see Him. Blessed is he that believes without seeing.

Although Peter came to me with sheaves of writing in every

pocket, which he either read aloud, or pressed upon me to read and study, he had not begun to write till late in life. All his writing, even his letters to me, were in phrased sentences, broken up to look like free verse. He used this device to compel attention, to make for more reflective reading but also because some of his writings had a swing, a rhythm like verse. He liked to consider himself a troubadour of Christ, singing solutions to the world's ills, insinuating them into men's ears with catchy phrases.

I do not remember with what essays he introduced himself to me. It might have been "The Dynamite of the Church" or "When the Irish Were Irish, a Thousand Years Ago."

I had been coffined in a bus for eight hours; I was anxious for quiet, for a cup of coffee. I was anxious to greet my child and Tessa and John. I am sure that first night I was no more than polite. In fact, had it not been for Tessa, with her unfailing hospitality, her ready attention to guests, I might not have met Peter at all. For my brother was a conventional American and Peter often gave the impression of being a dangerous and unbalanced radical when he began "indoctrinating" someone who was unprepared. I speak as the conventional American myself, in spite of years in the radical movement. Peter was the most persistent soul in the world and he was looking for apostles to share his work. When he read the articles I had written in *America, The Commonweal* and *The Sign,* he was convinced that I was the one who was to work with him. Before he knew me well he went about comparing me to a Catherine of Siena who would move mountains and have influence on governments, temporal and spiritual. He was a man of enthusiasm and always saw great talents in people.

When he came back the next day, for we did not share ideas at length that first night, he began at once on what he called my education. "Indoctrination" was his word. He not only wished to give me a Catholic outline of history—but he also wished to repeat over and over again his program of action; round-table discussions, houses of hospitality and agronomic universities. We were to popularize this program for immediate needs, which in itself would be the seed for a long-range program, a green revolution, by publishing a paper for the man in the street.

What Peter called round-table discussions I was already familiar enough with as meetings, whether indoors or from a soapbox. I could see the necessity for them, "for the clarification of thought," as he always said, and I knew that humanly speaking they would always go on. But he wanted more than supper-table conversations; he wanted to plan meetings too for the beginnings of a school, to bring the workers and scholars together.

Since I came from a newspaper family, with my two older brothers working on newspapers at that time, and my father still a writer though no longer an editor, I could see the need for such a paper as Peter described.

But how were we going to start it?

Peter did not pretend to be practical along these lines. "I enunciate the principles," he declared grandly.

"But where do we get the money?" I asked him, clinging to the "we," though he was making clear his role as theorist.

"In the history of the saints, capital was raised by prayer. God sends you what you need when you need it. You will be able to pay the printer. Just read the lives of the saints."

St. Francis de Sales scattered leaflets like any radical. St. John of God sold newspapers on the streets. We didn't have to do things on a big scale, Peter made it clear.

I had been reading the life of Rose Hawthorne not long before, how she started what has since become a chain of cancer hospitals in a four-room tenement apartment such as the one I was living in. Why not start a newspaper in the same way? I began to look on our kitchen as an editorial office, my brother as an assistant to write heads and to help with mechanical make-up. Tamar and I could go out to sell papers on the streets!

Peter was very optimistic in his expectations of people. At first he thought that his priest friend who had a large uptown parish would provide the basement of his church for an office, and a mimeograph machine for printing press. Since Father Scully provided him with a dollar a day for city expenses while he was working for him, he used to go to see him often in those early days of our acquaintance. I, too, wanted to meet Peter's friend and went one time to his rectory. He was away at the time, so I turned to the church next door and went in for a visit. There was Peter, the only other one besides myself in the church at that moment, and he did not see me come in, but sat there, before the Blessed Sacrament, motionless, quiet, absorbed, gazing altarward. Every now and then I saw his forefinger rise, count off a few points, and then stillness again.

I thought, as I looked at him there, how much he looked like pictures of St. John Bosco. St. John Bosco was an Italian peasant who became a priest and built up a tremendous number of boy's hospices and trade schools throughout the world. The conviction came over me that Peter too was a man of vision.

My impatience kept me from waiting longer for Father Scully —he was pastor of a big parish and dealt with educational affairs in the diocese besides running the camp at Mount Tremper as a hobby—truly a very busy man. My mind turned to printers. Finding that I could have twenty-five hundred copies of an eight-page tabloid printed for fifty-seven dollars by the Paulist Press, I decided to use two small checks I had just received for articles for the first printing bill, rather than for the rent or gas and electric. We would sell the paper, I decided, for a cent a copy, to make it so cheap that anyone could afford to buy.

Peter had his own ideas as to what was to be in that paper. When the first issue came out the following May Day with articles about labor, strikes, unemployment, factual accounts, columns, features, in addition to half a dozen of Peter's "Easy Essays," as John named them, he protested.

"Everybody's paper is nobody's paper," he said. And I realized that in his simplicity, in his lofty concept of his mission, he wanted nothing but his own essays to be printed, over and over, and broadcast throughout the country. He knew that he had a message. His confidence looked like conceit and vanity to the unknowing. He had a message, and he was filled with the glow of it, night and day. He lived for the work he was called to do, and the days were not long enough for research in the library, for the round-table discussions which took place wherever he happened to be, whether in coffee shop, on street corners, public squares, streetcar or bus.

It was amazing how little we understood each other at first. But Peter was patient. He wanted to call the paper *The Catholic Radical*, but with my Communist background, I insisted on calling it *The Catholic Worker*. Peter said, "Man proposes, but woman disposes." It was aways with humor, never with bitterness or malice, that we differed.

I did not fully realize why this was until much later, when I finally could pin him down to talking about himself. He was a Frenchman; I was an American. He was a man twenty years older than I and infinitely wiser. He was a man, I was a woman. We looked at things differently. He was a peasant; I was a city product. He knew the soil; I the city. When he spoke of workers, he spoke of men who worked at agriculture, building, at tools and machines which were the extension of the hand of man. When I spoke of workers, I thought of factories, the machine, and man the proletariat and slum dweller, and so often the unemployed.

He was born, he told us, in a small French community, two hundred miles from Barcelona, one of a family of twenty-three children. His own mother died, after giving birth to five children, and his father married again and there were eighteen more children. Among them now there are nuns and some of his brothers are religious.

"My mother's name," Peter said, "was Marie Pages. She died in 1885. Of her five children only I and Celestin, a brother who was eighteen months younger than I, and my sister Marie, two years younger than my brother, were left. My whole name was Aristide Pierre. Pierre was my grandfather and my godfather. He died at the age of ninety-four and he was never sick. He worked in the fields until he was eighty-five, and when he could no longer because of his eyes, stayed home and made baskets and recited his rosary. He liked to work for he knew it was good for him.

"The last I heard of my brother he was the head of a school in Paris, St. Clotilde's, a parish school. He had been a Christian

Brother, but when they were secularized they no longer wore the garb but did continue to teach just the same. One of my half brothers taught for the Christian Brothers' School and he was married to a schoolteacher, who taught in the public school. In the last war he had a bullet in his body seventy-one days when he was taken prisoner by the Germans. I was with the Christian Brothers for about five years.

"Celestin was teaching in Pueblo, Mexico, when the First World War broke out, and he returned to France, and because he had not served his time in the army, he was put in the medical corps. He was buried alive by one shell bursting near him, and unburied by another. Another half brother was lost in the war and there were five others in that war and maybe some in this second.

"My youngest half sister was a weakling but got stronger as she grew older. She studied in England and she is a nun, I don't know what order. She is head of a school in Bolivia."

Once as we sat around the table at dinner Peter was giving us slogans and he proposed this one: "Eat what you raise and raise what you eat." We asked him what they ate in his family when he was a boy.

"We did not eat the calves, we sold them," he said. "We ate salt pork every day. We raised no hops, and there was no beer. We raised no grapes, so no wine. We had very little meat. We had plenty of bread—there was a communal oven. We had plenty of butter; we had eggs. We had codfish from the Brittany fishermen. They went all the way to Newfoundland and Iceland to fish. We had vegetable soups, salads and cheese.

"It was in 1882 when the public-school system started (I was five years old). It was obligatory in every village. My mother and father could not speak French, only a dialect like Catalan. (Joffre was born in French Catalonia and Foch in Basque. Catalonian is spoken in Barcelona.) Our home language was more Latin than French. The name of our town was a Latin one, Oultet.

"The seat of our diocese was twelve miles away, and our parish church two miles. Oultet had fifteen families and in the parish there were ten villages. There were two priests who worked very hard. To help earn their livelihood they worked in the garden. The villagers provided them with wood, and they got some pay from the state, a compensation which was regulated by the concordat made by Napoleon.

"My family owned eighty sheep and there was one herder for all the village. He had a helper in summer. There were probably three thousand sheep in the flock and they grazed off what was still communal land. It was very cold in winter. We used branches from the trees for fuel, cutting them every three years. The leaves were for the sheep and the branches for firewood. We cooked at an open fireplace.

"My father is dead, and my stepmother must be seventy-five by now. Her name was Rosalie. She was nineteen when she married my father. Last I heard, my brother was still farming and dealing in cattle.

"I lived there in the southern part of France, a peasant, on the soil, until I was fourteen. After that for a time I was a cocoa salesman traveling around France. Then while I was teaching at the Christian Brothers' School I was a member of a study club in Paris. At the same time Charles Peguy was there, but I did not know him, nor was I influenced by him, though people say I write like him. Instead I was interested in a group which published a paper twice a week, called *Le Sillon*. It had nothing to do with the decentralist movement, no, but it was interested in ethics. It understood the chaos of the times. Marc Sangnier was editor and backer of the paper. Later my friends got out a weekly paper called *The Spirit of Democracy*. They were looking for an ideology. They were preoccupied about the idea of an elite in a democracy.

"I did not like the idea of revolution. I did not like the French Revolution, nor the English Revolution. I did not wish to work to perpetuate the proletariat so I never became a member of a union. Besides I was an unskilled worker. I was always interested in the land and men's life on the land.

"That is why I went homesteading to Canada in 1909, but after two years, when my partner was killed, I moved about the country with work gangs and entered this country in 1911, where I have been ever since."

Probably it was the sight of the poverty of Paris slums, and the thought of his peasant background, and the reading of Prince Kropotkin, that first led Peter to think of moving to Canada to settle on the land.

The old Biblical dictim of not letting the sun set either on wrath or on an unpaid workman is not in practice in our industrial system. Once Peter went to jail in Illinois when he was working for the railroad. The job finished, he set out for Chicago where he was to be paid. The "gandy dancers," as these workers were called, had to ride freight trains, which was illegal, in order to get back to the city. They were often taken off, arrested and confined to jail as vagrants and set loose again, either to repeat their misdemeanor or to walk the long trek into the city. Yes, Peter was well acquainted with poverty, and injustice, rudeness and abuse.

He worked on farms, in brickyards, in steel mills, at every kind of unskilled labor, from Chicago to New York. He settled in Chicago for a time and gave French lessons, using the methods, so I understand, of the Berlitz School, and was successful at it. He read constantly, he worked and he taught. He was always the teacher. When he could not get people to listen, he wrote out his ideas in neat, lettered script, duplicated the leaflets and distributed them himself on street corners, an undignified apostolate.

For the seven years before I met him, he had worked as caretaker in New York State at a boys' camp during the winter. As far as I could gather, he lived with the horse in the barn. He mended the roads, broke rock and cut ice.

Peter was vehemently opposed to the wage system, so he received in return for his labor, which he pointed out was voluntarily "given," the return "gift" of enough food and clothing from the village store to supply his needs, a place to sleep and the use of the priest's library, without which he never would have stayed upstate so long. During slack seasons he came to New York and indoctrinated in Union Square, sleeping on the Bowery in Uncle Sam's Hotel, on the corner of Houston Street, in a bed which cost him forty cents a night. Often he sat up in coffee houses, or in the park, because his "brother" had come to him with a greater need than his own. He never refused to give alms, no matter how poor he was. He believed in poverty and loved it and felt it a liberating force. He differentiated between poverty and destitution, but the two often came close together in his life, when to give to others he had to strip himself.

He never had more than the clothes on his back, but he took the Gospel counsel literally—"if anyone asks for thy coat give him thy cloak too." That is, if he encountered anyone needing a coat, and he had already given his own away, he would take the person to some friend and ask for a coat for him. He went in all simplicity to men like Thomas Woodlock of the *Wall Street Journal*, and John Moody of the Moody Investment Service, and not only asked them for things, but also discussed finance capitalism, unemployment and usury with them.

He ate on the Bowery when he was in New York, at cheap restaurants and of poor fare. If he had no money he went without food. He always advised people to beg if they were in need. But I know he did not like to beg himself. He preferred to go without. I used to taunt him gently with this.

"That is why people prefer going on relief, getting aid from the state," I told him. "They prefer that to taking aid from their family. It isn't any too easy, you know, to be chided by your family for being a failure. People who are out of work are always considered failures. They prefer the large bounty of the great, impersonal mother, the state."

But the fact remained, he always reminded me, no matter what people's preferences, that we are our brother's keeper, and the unit of society is the family; that we must have a sense of personal responsibility to take care of our own, and our neighbor, at a personal sacrifice. "That is a first principle," he always said. "It is not the function of the state to enter into these realms. Only in times of great crisis, like floods, hurricane, earthquake or drought, does public authority come in. Charity is personal. Charity is love." He admitted we were in a crisis then, but he wanted none of state relief. While other papers, monthly, weekly and daily, displayed the "blue eagle" of the National Recovery Administration, he would have no part in co-operating with the state.

Peter saw only the land movement as the cure for unemployment and irresponsibility, and the works of mercy as the work at hand, ignoring the immediate needs of the workers in the unions, their conflicts and demands. I comforted myself by saying, "Men are more single-minded. They are the pure of heart." But I continued to think in terms of unions and strikes as an immediate means of bettering the social order. I could not blind myself to the conflict between us, the conflict that would continue between one or another who came to join in the movement later. When Peter said, "Everybody's paper is nobody's paper," when he protested the coverage of strike news, or the introduction of the personal element into the work by feature story, he was envisaging a sheet carrying nothing but his own phrased writings, regrouped, rewritten principles to apply to whatever situation came up, local, federal or world crisis. He had lived alone for so long, had for so long been a single apostle, that he did not realize how grim the struggle was going to be.

On two occasions indeed he was ready to give it up, to retire, to become silent in the face of opposition. Once it was when some of our young workers wanted whatever money contributed to us to be used for propaganda, printing, and the support of the editors rather than the feeding of the poor who came to our door. The opposition that went on over breadlines and the housing of what this young group called "the derelicts," the "rotten lumber," the "deadwood," was such that Peter got up from the table one evening and turning to me said, "Come, let us go. Let us leave the paper and the house to them." I refused to give it up and after two years the others left and they in turn founded their own journal and bought a piece of property to be used as a summer school. Both failed after a few years.

The other occasion was during the beginning of World War II, when we had already been suffering grave criticism for our stand on the Ethiopian and the Spanish wars. "Perhaps silence would be better for a time than to continue our opposition to war. Men are not ready to listen," Peter said. Again I would not give up, and though we opposed the war and upheld the stand of the conscientious objector and the absolutist who advocated nonpayment of taxes and nonregistration we were able to continue and there was no attempt made on the part of Church or state to suppress us. Peter may have been right on both occasions; silence may have been better. We have always acknowledged the primacy of the spiritual, and to have undertaken a life of silence, manual labor and prayer might have been the better way. But I do not know. God gives us our temperaments, and in spite of my pacifism, it is natural for me to stand my ground, to continue in what actually amounts to a class war, using such weapons as the works of mercy for immediate means to show our love and to alleviate suffering.

And the weapons of journalism! My whole life had been in journalism and I saw the world in terms of class conflict. I did not look upon class war as something to be stirred up, as the Marxist did. I did not want to increase what was already there but to mitigate it. When we were invited to help during a strike, we went to perform the works of mercy, which include not only feeding the hungry, visiting the imprisoned, but enlightening the ignorant and rebuking the unjust. We were ready to "endure wrongs patiently" for ourselves (this is another of the spiritual works of mercy) but we were not going to be meek for others, enduring *their* wrongs patiently.

When I was afterward accused of class-war tactics I retorted with St. Augustine, "The bottle always smells of the liquor it once held." But I did not feel the criticism just.

Peter used to say when we covered strikes and joined picket lines, "Strikes don't strike me." Yet he took the occasion to come out on the picket line to distribute leaflets upon which some single point was made. "To change the hearts and minds of men," he said. "To give them vision—the vision of a society where it is easier for men to be good."

PAPER, PEOPLE AND WORK

WE STARTED publishing *The Catholic Worker* at 436 East Fifteenth Street in May, 1933, with a first issue of 2,500 copies. Within three or four months the circulation bounded to 25,000, and it was cheaper to bring it out as an eight-page tabloid on newsprint rather than the smaller-sized edition on better paper we had started with. By the end of the year we had a circulation of 100,000 and by 1936 it was 150,000. It was certainly a mushroom growth. It was not only that some parishes subscribed for the paper all over the country in bundles of 500 or more. Zealous young people took the paper out in the streets and sold it, and when they could not sell it even at one cent a copy, they gave free copies and left them in streetcar, bus, barber shop and dentist's and doctor's office. We got letters from all parts of the country from people who said they had picked up the paper on trains, in rooming houses. One letter came from the state of Sonora in Mexico and we read with amazement that the reader had tossed in an uncomfortable bed on a hot night until he got up to turn over the mattress and under it found a copy of *The Catholic Worker*. A miner found a copy five miles underground in an old mine that stretched out under the Atlantic Ocean off Nova Scotia. A seminarian said that he had sent out his shoes to be half-soled in Rome and they came back to him wrapped in a copy of *The Catholic Worker*. These letters thrilled and inspired the young people who came to help, sent by Brothers or Sisters who taught in the high schools. We were invited to speak in schools and parishes, and often as a result of our speaking others came in to help us. On May Day, those first few years, the streets were literally lined with papers. Looking back on it, it seemed like a gigantic advertising campaign, entirely unpremeditated. It grew organically, Peter used to say happily, and not through organization. "We are not an organization, we are an organism," he said.

First there was Peter, my brother and I. When John took a job at Dobb's Ferry, a young girl, Dorothy Weston, who had been studying journalism and was a graduate of a Catholic college, came to help. She lived at home and spent her days with us, eating with us and taking only her carfare from the common fund. Peter brought in three young men from Columbus Circle, whom he had met when discussing the affairs of the world there, and of these one became bookkeeper (that was his occupation when he was employed), another circulation manager, and the third married Dorothy Weston. Another girl came to take dictation and help with mailing the paper, and she married the circulation manager. There were quite a number of romances that first year—the paper appealed to youth. Then there were the young intellectuals who formed what they called Campion Committees in other cities as well as New York, who helped to picket the Mexican and German consulates and who distributed literature all over the city. Workers came in to get help on picket lines, to help move dispossessed families and make demonstrations in front of relief offices. Three men came to sell the paper on the street, and to eat their meals with us. Big Dan had been a truck driver and a policeman. The day he came in to see us he wanted nothing more than to bathe his tired feet. That night at supper Peter indoctrinated him on the dignity of poverty and read some of Father Vincent McNabb's *Nazareth or Social Chaos*. This did not go over so well, all of us being city people, and Father McNabb advocating a return to the fields, but he made Dan Orr go out with a sense of a mission, not worrying about shabby clothes or the lack of a job. Dan began to sell the paper on the streets and earned enough money to live on. He met others who had found subsistence jobs, carrying sandwich signs or advertising children's furniture by pushing a baby carriage, a woman who told fortunes in a tea shop, a man who sold pretzels, which were threaded on four poles one on each corner of an old baby carriage. He found out their needs, and those of their families, and never left the house in the morning without bundles of clothes as well as his papers.

Dan rented a horse and wagon in which to deliver bundles of the paper each month. (We had tried this before he came but someone had to push the horse while the other led it. We knew nothing about driving a wagon.) Dan loved his horse. He called it Catholic Action, and used to take the blanket off my bed to cover the horse in winter. We rented it from a German Nazi on East Sixteenth Street, and sometimes when we had no money he let us have the use of it free for a few hours. It rejoiced our hearts to move a Jewish family into their new quarters with his equipment.

Dan said it was a pious horse and that when he passed St. Patrick's Cathedral, the horse genuflected. He liked to drive up Fifth Avenue, preferably with students who had volunteered their help, and shout, "Read *The Catholic Worker*" at the top of his lungs. He was anything but dignified and loved to affront the dignity of others.

One time he saw me coming down the street when he was selling the paper in front of Gimbel's and began to yell, "Read *The Catholic Worker!* Romance on every page." A seminarian from St. Louis, now Father Dreisoner, took a leaf from Dan's book and began selling the paper on the corner of Times Square and at union meetings. He liked to stand next to a comrade selling *The Daily Worker,* and as the one shouted "Read *The Daily Worker*," he in turn shouted, "Read *The Catholic Worker* daily." Between sales they conversed.

Another of Peter's friends was an old Armenian who wrote poetry in a beautiful mysterious script which delighted my eyes. He carried his epic around with him always. He was very little and wore a long black overcoat which reached to his heels and a black revolutionary hat over his long white hair. He had a black cat whom he called Social Justice, mimicking Big Dan. She was his constant companion. He used my washrag to wipe her face with after eating. He prepared dishes for us with rice and meat wrapped in grape leaves, held together with toothpicks. He slept on a couch in the kitchen for a time. Once when Tamar was tearing around the house playing with Freddy Rubino, the little boy who lived upstairs, and I told her to be a little more quiet, that Mr. Minas was asleep in the next room, she said mischievously, "I don't care if the Pope is asleep in the next room, we want to play and make noise." Day and night there were many meetings in the converted barber shop which was our office, and Tamar heard plenty of noise from us. When someone asked her how she liked *The Catholic Worker* she wrinkled up her nose and said she liked the farming-commune idea, but that there was too much talk about all the rest.

Peter, the "green" revolutionist, had a long-term program which called for hospices, or houses of hospitality, where the works of mercy could be practiced to combat the taking over by the state of all those services which could be built up by mutual aid; and farming communes to provide land and homes for the unemployed, whom increasing technology was piling up into the millions. In 1933, the unemployed numbered 13,000,000.

The idea of the houses of hospitality caught on quickly enough. The very people that Peter brought in, who made up our staff at first, needed a place to live. Peter was familiar with the old I.W.W. technique of a common flophouse and a pot of mulligan on the stove. To my cost, I too had become well acquainted with this idea.

Besides, we never had any money, and the cheapest, most practical way to take care of people was to rent some apartments and have someone do the cooking for the lot of us. Many a time I was cook and cleaner as well as editor and street seller. When Margaret, a Lithuanian girl from the mining regions of Pennsylvania came to us, and took over the cooking, we were happy indeed. She knew how to make a big pot of mashed potatoes with mushroom sauce which filled everyone up nicely. She was a great soft creature with a little baby, Barbara, who was born a few months after she came to us. Margaret went out on May Day with the baby and sold papers on the street. She loved being propagandist as well as cook. When Big Dan teased her, she threatened to tell the "pasture" of the church around the corner.

To house the women we had an apartment near First Avenue which could hold about ten. When there were arguments among them, Margaret would report them with gusto, giving us a blow-by-blow account. Once when she was telling how one of the women abused her so that she "felt as though the crown of thorns was pressing right down on her head" (she was full of these mystical experiences), Peter paused in his pacing of the office to tell her she needed to scrub the kitchen floor. Not that he was ever harsh, but he was making a point that manual labor was the cure of all such quarreling. Margaret once told Bishop O'Hara of Kansas City that when she kissed his ring, it was just like a blood transfusion—she got faint all over.

Jacques Maritain came to us during these early days and spoke to the group who were reading *Freedom and the Modern World* at that time. He gave special attention to the chapter on the purification of means. Margaret was delighted with our distinguished guest, who so evidently loved us all, and made him a box of fudge to take home with him when he sailed for France a few weeks later.

Ah, those early days that everyone likes to think of now since we have grown so much bigger; that early zeal, that early romance, that early companionableness! And how delightful it is to think that the young ones who came into the work now find the same joy in community. It is a permanent revolution, this Catholic Worker Movement.

In New York we were soon forced by the increasing rent of three apartments and one store to move into a house on the West Side. We lived on West Charles Street, all together, men and women, students and workers, about twenty of us. In the summer young college girls and men came for months to help us, and, in some cases, returned to their own cities to start houses of hospitality there. In this way, houses started in Boston, Rochester, Milwaukee, and other cities. Within a few years there were thirty-three houses of hospitality and farms around the country.

One of the reasons for the rapid growth was that many young men were coming out of college to face the prospect of no job. If they had started to read *The Catholic Worker* in college, they were ready to spend time as volunteers when they came out. Others were interested in writing, and houses in Buffalo, Chicago, Baltimore, Seattle, St. Louis and Philadelphia, to name but a few cities, published their own papers and sold them with the New

York *Catholic Worker*. A *Catholic Worker* was started in Australia and one in England. Both papers are still in existence, but the New York *Catholic Worker* is the only one published in the United States. The English and Australian papers are neither pacifist nor libertarian in their viewpoint, but the Australian paper is decentralist as well as strongly pro-labor. The English paper concentrates on labor organization and legislation. "These papers have part of the program," Peter said, "but ours makes a synthesis—with vision."

The coming of war closed many of the houses of hospitality, but with new ones reopening there are still more than twenty houses and farms. When the young men in the work were released from service, most of them married and had to think in terms of salaries, jobs to support their growing families. The voluntary apostolate was for the unwilling celibate and for the unemployed as well as for the men and women, willing celibates, who felt that running hospices, performing the works of mercy, working on farms, was their vocation, just as definitely a vocation as that of the professed religious.

Voluntary poverty means a good deal of discomfort in these houses of ours. Many of the houses throughout the country are without central heating and have to be warmed by stoves in winter. There are back-yard toilets for some even now. The first Philadelphia house had to use water drawn from one spigot at the end of an alley, which served half a dozen other houses. It was lit with oil lamps. It was cold and damp and so unbelievably poverty-stricken that little children coming to see who were the young people meeting there exclaimed that this could not be a *Catholic* place; it was too poor. We must be Communists. They were well acquainted with the Communist point of view since they were Puerto Rican and Spanish and Mexican and this was at the beginning of the Spanish Civil War.

How hard a thing it is to hear such criticisms made. Voluntary poverty was only found among the Communists; the Negro and white man on the masthead of our paper suggested communism; the very word "worker" made people distrust us at first. We were not taking the position of the great mass of Catholics, who

were quite content with the present in this world. They were
quite willing to give to the poor, but they did not feel called
upon to work for the things of this life for others which they
themselves esteemed so lightly. Our insistence on worker-owner-
ship, on the right of private property, on the need to de-pro-
letarize the worker, all points which had been emphasized by the
Popes in their social encyclicals, made many Catholics think we
were Communists in disguise, wolves in sheep's clothing.

The house on Mott Street which we occupied for many years
began to loom up in our lives as early as 1934, through Mary
Lane. She was one of our readers, who lived in a small tenement
apartment on the upper West Side on her telegrapher's pension.
She was very holy, and when she first saw a copy of the paper
with its stories of human misery, she who also saw poverty at
first hand began collecting clothes for us. The first time she came
down she stood at the door dramatically and said to me abruptly,
"Do you have ecstasies and visions?" Poor dear, so hungry for
mystical experience, even if secondhand, after a long life of faith.

I was taken aback. "Visions of unpaid bills," I said abruptly.
Her warmth, her effusivenes, were embarrassing but I soon
learned to take them for what they were, an overflowing of an
ardent soul, ready to pour itself out in love.

She became our faithful friend. She was lame, half blind, old,
yet she stinted herself and gave us five dollars a month of her
pension. She had a well-to-do friend named Gertrude Burke, the
only daughter of an invalid widowed mother. Gertrude took care
of her mother until she died and then began to give her property
away to the Church. She went to live at the House of Calvary, a
cancer hospital for the poor, which was one of her pet charities.
This had been founded by a small group of widows, a "lay institute" according to the terminology of the Church. They were
not a religious order. Neither wife nor virgin could belong,
though either could help. Miss Burke's uptown house was given
to the order of the Good Shepherd. The house on Mott Street had
been built by an old uncle back in 1860. His name was Kerrigan
and it was said he had defended old St. Patrick's Cathedral on

Mott Street during the Know Nothing riots, standing on the steps with a gun in his hand.

At 115 Mott Street, there was a rear house which had been the original house, and had had a long yard in front; there also was the front house, twice as deep, four rooms on either side of a long narrow hall. The rear house had two rooms on either side with one toilet between them, open fireplaces, a sink and a washtub in each kitchen. In these primitive, unheated, bathless flats, made up of a kitchen and bedroom, the Irish first came to live and then the Italians. Katie, the vegetable woman on the corner, told me her mother had lived in the first floor of the rear building and that St. Francis Cabrini had visited her there. That two-room flat was dark and airless, surrounded as it was by five-story buildings on every side. The sun never reached the rear room whose long window looked out on another five-story building, one foot away. Yet when the priest came to read the prayers for the dying in that dark room, a ray of sunlight fell on his book so that the candle held by Katie herself was no longer needed!

This entire rear house was empty when I first saw it. Half of the apartments in the front building were also empty. Miss Burke offered us the use of the empty apartments provided we would collect the rents on the rest and be caretakers. It was so much worse a neighborhood than Fifteenth Street that I was appalled at the idea. I asked Rose Clafani, whom I met on the stairs, if she had lived there long and she said stormily, "I was born in this g—— d—— place!" And that was all I got out of her! I found afterward that she was afraid we were going to buy the building and evict them, and her heart was there. She loved her home.

I turned down the offer then but within a few years I regretted it. I felt it was wrong to take rent for such a place—that it had far better be torn down, or given rent free to the poor. I might easily have expressed myself along these lines, so imprudent am I, so hasty in speeech.

When we had found the house on Charles Street too small

for us, I telephoned Mary Lane and asked her to intercede for us with Miss Burke, to tell her that we had reconsidered and would be most grateful for the use of the rear house at 115 Mott Street. We would not, however, collect rents on the front building. There was one store empty at that time and we asked for that too. Miss Burke reminded us of the fact that we refused the house when we could have had it—-we had not understood her previous offer in this way—and that now she had given the place to the House of Calvary. However, she would ask them if we could use it. The housing crisis was not on us at that time. So, finally we obtained the use of the house and moved in. The other store in front was a speakeasy, run as a dry-goods store. When the tenants moved out we took that as an office. As the apartments became vacant, we rented them for eighteen dollars each. We ended by having twelve rooms in the front house for women, another four for men, which with those in the rear house made twenty-four rooms for men. Four were used for laundry and storerooms. We did not use the basement because of rats and defective plumbing. The neighbors used one cellar of the rear building for wine-making, and hogsheads of wine were stored there. Once, one of our workers, a former seaman, went down in the cellar and in trying to obtain wine, let much of it escape. We had to pay for it. These apartments and stores, on this narrow, pushcart-lined street, were our home for fourteen years.

The people who worked with us! For the first six months that we published *The Catholic Worker,* we longed for an artist who could illustrate Peter's ideas. An answer to our prayers came in the form of a young girl just out of high school who signed her work, A. de Bethune. Her woodcuts were of worker-saints, St. Peter the fisherman, St. Paul writing in prisons, walking the roads and indoctrinating St. Timothy, St. Crispin the shoemaker, St. Conrad and a host of minor saints, if any saints could be called minor who gave their lives for the faith, whose hearts burned with so single-hearted a fire.

"A picture," Ade reminded us, "was worth ten thousand words." Through a misunderstanding as to her name, we signed her pictures Ade Bethune and so she was called by all of us. She was Belgian and it was only some years later that we knew her title, which her mother continued to use, Baronne de Bethune. The aristocrat and the peasant Peter got on famously. "Our word is tradition," he said happily, and wrote a little essay, "Shouting a Word."

Mrs. Bethune and her daughter illustrated for Peter many ideas besides *noblesse oblige*. He liked to illustrate his ideas by calling attention to people who exemplified them. The Bethune family performed all the works of mercy out of slender resources, earned by the labor of their hands. They had come to this country at the close of World War I. They exemplified voluntary poverty and manual labor and the love of neighbors to the highest degree.

When Ade built up her studio in Newport where the family moved soon after we met them, she took in apprentices, young girls from different parts of the country who could not have afforded to pay tuition or to support themselves. Two of her apprentices married and went to live on Catholic Worker farms, and are now mothers of large families. My own daughter went to her when she was sixteen and stayed a year, learning the household arts. For to Ade, as to Eric Gill and Peter Maurin, the holy man was the whole man, the man of integrity, who not only tried to change the world, but to live in it as it was.

Whenever I visited Ade I came away with a renewed zest for life. She has such a sense of the sacramentality of life, the goodness of things, a sense that is translated in all her works whether it was illustrating a missal, making stained-glass windows or sewing, cooking or gardening. To do things perfectly was always her aim. Another first principle she always taught was to aim high. "If you are going to put a cross bar on an H," she said, "you have to aim *higher* than your sense of sight tells you."

Dom Vitry, a Benedictine monk from Mared-sous, said this same thing in regard to music, "Aim higher than the note you wish to reach, and you will come down on it."

Ade came to learn from us as well as give us her woodcuts and we have learned from her. Peter taught her, and she translated his teachings into pictures which we used again and again in the paper.

Once I was attending a steelworker's open-air meeting in Pittsburgh, and when we had distributed the papers we brought, I was amused and delighted to see a huge Slovak or Hungarian worker pointing to the pictures of the working saints and laughing with the joy of discovery.

Ade not only drew for our paper—she allowed her work to be copied by papers all over the world, Catholic and non-Catholic. We saw reproductions of her woodcuts in Japanese papers, Portuguese papers, Indian papers, to mention but a few.

Before she was mid-twenty she had designed and with unemployed steelworkers helped build a church in the outskirts of Pittsburgh. She made the stained-glass windows in the Church of the Precious Blood in Brooklyn and recently finished mosaics in a church in the Philippines. In addition to her work of painting, carving, et cetera, she edits a Catholic art quarterly and is a trustee of St. Benedict's farm in Massachusetts, one of the Catholic Worker centers.

On that farm where four families live, one family is made up of seven boys, a father who must go out to work and a mother who has been hospitalized for some years. Ade and her mother have helped this family, as they have helped a number of others in many ways. Not only money and clothes but hard manual labor made up their contributions. Every week a bundle of clothes was sent—and this went on for years—to the Baronne de Bethune in Newport, and she washed, ironed and mended these clothes and sent them back.

It is wonderful to think of and to write of such good works. Hundreds of pairs of socks for men on our breadlines, funds collected—she was always the great lady with special projects into which she drew many others.

I like to speak of her nobility because in her case that is actually what the word connotes. We emphasize the "Prince" when referring to Kropotkin precisely because he gave up titles and estates to be with the poor. We can recognize too our own country's claim to greatness in that here titles are naturally discarded in an attempt to reach the highest principle of human brotherhood.

The de Bethune family lost much in World War I, but when they came here their philosophy of work was so vital that they made what Eric Gill called a cell of good living.

It is amazing how quickly one can gather together a family. Steve Hergenhan came to us from Union Square. He was a German carpenter, a skilled workman who after forty years of frugal living had bought himself a plot of ground near Suffern, New York, and had proceeded to build on it, using much of the natural rock in the neighborhood. He built his house on a hillside and used to ski down to the village to get groceries. He did not like cars and would not have one. He thought that cars were driving people to their ruin. Workers bought cars who should buy homes, he said, and they willingly sold themselves into slavery and indebtedness for the sake of the bright new shining cars that speeded along the super highways. Maybe he refused to pay taxes for the roads that accommodated the cars. Maybe he was unable to. At any rate, he lost his little house on the side of the hill and ended up in New York, on a park bench during the day, telling his grievances to all who would listen, and eating and sleeping in the Municipal Lodging House, which then maintained the largest dormitory in the world, seven hundred double-decker beds.

Peter loved the articulate, and after having one of his "round-table discussions" with Steve in Union Square, he invited him to come and stay with us. The technique of the Square then was for two people to have a discussion together with no one interrupting until he was given permission by one of the two speakers, who might cede "the floor" to another.

Both Peter and Steve were agreed on a philosophy of work and the evils of the machine—they followed the writings of the distributists of England and the Southern agrarians in this country. But Steve differed from Peter on works of mercy. He declaimed loudly with St. Paul, "He who does not work, neither let him eat." And no physical or mental disability won his pity. Men were either workers or shirkers. It was the conflict between the worker and scholar that Peter was always talking about. Steve considered himself both a worker and a scholar.

He did not attend church but he used to say scornfully, when he was living with us on our hilltop farm near Easton, Pennsylvania, "If I believed as you do, that Christ Himself is present there on the altar, nothing in this world would keep me from it." He heard just enough of the discussion about the sacrament of duty and the self-imposed obligation of daily Mass and communion to know which side to take. He was a carper and constant critic and sometimes his language was most immoderate. He aimed to goad, to irritate, and considered it the most effective agitation. Peter never irritated but if Hergenhan became too vituperative he would walk away.

When he came to us, Peter begged him to consent to be used as a foil. Steve was to present the position of the Fascist, the totalitarian, and Peter was to refute him. They discoursed at our nightly meetings, in Union Square and Columbus Circle, and in Harlem, where we had been given the use of another store for the winter. They were invited to speak by Father Scully at a Holy Name meeting, and a gathering of the Knights of Columbus. How they loved these audiences in the simplicity of their hearts. Steve the German, Peter the Frenchman, both with strong accents, with oratory, with facial gesture, with striking pose, put on a show, and when they evoked laughter, they laughed too, delighted at amusing their audience, hoping to arouse them. "I am trying to make the encyclicals click," Peter used to say joyfully, radiant always before an audience. They never felt that they were laughed at. They thought they were being laughed with. Or perhaps they pretended not to see. They were men of poverty, of hard work, of Europe and America; they were men of vision; and they were men, too, with the simplicity of children.

But Hergenhan had bitterness too. The articles he wrote for *The Catholic Worker* about life in the Municipal Lodging House and the quest for bread of the homeless were biting. After the first one appeared, one of the city officials drove up with some companions in a big car and with unctuous flattery praised the work we were doing and asked us why we did not come to them first rather than print such articles about the work of the city.

"I tried to tell you," Hergenhan said. "I tried to tell you of the graft, the poor food, the treatment we received, the contempt and kicking around we got. But you threatened me with the psychopathic ward. You treated me like a wild beast. You gave me the bum's rush."

Perhaps he looked to them like a dangerous radical, like a wild beast. In the helpless resentment of these men there was a fury which city authorities were afraid would gather into a flood of wrath, once they were gathered into a mob. So among every group in the public square, at the meetings of the unemployed, there were careful guardians of law and order watching, waiting to pounce on these gray men, the color of the lifeless trees and bushes and soil in the squares in winter, who had in them as yet none of the green of hope, the rising sap of faith.

Both Peter and Steve tried to arouse that hope. Both of them were personalists, both were workers. They did not want mass action, or violence. They were lambs in the simplicity of their program. They wanted to see the grass spring up between the cobbles of the city streets. They wanted to see the workers leave the cities with their wives and children and take to the fields, build themselves homes, where they would have room to breathe, to study, to pray, where there would be work for all.

"There is no unemployment on the land," Peter used to shout, and he would be met by jeers. "What about the migrants, the tenant farmers. They either work like slaves for the bosses, or they rot like the men in Tobacco Road."

"Fire the bosses," Peter used to say.

The trouble was that he never filled in the chasms, the valleys, in his leaping from crag to crag of noble thought.

He wanted men to think for themselves. Voluntary poverty, the doing without radios, cars, television sets, cigarettes, movies, cosmetics, all these luxuries, would enable men to buy the necessities. In a village community there would be work, even work in the gardens for the invalids, the children, the old, the crippled, the men and women who hung around the street corners and the market places, waiting for someone to hire them.

"Personalism and communitarianism," was Peter's cry.

Steve wanted to flog men into action. His impatience was ferocious.

We were put out of the store in Harlem by the owner, who did not agree with our pacifism. As a member of the National Guard, he thought we were subversive. But not before there had been a riot in Harlem which wrecked store fronts, and resulted in some casualties to man and property. During the long night of the rioting, the Negroes who made up the mobs passed us by. "Don't touch this place," Steve and Peter and the old professor who inhabited the store heard them say. "These folks are all right," and the windows smashed all around them and the roaring of the mobs passed down the avenue. It was a fearful night, the men said, and it but reinforced their conviction of the futility of violence.

To build a new society within the shell of the old! It was the old I.W.W. slogan.

Soon we rented a twelve-room house with a big attic, in Huguenot, Staten Island, right on the water, and there Steve planted a garden which was a model to all who came to participate in week-end conferences. Groups of young people came and speakers from Columbia University, from the Catholic University, from colleges in the Midwest, for these retreats and colloquiums. But as usual in groups working together, they went off on tangents and spent hours discussing rubrics and whether or not to say "compline" in English or Latin and there was discussion too of machines and the land, organization and organism, the corporative order and the corporative state and the rising tide of fascism and nazism.

They all talked, and Steve talked with the best of them, but they were young and he was past fifty; they were young students, second- or third-generation Italian, German, French, Irish, and Peter and Steve were first generation. They listened to Peter because he never turned on them. Steve hated their avoidance of work, and after a good deal of recrimination turned from them to cultivate his garden.

The young fellows picketed the German consulate in protest against nazism; they gave out literature at the docking of the

Bremen and became involved in a riot when some Communists who called themselves Catholic workers tore down the swastika from the ship and were arrested. But Hergenhan just vented his scorn on youth in general and brought in great baskets of Swiss chard, tomatoes, beans and squash for us to admire and eat. It choked him to see the young people eat them. He wanted disciples who would listen to him and work with him.

The next year we received a letter from a Baltimore school-teacher who wished to invest in community. She offered us a thousand dollars provided we would build her a house and deed her three acres of the farm near Easton, Pennsylvania to be purchased with her down payment. She would provide second-hand materials for the house.

We tried to dissuade her from coming to us, telling her of our dissensions, warning her she would be disappointed, but she insisted on contributing the money. She was disappointed of course, but when she sold her little house some ten years later, she got out of it a great deal more than she put into it. That didn't prevent her from writing to the Archbishop of Baltimore telling him that she had been lured to contribute to our farming commune by promises of community, which promises had proved false.

Steve always insisted that he had built her house singlehanded. But Peter, and John and Paul Cort helped clean secondhand brick, pull nails out of the secondhand lumber, cart water up the hill from the spring and cisterns and dig the cellar, and there were many others who contributed many man hours of labor. Of course much discussion went on with the building and digging. Hergenhan lived in a little shanty on the edge of the woods and came down to the farmhouse for his meals. He worked with great satisfaction on the house for two years. He was starting off the Catholic Workers with their first farming commune. He was showing them how to work, how to build, and he had great satisfaction in his toil. It was a spot of unutterable beauty looking down over the Delaware and the cultivated fields of New Jersey. Two and a half miles away at the foot of the hills were the twin cities of Easton and Philipsburg, one on either side of the river.

Easton is a railroad center and a place of small factories, an old town with many historic buildings, and a college town, with Lafayette College perched upon a hill. There were Syrian, Lithuanian, German, Italian and Irish churches, and we had all these nationalities among us too.

Hergenhan built his house and then returned to the city to indoctrinate. He got tired of being considered the worker, and wanted to be a scholar for a time. But his bitterness had increased. In protest against our policies, specifically our works of mercy, he went to Camp La Guardia, a farm colony for homeless men run by the city. He wanted efficient and able-bodied workers building up village communities. We were clogged up with too much deadwood, with sluggish drones—it was the same old argument again, only this time it was a true worker and not just a young intellectual who was arguing the point.

He became ill and returned to us at Mott Street. We were his family after all. He was by then fifty-six. When he was examined the doctors discovered cancer, and after an operation he was taken to St. Rose's Cancer Hospital on the East Side, to die.

"Abandon hope all ye who enter here," he cried out when I came to visit him. He had not known of his cancer—they had talked of an intestinal obstruction at the hospital where the operation was performed—and when he was brought to St. Rose's he saw written over the door, HOME OF THE CANCEROUS POOR.

His was a little room on the first floor; all day one could look into the garden and past that to the river where tugs and tankers steamed up and down the tidal river and clouds floated over the low shore of Brooklyn. The world was beautiful and he did not want to die. There was so much work he wanted to do, so small a part he had been allowed to play.

Peter and I used to go to see him every day. By that time I had just made what came to be known as our retreat and was filled with enthusiasm and ready to talk to anyone who would listen on the implications of the Christian life—and Steve always loved to converse, provided one gave him a chance to get in his share of the conversation.

I went to St. Rose's each day with my notes, and read them

to him. He gradually became happy and reconciled. He had said, "There is so much I wanted to do." And I told him how Father John Hugo had talked of work, "that physical work was hard, mental work harder, and spiritual work was the hardest of all." And I pointed out that he was now doing the spiritual work of his life, lying there suffering, enduring, sowing all his own desires, in order to reap them in heaven. He began to realize that he had to die in order to live, that the door would open, that there was a glorious vista before him, "that all things were his."

"All things are yours," St. Paul wrote, "whether it be Paul or Apollo or Cephas, or the world, or life, or death, or things present, or things to come. For all are yours. And you are Christ's. And Christ is God's."

I read Bede Jarrett's *No Abiding City* to him, and some of Father Faber's conferences on death, and he enjoyed them all. They offered him the richness of thought that he craved, and when the Sister who cared for him asked him if he did not want Baptism, he shouted wholeheartedly, "Yes!"

Peter and I were his sponsors, and to me it was a miracle of God's grace that the lack of dignity with which the Sacrament was conferred did not affront Steve, who was always hyper-critical. He was baptized with speed and his confession listened to. He received Viaticum. I remember his anointing most vividly. Three other men were lined up on the bed at the same time, sitting there like gaunt old crows, their simple solemn faces lifted expectantly, childlike, watching every move of the priest, as he anointed their eyes, nose, mouth, ears, their clawlike hands stretched out to receive the holy oil, their feet with horny toes to which the priest bent with swift indifference.

He finished the job, he performed the outward signs, he re-cited the Latin prayers in a garbled monotone in the back of his throat, and despite the lack of grace in the human sense, Grace was there, souls were strengthened, hearts were lifted.

Ritual, how could we do without it! Though it may seem to be gibberish and irreverence, though the Mass is offered up in such haste that the sacred sentence, "hoc est corpus meus" was abbreviated into "hocus-pocus" by the bitter protestor and has come down into our language meaning trickery, nevertheless there is a sureness and a conviction there. And just as a husband may embrace his wife casually as he leaves for work in the morning, and kiss her absent-mindedly in his comings and goings, still that kiss on occasion turns to rapture, a burning fire of tenderness and love. And with this to stay her she demands the "ritual" of affection shown. The little altar boy kissing the cruet of water as he hands it to the priest is performing a rite. We have too little ritual in our lives.

Steve was baptized and anointed but he did not rally. Daily he became weaker and weaker and sometimes when I came I found him groaning with pain. Earlier at Roosevelt Hospital they had given him a brown-paper bag to blow into when he had an attack of pain. He would go through this ridiculous gesture as though he were going to break the bag explosively, as children do, but it was a desperate device like a woman's pulling on a roped sheet attached to the foot of the bed in the agonies of childbirth. Perhaps the intensity of pain and the intensity of pleasure are both somehow shameful because we so lose control, so lose ourselves, that we are no longer creatures of free will, but in the control of our blind flesh. "Who will deliver me from the body of this death?"

Steve died suddenly one morning, and there was no one with him. We found in his papers afterward notations which indicated his bitterness at not being more used, as writer, speaker, teacher. That has been the lament of so many who have died with us. Just as they are beginning to open their eyes to the glory and the potentialities of life their life is cut short as a weaver's thread. They were like the grass of the field. "The spaces of this life, set over against eternity, are most brief and poor," one of the desert fathers said. It is part of the long loneliness.

There was the French professor who could speak many languages, and who was inventing a universal language. He had been a drug addict and had been cured. Now he had begun to drink, but it was only occasionally. He loved to go on nature walks, up along the Palisades and through Bear Mountain Park, with others who came together by correspondence. This was a part of his life we knew little about. He liked to translate articles for us, not for publication, but for our information. He would write them out in notebooks in a small fine hand, but when he gave them in, it was always with the expectation of money for something to drink. Since we passed many a day with little or no money on hand, and often had to run up gigantic grocery bills (our bill has gone as high as $6,000) he did not often get the fifty cents or a dollar he was expecting. Fifty cents was enough to start him off because he could buy a pint of wine on the Bowery for thirty-five cents.

One of our readers in Burlington, Vermont, a woman doctor who admired Peter Maurin very much, once told him that he could charge books to her account at Brentano's. For a while Peter had a field day. He was buying books for all his friends, even ordering them from England and from France. The professor found a way to increase his pay by asking Peter for dictionaries, German, Italian, French, Latin, Greek, et cetera. The friend in Burlington probably thought we were becoming impossibly intellectual, but she did not protest until bills came in for three French dictionaries. She wrote to us then saying that she could understand the need for one, but not for three. The professor had been selling them all. After that Peter limited his book-buying to one volume a week, and that for himself. It was a luxury, but also a necessity. It was the one luxury he enjoyed, and he shared it with young students who could not afford books and with others whom he tried to induce to read.

But as one young man who shared a room with Peter said, "Peter is always asking you to read his list of essential books, but when you settle down for a long evening of reading, he finds that an opportunity to talk." He liked catching you alone, serious and ready to think. He thought the role of teacher more effective than that of author.

There were these friends of Peter, some of them writing for the paper from the depths of their own experience. There were Margaret and Charlie and Francis who also wrote for the paper— Margaret, the Lithuanian girl, and Charlie, the convert Jew who used to sell gardenias on street corners, and Francis, who had

been in Sing Sing for robbery with a Brooklyn gang. We knew
many youths who had been in jail for robbery. The Italians love
to gamble and the stakes often reach into the thousands. Families
have to mortgage homes, take up collections among themselves
to pay off. If other payment fails the youths are given "jobs" to
do, and they find themselves part of a gang. They have seen the
penalty for nonpayment of gambling debts in the slums in many
a gang killing. One time, John Cort coming home from Mass
saw a man lying dead in the center of the street, while the car
from which the shooting was done sped away. John took the
number on the license plates, though it was as much as his life
was worth, but nothing ever came of this that we knew of.
Women rushing out from tenements all around feared for their
own. On this occasion, the young girl who lived in our house said
to me bitterly, "There isn't a house on this block that hasn't
got a son in Sing Sing."

Many college students and graduates came to live with us and
to help us. It was usually the war or marriage which caused them
to leave, or other opportunities for interesting work. But they
always left with what they called their positions, their basic principles, firmly fixed in their minds, their faith confirmed, their
lives in a way integrated. They did not go away to make a material success. And certainly there were many happy marriages.
At *The Catholic Worker* there is always work for people to do.
Peter glorified manual labor and taught what he liked to call his
philosophy of labor. Ed Marciniak, one of the Chicago *Catholic
Worker* group began a Labor weekly called *Work*. Ade Bethune
wrote a pamphlet WORK, the size of a small book, which has run
through many editions. Father Rembert Sorg, the Benedictine
from St. Procopius Abbey in Chicago, had written a book called
Towards a Theology of Manual Labor which has much in it from
the early Fathers of the Church. This emphasis on the manual
work of the world, which will go on no matter how many
machines we may have to lighten labor, made students eager to
help with hauling, cleaning, moving, cooking and washing, all
the multitude of household tasks that come up about a hospice.

In the early days, every afternoon saw visitors engaged in the work of moving evicted families. Now there are only occasional apartments for rent and occasional movings, but Helen Adler, one of the girls working with us, spent a number of months hunting apartments for women and children who were in the Municipal Lodging House. Charles McCormick, another of our staff, not only moved them but collected furniture from all over Greater New York, to supplement our own old furniture and also to help furnish the homes of the poor. He is kept busy driving to pick up food at the Essex Market, fish at the Fulton Market, or transporting supplies and our home-baked bread from our Staten Island farm to the city.

Selling the paper in front of Macy's or St. Francis Church, or in Times Square or in front of Grand Central Station made one indeed look the fool. It was more natural to sell it along Fourteenth Street or Union Square where people were always selling or giving out literature. Once when we distributed along the water front to longshoremen, publicizing a meeting for longshoremen and seamen, one of them said, "They're always poking stuff at us, papers, posters, leaflets; first it's the Communists and then it's the Jehovah's Witnesses, and now it's the Catholics."

It was a difficult job, giving out literature, or selling the paper on the streets, but when one got used to it there was joy and freedom in it too, and the camaraderie of those who live on the streets and talk to each other freely. We learned their point of view. We were constantly confronted with the fact that on the one hand our daily papers, radio commentators and now television were shaping the minds of the people, and yet they were still responsive to basic and simple religious truths. They were attracted to the good; they were hard-working, struggling human beings living for the day, and afraid of the unknown.

Once that sense of fear of the unknown was overcome, brotherly love would evoke brother love, and mutual love would overcome fear and hatred.

The Communists recognized the power of the press, and also that the simple maxim "go to the people" meant literally going to them. The first time Trotsky was arrested it was for distributing literature at factory gates. When some of our friends were arrested in Chicago at stockyards during an organizational drive, we felt truly revolutionary and effective since organized industry, through the hands of the law which they controlled, had reached out to stop us.

It is easy enough to write and publish a paper and mail it out with the help of volunteers to the four corners of the earth. But it becomes an actual, living thing when you get out on the street corners with the word, as St. Paul did in the early days of Christianity.

LABOR

The Catholic Worker, as the name implied, was directed to the worker, but we used the word in its broadest sense, meaning those who worked with hand or brain, those who did physical, mental or spiritual work. But we thought primarily of the poor, the dispossessed, the exploited.

Every one of us who was attracted to the poor had a sense of guilt, of responsibility, a feeling that in some way we were living on the labor of others. The fact that we were born in a certain environment, were enabled to go to school, were endowed with the ability to compete with others and hold our own, that we had few physical disabilities—all these things marked us as the privileged in a way. We felt a respect for the poor and destitute as those nearest to God, as those chosen by Christ for His compassion. Christ lived among men. The great mystery of the Incarnation, which meant that God became man that man might become God, was a joy that made us want to kiss the earth in worship, because His feet once trod that same earth. It was a mystery that we as Catholics accepted, but there were also the facts of Christ's life, that He was born in a stable, that He did not come to be a temporal King, that He worked with His hands, spent the first years of His life in exile, and the rest of His early manhood in a crude carpenter shop in Nazareth. He fulfilled His religious duties in the synagogue and the temple. He trod the roads in His public life and the first men He called were fishermen, small owners of boats and nets. He was familiar with the migrant worker and the proletariat, and some of His parables dealt with them. He spoke of the living wage, not equal pay for equal work, in the parable of those who came at the first and the eleventh hour.

He died between two thieves because He would not be made an earthly King. He lived in an occupied country for thirty years without starting an underground movement or trying to get out from under a foreign power. His teaching transcended all the wisdom of the scribes and pharisees, and taught us the most effective means of living in this world while preparing for the next. And He directed His sublime words to the poorest of the poor, to the people who thronged the towns and followed after John the Baptist, who hung around, sick and poverty-stricken at the doors of rich men.

He had set us an example and the poor and destitute were the ones we wished to reach. The poor were the ones who had jobs of a sort, organized or unorganized, and those who were unemployed or on work-relief projects. The destitute were the men and women who came to us in the breadlines and we could do little with them but give what we had of food and clothing. Sin, sickness and death accounted for much of human misery. But aside from this, we did not feel that Christ meant we should remain silent in the face of injustice and accept it even though He said, "The poor ye shall always have with you."

In the first issue of the paper we dealt with Negro labor on the levees in the South, exploited as cheap labor by the War Department. We wrote of women and children in industry and the spread of unemployment. The second issue carried a story of a farmers' strike in the Midwest and the condition of restaurant workers in cities. In the third issue there were stories of textile strikes and child labor in that industry; the next month coal and milk strikes. In the sixth issue of the paper we were already combatting anti-Semitism. From then on, although we wanted to make our small eight-page tabloid a local paper, that is, covering the American scene, we could not ignore the issues abroad. They had their repercussions at home. We could not write about these issues without being drawn out on the streets on picket lines, and we found ourselves in 1935 with the Communists picketing the German consulate at the Battery.

It was not the first time we seemed to be collaborators. During the Ohrbach Department Store strike the year before I ran into old friends from the Communist group, but I felt then, and do now, that the fact that Communists made issue of Negro exploitation and labor trouble was no reason why we should stay out of the situation. "The truth is the truth," writes St. Thomas, "and proceeds from the Holy Ghost, no matter from whose lips it comes."

There was mass picketing every Saturday afternoon during the Ohrbach strike, and every Saturday the police drove up with patrol wagons and loaded the pickets into them with their banners and took them to jail. When we entered the dispute with our slogans drawn from the writings of the Popes regarding the condition of labor, the police around Union Square were taken aback and did not know what to do. It was as though they were arresting the Holy Father himself, one of them said, were they to load our pickets and their signs into their patrol wagons. The police contented themselves with giving us all injunctions. One seminarian who stood on the side lines and cheered was given an injunction too, which he cherished as a souvenir.

Our readers helped us when they responded to our call not to trade with a store which paid poor wages and forced workers to labor long hours, and we helped defeat the injunction, one of the usual weapons used by employers to defeat picketing, which was handled down against the strikers. Now there is the Taft-Hartley law.

At that time one of the big Catholic high schools in the city each month received a bundle of three thousand copies of our paper for their students. I had spoken there of the work for the poor and some of the students had worked with us. When we picketed the Mexican consulate to protest the religious persecution which was revived in 1934, the students came and joined us more than two thousand strong. We had set out, half a dozen of us, and, although we had printed an invitation in the paper, we did not expect such a hearty response. The police again were stunned at this demonstration, having met only with Communists in such mass demonstrations before. The students sang, marched and rejoiced in the fact that their pictures appeared on the front page of the *Daily News* the next morning.

Among other readers who joined us that day was a young mate on a Standard Oil tanker who said he first read our paper while sailing in the Gulf. From then on he visited the office between trips and contributed half his salary to the work. Other picketers were Margaret, our cook, and her baby, and my daughter. Most belligerent was a young woman who had been sent to us from a hospital after an unsuccessful operation for tumor on the brain. She was not too well informed as to issues and principles, and when one of the passers-by asked her what the picketing was about, she answered tartly, "None of your business."

She was one of those who liked to get out on the streets and sell the paper with Big Dan and a few others. There were many protests from the young intellectuals that these should seem to the public to represent the work. But they were certainly a part of it—"they belonged"—and they felt it and were fiercely loyal, though often they could make no answer for the faith that was in them.

The picketing of the Mexican consulate went well with the good Sisters who taught in a great Catholic high school, but when the students wanted to go on a picket line in a strike for the unionization of workers and better wages and hours, and were logical enough to extend their sympathy by boycotting the National Biscuit Company products and to inform their family grocers and delicatessens of this intention, then it was time for a stop. We were politely told that individuals could take the paper, but that the bundle order of three thousand must be canceled. There were too many people protesting against our activities with the students.

(On another occasion when I spoke to a high school group in Philadelphia, before I even returned to New York, a cancelation came in. "You must have done a good job down there," our circulation manager said grimly. "They used to take two thousand copies and now they've dropped them.")

Other readers who owned stock in N.B.C. sold their shares and informed the corporation. These acts helped settle the strike. The most spectacular help we gave in a strike was during the formation of the National Maritime Union. In May, 1936, the men appealed to us for help in housing and feeding some of the strikers, who came off the ships with Joe Curran in a spontaneous strike against not only the shipowners but also the old union leaders.

We had then just moved St. Joseph's house to 115 Mott Street and felt that we had plenty of room. Everyone camped out for a time while seamen occupied the rooms which they made into dormitories. There were about fifty of them altogether during the course of the next month or so, and a number of them became friends of the work.

There were O'Toole, a cook on the United States Lines, and Mike, a Portuguese engineer who carried copies of *The Catholic Worker* to Spain when he shipped out later, bringing us back copies of papers and magazines from Barcelona. This same friend brought us a bag full of earth from Mount Carmel after his ship had touched at the Holy Land. Once he asked me what I wanted from India, and I told him the kind of a spindle which Gandhi had sent to Chiang Kai-shek, as a gift and a warning, perhaps against United States industrialism. He and a shipmate searched in several Indian ports for what I wanted and finally found three spindles in Karachi which they brought to me. One was a metal hand spinner shaped like those shown in old pictures which could be carried about in a little box; the other two were most peculiar contraptions, one of them looking like a portable phonograph.

The seamen came and went and most of them we never saw again, but three remained for years and joined in our work. That first strike was called off, but in the fall, after the men built up their organization, the strike call went out again. For the duration of the strike we rented a store on Tenth Avenue and used it as a reading room and soup kitchen where no soup was served, but coffee and peanut butter and apple butter sandwiches. The men came in from picket lines and helped themselves to what they needed. They read, they talked, and they had time to think. Charlie O'Rourke, John Cort, Bill Callahan and a number of seamen kept the place open all day and most of the night. There was never any disorder; there were no maneuverings, no caucuses, no seeking of influence or power; it was simply a gesture of help, the disinterested help of brothers, inspired in great part by our tanker friend, Jim McGovern, who had written an article for the paper telling how he had been treated as a seaman in Russia and the kind of treatment these same men got here.

Jim was a college graduate, had fallen away from his early faith but regained it by reading Claudel. He was so painfully shy that he was no good at all in contacts with the rank and file. He went to sea because he loved it; he loved the ship he served and the responsibility it entailed. Perhaps there was much of romance and youth in his attitude. He wrote to us of the clubs in the Russian port, and how the men were treated as men, capable of appreciating lectures, concerts, dances and meetings with student groups. In this country, he said, the seamen were treated as the scum of the earth; port towns and the port districts in these towns were slums and water-front streets made up of taverns and pawnshops and houses of prostitution. He felt that the Russians treated their American comrades as though they were creatures of body and soul, made in the image and likeness of God (though atheism was an integral part of Marxism) and here in our professedly Christian country they were treated like beasts, and often became beasts because of this attitude.

Our headquarters were a tribute to the seaman's dignity as a man free to form association with his fellows, to have some share in the management of the enterprise in which he was engaged.

On another occasion, when the Borden Milk Company attempted to force a company union on their workers, *The Catholic Worker* took up their cause, called public attention to the

use of gangsters and thugs to intimidate the drivers and urged
our readers to boycott the company's products while unfair
conditions prevailed. As a result of the story the company attacked *The Catholic Worker* in paid advertisements in the
Brooklyn *Tablet* and the *Catholic News*.

Many times we have been asked why we spoke of *Catholic*
workers, and so named the paper. Of course it was not only
because we who were in charge of the work, who edited the
paper, were all Catholics, but also because we wished to influence
Catholics. They were our own, and we reacted sharply to the
accusation that when it came to private morality the Catholics
shone but when it came to social and political morality, they
were often conscienceless. Also Catholics were the poor, and
most of them had little ambition or hope of bettering their condition to the extent of achieving ownership of home or business,
or further education for their children. They accepted things as
they were with humility and looked for a better life to come.
They thought, in other words, that God meant it to be so.

At the beginning of the organizing drive of the Committee
(now the Congress) for Industrial Organization, I went to
Pittsburgh to write about the work in the steel districts. Mary
Heaton Vorse was there at the time and we stayed at Hotel Pitt
together in the cheapest room available, at a dollar and a half a
day. It was before we had the house of hospitality in Pittsburgh
which now stands on the top of a hill in the Negro district. A
student reader of the paper drove us around to all the little
towns, talking of his soul, much to Mary's distress; she was
especially distracted when he told of practicing penances on our
Easton farm by going out at night and rolling in some brambles.
He had no interest in the struggles of the workers—it was the
spiritual side of our work which appealed to him—and he was
driving us through all the complicated districts on either side of
rivers not so much to help us, as to help himself. He wanted to
talk to us about his problems. There was not the quiet and peace
on such trips to make such talk very fruitful.

There had been the big strike in 1919 led by William Z.
Foster, which Mary had covered, and she knew some of the old

priests who had helped the people by turning the basements of their churches into relief centers. We went to see them, and we attended open-air meetings along the Monongahela and the Allegheny and Ohio Rivers, where we distributed papers.

On that visit Bishop Hugh Boyle said to me, "You can go into all the parishes in the diocese with my blessing, but half the pastors will throw you out." He meant that they did not have that social consciousness which I was seeking among Catholics and that they felt all organizations of workers were dominated by Communists and were a danger to be avoided.

Later in the big steel strikes in Chicago and Cleveland, when "Little Steel" fought it out with the workers, there was tragedy on the picket lines. In what came to be called the Memorial Day massacre, police shot down hundreds out on the prairies in front of the Republic Steel plants in South Chicago. Ten men died, and others were disabled for life. I had just visited their soup kitchens and strike headquarters; in addition to recognizing that the majority of the workers were Catholics, I also recognized an old friend, Elizabeth, the wife of Jack Johnstone, one of the Communist party leaders in this country. Elizabeth and Jack had brought me roast chicken and ginger ale one night as I lay sick with influenza in NewYork, and Elizabeth had taken care of Tamar for me so that I could go to Mass, and I had taken care of her young son. Elizabeth, whom I had last seen in New York, was there to write a pamphlet on "Women in Steel," a call to the wives and mothers to help their men organize. Her husband had been organizing in India, and they were accustomed to long separations during which both of them worked for the party. Elizabeth used to tease me by saying that it was due to me that she had become a member of the party and had met Jack, because I had obtained a job for her with the Anti-imperialist League, where I was working at the time.

Elizabeth in Chicago, Jack in India—these wives of Communists, dedicated to revolution as Rayna was! Rayna's husband had worked in the Philippines while she was in Hankow. They went where they were sent, had a sense of their world mission and accepted any hardship that it entailed. If I could only arouse

Catholics to such zeal, with the spiritual weapons at their disposal, I thought! If they could only be induced to accept voluntary poverty as a principle, so that they would not fear the risk of losing job, of losing life itself. Organizing sometimes meant just that.

It was not only the Communists, however, who had this courage. One winter I had a speaking engagement in Kansas and my expenses were paid, which fact enabled me to go to Memphis and Arkansas to visit the Tenant Farmers' Union, which was then and is still headed by a Christian Socialist group. The headquarters were a few rooms in Memphis, where the organizers often slept on the floor because there was no money for rent other than that of the offices. Those days I spent with them I lived on sandwiches and coffee because there was no money to spend on regular meals either. We needed to save money for gas to take us around to the centers where dispossessed sharecroppers and tenant farmers were also camping out, homeless, in railroad stations, schools and churches. They were being evicted wholesale because of the purchase of huge tracts of land by northern insurance agencies. The picture has been shown in *Tobacco Road*, *In Dubious Battle* and *Grapes of Wrath*—pictures of such desolation and poverty and in the latter case of such courage that my heart was lifted again to hope and love and admiration that human beings could endure so much and yet have courage to go on and keep their vision of a more human life.

During that trip I saw men, women and children herded into little churches and wayside stations, camped out in tents, their household goods heaped about them, not one settlement but many—farmers with no land to farm, housewives with no homes. They tried with desperate hope to hold onto a pig or some chickens, bags of seed, some little beginnings of a new hold on life. It was a bitter winter and frame houses there are not built to withstand the cold as they are in the north. The people just endure it because the winter is short—accept it as part of the suffering of life.

I saw children ill, one old man dead in bed and not yet buried, mothers weeping with hunger and cold. I saw bullet holes in the frame churches, and their benches and pulpit smashed up and windows broken. Men had been kidnaped and beaten; men had been shot and wounded. The month after I left, one of the organizers was killed by a member of a masked band of vigilantes who were fighting the Tenant Farmers' Union.

There was so little one could do—empty one's pockets, give what one had, live on sandwiches with the organizers, and write, write to arouse the public conscience. I telegraphed Eleanor Roosevelt and she responded at once with an appeal to the governor for an investigation. The papers were full of the effrontery of a northern Catholic social worker, as they called me, who dared to pay a four-day visit and pass judgment on the economic situation of the state. The governor visited some of the encampments, and sarcastic remarks were made in some of the newspaper accounts about the pigs and chickens. "If they are starving, let them eat their stock," they wrote.

I spoke to meetings of the unemployed in California, to migrant workers, tenant farmers, steelworkers, stockyard workers, auto workers. The factory workers were the aristocrats of labor. Yet what a struggle they had!

There was that migrant worker I picked up when I drove in a borrowed car down through the long valley in California, writing about government aid to the agricultural workers. "Nothing I love so much as jest to get out in a field and chop cotton," he said wistfully.

There was that old Negro living in a little shack in Alabama where the rain fell through on the rags that covered him at night. While I talked to him a little boy ran up and gave him a bone and some pieces of cornbread; the old man was so excited talking to me and the priest who was with me that he dropped the bone on the ground and a hound dog started licking it. The little boy stood by him, pulling at his sleeve and crying. It was his dinner too, his only dinner, and it was being devoured by a dog. If the old man had more, the children would have less. And there was so little.

There was that little girl in Harrisburg, and another in Detroit, sent out by their parents to prostitute themselves on the street. While I talked to the family in Harrisburg, all of whom lived in one room, the little girl sat reading a tattered book, *Dorothy Vernon of Haddon Hall*.

There was Paul St. Marie, who was president of the first Ford local, a tool and die maker, with a wife and eight children. He suffered from unemployment, from discrimination when he was hired. He worked the graveyard shift from twelve to eight, walked a mile from gate to plant, and worked in the cold on stone floors. He fell ill with rheumatic fever at the age of forty-five and died. He knew poverty and insecurity and living on relief—he and his wife were heroic figures in the labor movement, thinking of their fellows more than of themselves. Paul took me around the auto plants and showed me what the assembly line meant. I met the men who were beaten to a pulp when they tried to distribute literature at plant gates, and I saw the unemployed who had fire hoses turned on them during an icy winter when they hung around the gates of the Ford plant looking for work.

"How close are you to the worker?" Pitirim Sorokin asked me when I was talking with him at Harvard. He himself was the son of a peasant woman and a migrant worker and was imprisoned three times under the Czars and three times under the Soviets. He too had suffered exile in the forests, hunger and imprisonment; he had lived under the sentence of death and was, through some miracle, and probably because of his doctrine of love in human behavior, allowed to go abroad. He had a right to ask such a question and it was a pertinent one.

Going around and seeing such sights is not enough. To help the organizers, to give what you have for relief, to pledge yourself to voluntary poverty for life so that you can share with your brothers is not enough. One must live with them, share with them their suffering too. Give up one's privacy, and mental and spiritual comforts as well as physical.

Our Detroit house of hospitality for women is named for St. Martha. We are always taking care of migrant families in that house, southern families who are lured to the North because they hear of the high wages paid. It is a house of eight large rooms, and each of the bedrooms has housed a family with children, but the congestion has meant that the husbands had to go to the men's house of hospitality named for St. Francis. Sometimes the families overflow into a front parlor and living room downstairs. The colored take care of the white children, and the white the colored, while the parents hunt for homes and jobs. Such an extreme of destitution makes all men brothers.

Yes, we have lived with the poor, with the workers, and we know them not just from the streets, or in mass meetings, but from years of living in the slums, in tenements, in our hospices in Washington, Baltimore, Philadelphia, Harrisburg, Pittsburgh, New York, Rochester, Boston, Worcester, Buffalo, Troy, Detroit, Cleveland, Toledo, Akron, St. Louis, Chicago, Milwaukee, Minneapolis, Seattle, San Francisco, Los Angeles, Oakland, even down into Houma, Louisiana where Father Jerome Drolet worked with Negroes and whites, with shrimp shellers, fishermen, longshoremen and seamen.

Just as the Church has gone out through its missionaries into the most obscure towns and villages, we have gone too. Sometimes our contacts have been through the Church and sometimes through readers of our paper, through union organizers or those who needed to be organized.

We have lived with the unemployed, the sick, the unemployables. The contrast between the worker who is organized and has his union, the fellowship of his own trade to give him strength, and those who have no organization and come in to us on a breadline is pitiable.

They are stripped then, not only of all earthly goods, but of spiritual goods, their sense of human dignity. When they are forced into line at municipal lodging houses, in clinics, in our houses of hospitality, they are then the truly destitute. Over and over again in our work, many young men and women who come as volunteers have not been able to endure it and have gone away. To think that we are forced by our own lack of room, our lack of funds, to perpetuate this shame, is heartbreaking.

"Is this what you meant by houses of hospitality," I asked Peter.

"At least it will arouse the conscience," he said.

Many left the work because they could see no use in this gesture of feeding the poor, and because of their own shame. But enduring this shame is part of our penance.

"All men are brothers." How often we hear this refrain, the rallying call that strikes a response in every human heart. These are the words of Christ, "Call no man master, for ye are all brothers." It is a revolutionary call which has even been put to music. The last movement of Beethoven's Ninth Symphony has that great refrain—"All men are brothers." Going to the people is the purest and best act in Christian tradition and revolutionary tradition and is the beginning of world brotherhood.

Never to be severed from the people, to set out always from the point of view of serving the people, not serving the interests of a small group or oneself. "To believe in the infinite creative power of the people," Mao Tse-tung, the secretary of the Communist party in China, wrote with religious fervor. And he said again in 1943, "The maxim 'three common men will make a genius' tells us that there is great creative power among the people and that there are thousands and thousands of geniuses among them. There are geniuses in every village, every city." It is almost another way of saying that we must and will find Christ in each and every man, when we look on them as brothers.

At a group meeting in New York, part of the Third Hour movement, made up of Catholics, Russian Orthodox, and Protestants of all denominations, a Socialist said to me that the gesture of going to the people was futile and that it had been tried in Russia and failed. We had a long discussion on the validity of such efforts to achieve brotherhood, and I kept repeating that the Christian point of view was to keep in mind the failure of the Cross. Then thinking I might be talking to someone with a Jewish background, I spoke of the natural order itself, how the seed must fall into the ground and die in order to bear fruit. In the labor movement every strike is considered a failure, a loss of wages and man power, and no one is ever convinced that understanding between employer and worker is any clearer or that gains have been made on either side; and yet in the long history of labor, certainly there has been a slow and steady bettering of conditions. Women no longer go down into the mines, little children are not fed into the mills. In the long view the efforts of the workers have achieved much.

At the close of the evening, I learned that I had been talking to Alexander Kerensky, one of the greatest failures in history.

My trips around the country were usually to visit our houses of hospitality, which were springing up everywhere, and also to speak at schools. I took advantage of theses trips to cover strikes and the new organizational drive of the Congress of Industrial Organizations.

Father James G. Keller, head of the Christopher Movement, called me one day and said that Archbishop McNicholas would like to talk to me, so I took a train to Cincinnati. Usually I travel by bus in order to economize. But this time the Archbishop sent a ticket and I traveled comfortably. I spent the day with him and with several other bishops of the Midwest, discussing the condition of the unemployed and the strikes that were going on in the auto plants. We were served magnificently at the bishops' table but the Archbishop himself dined modestly on a few vegetables and milk. I could not help thinking, of course, of our breadlines, and our cramped quarters. It is not only the Archbishop's palace which is a contrast, but every rectory in our big cities, and even in country sections. Only in the mission fields is the rectory as poor as the homes of the workers round about. One can understand the idea of a functional society and the needs of doctors for cars and telephones and of the lawyer and teacher for books and space, but the ordinary family has need of space too for his little church which is his family.

For Christ Himself, housed in the tabernacles in the Church no magnificence is too great, but for the priest who serves Christ, and for the priesthood of the laity, no such magnificence, in the face of the hunger and homelessness of the world, can be understood.

And yet I do know too that if any bishop or archbishop

started to take the poor into his palace, or moved out of his palace to live with the poor, he would be considered mad. And he would suffer the fate of the fool.

Bishops and priests may long to make that gesture, but their own humility no doubt restrains them. Some day may God put His hand upon them so unmistakably that they know they are called to this gesture, to this madness. We begin to see a little of it in Archbishop Stepinac, who told C. L. Sulzberger of the *New York Times* that he would not be other than where he was, in a prison cell, doing penance for the Church.

"The Church is the Cross on which Christ was crucified, and who can separate Christ from His cross," Guardini has written.

On that happy occasion when I enjoyed the day with the Archbishop, who, like so many others, lived in poverty in the midst of wealth, Father Keller and I listened to him read a pastoral letter he had just written. It was about the condition of capital and labor, and I felt it was a noble piece of writing. But Father Keller thought the archbishop was a trifle harsh to the rich.

That night when I discussed going to Detroit to cover the situation of the sit-down strikers in the Flint auto plants, the Archbishop urged me to go to them, to write about them. He had one of his priests reserve and pay for a Pullman berth for me so that I would be fresh the next day for my work.

It was a friendly and a happy day of talk about the needs of the workers and the poor. It made me unhappy later when the Archbishop became so uneasy about *The Catholic Worker's* editorial position on the Spanish Civil War that he asked pastors in his diocese to discontinue getting it for their churches or schools, though he did not suggest that they cease taking it themselves.

On another occasion he issued a call in one of his public statements, for a mighty army of conscientious objectors if we embarked upon a war with Russia as an ally. Those of our associates around the country who swelled the ranks of the Catholic conscientious objectors looked ruefully on the anything-but-mighty army. They also felt that they were conscientious objectors for the same reason that they opposed the war in Spain, or class war or race war or imperialist war, not because Russia was our ally.

The Archbishop gave us three hundred dollars as a contribution toward our camp for conscientious objectors, and we deeply appreciated this first gesture of ecclesiastical friendship in our hitherto unheard-of position. Before he died he sent us his blessing again.

But I am trying to write about the bishops in connection with the labor movement. Archbishop Schrembs of Cleveland was always friendly when I visited him at those times I was invited to speak at congresses and social-action meetings. I visited strike headquarters during the Little Steel strike and talked with the men. They were worn with the protracted conflict and worried about losing the homes they had managed to buy after years of saving, and the food and clothing needed for their children if they lost both strike and job as had happened on other occasions in the past. The next day when I visited Archbishop Schrembs he told me that during the morning a representative of Associated Industries had called on him and told him of my presence at strike headquarters the day before.

In New York the Chancery office had also been informed of our activities, and when a priest came to see us in our Tenth Avenue headquarters during the seamen's strike the visit was immediately reported. This happened often enough to indicate to me that there were spies from the employers among the strikers and that the employers felt that the Church was on their side in any industrial dispute. The worker present at Mass was in the eyes of bishop and priest just like any member of Knights of Columbus or Holy Name Society, but as soon as he went on strike he became a dangerous radical, and the publicity he got linked him with saboteurs and Communists.

We met other bishops who visited our offices and told us about the work in their dioceses, in the co-operative movement, parish credit unions, circulating libraries and other activities among the laity. They sat down to eat with us—Bishop O'Hara, Bishop Waters, Bishop Busch—and abbots of monasteries, who are also princes of the Church, came too. Every six months when we sent out our appeals, there were a number of bishops who always responded, even those who disagreed so strongly on some aspects of our work that they would not permit meetings in their dioceses and certainly not houses of hospitality. However, some houses opened up not specifically associated with *The Catholic Worker,* but owing their inspiration to it. Those who run these houses feel themselves to be children of the movement since they work with the poor and dispossessed. However, they do not hold to the distributist or anarchist or pacifist positions that are taken editorially in *The Catholic Worker.* They leave the discussion of these issues to others, and do the immediate work of showing their love for their brothers in the simple practical method of the corporal works of mercy.

The spiritual works of mercy include enlightening the ignorant, rebuking the sinner, consoling the afflicted, as well as bearing wrongs patiently, and we have always classed picket lines and the distribution of literature among these works.

During the course of writing about labor and capital, we began a study club at the Mott Street headquarters. It was an outgrowth of the seamen's strike and was started by John Cort, a young Harvard graduate who was working with us at the time, and Martin Wersing, a union official in the electrical workers. Father John Monaghan and a group of other union men joined with them in forming what they called the Association of Catholic Trade Unionists. After it had obtained its start under our auspices, the group moved to Canal Street so that they would have room for their meetings and could handle the avalanche of inquiry which came to them, once they were under way.

Their aim and endeavor was to assist the worker to organize and to enlighten the Catholic in the existing unions as to the teachings of the Popes in regard to labor. They set out at once to oppose the Communist and gangster elements (two separate problems) in the longshoreman and other unions, and their policy came into conflict with ours.

As Peter pointed out, ours was a long-range program, looking for ownership by the workers of the means of production, the abolition of the assembly line, decentralized factories, the restoration of crafts and ownership of property. This meant, of course, an accent on the agrarian and rural aspects of our economy and a changing of emphasis from the city to the land.

The immediate job at hand was enough for the Association. They disagreed too with our indiscriminate help in strikes where there was strong Communist influence, and our loss of the opportunity to get our own men into positions of vantage in order to influence others.

Peter, however, talked about Christ's technique, of working from the bottom and with the few, of self-discipline and self-organization, of sacrifice rather than enlightened self-interest, and of course, of the synthesis of cult, culture and cultivation. How he loved the roll of that phrase. Once when he spoke to the seamen at the Tenth Avenue strike headquarters he attacked communism, but it was by reviewing a book by André Gide and by talking of his disillusionment with the Russian regime. I supposed he considered the meeting from the standpoint of culture, most of the seamen never having heard of André Gide, or if they had, only of the unsavory aspects of his erotic life. Sometimes we used to sigh over Peter's idea as to what would be dynamic thought for the workers.

There is so much more to the Catholic Worker Movement than labor and capital. It is people who are important, not the masses. When I read Pope Pius XII's Christmas message, in which he distinguished between the masses and the people, I almost wished I had named our publication *The People*, instead of *The Catholic Worker*.

We published many heavy articles on capital and labor, on strikes and labor conditions, on the assembly line and all the other evils of industrialism. But it was a whole picture we were presenting of man and his destiny and so we emphasized less, as the years went by, the organized-labor aspect of the paper.

It has been said that it was *The Catholic Worker* and its stories of poverty and exploitation that aroused the priests to start labor schools, go out on picket lines, take sides in strikes with the worker, and that brought about an emphasis on the need to study sociology in the seminaries.

And many a priest who afterward became famous for his interest in labor felt that we had in a way deserted the field, had left the cause of the union man. Bishops and priests appearing on the platforms of the A.F. of L. and C.I.O. conventions felt that we had departed from our original intention and undertaken work in the philosophical and theological fields that might better have been left to the clergy. The discussion of the morality of modern war, for instance, and application of moral principle in specific conflicts. Labor leaders themselves felt that in our judgment of war, we judged them also for working in the gigantic armaments race, as indeed we did. Ours is indeed an unpopular front.

When we began our work there were thirteen million unemployed. The greatest problem of the day was the problem of work and the machine.

The state entered in to solve these problems by dole and work relief, by setting up so many bureaus that we were swamped with initials. NIRA gave plan to NRA, and as NRA was declared unconstitutional another organization, another administration was set up. The problem of the modern state loomed up as never before in American life. The Communists, stealing our American thunder, clamored on the one hand for relief and on the other set up Jeffersonian schools of democracy.

Peter also quoted Jefferson—"He governs best who governs least." One of his criticisms of labor was that it was aiding in the creation of the Welfare State, the Servile State, instead of aiming for the ownership of the means of production and acceptance of the responsibility that it entailed.

COMMUNITY

ONE of the great German Protestant theologians said after the end of the last war that what the world needed was community and liturgy.

The desire for liturgy, and I suppose he meant sacrifice, worship, a sense of reverence, is being awakened in great masses of people throughout the world by the new revolutionary leaders. A sense of individual worth and dignity is the first result of the call made on them to enlist their physical and spiritual capacities in the struggle for a life more in keeping with the dignity of man. One might almost say that the need to worship grows in them with the sense of reverence, so that the sad result is giant-sized posters of Lenin and Stalin, Tito and Mao. The dictator becomes divine.

We had a mad friend once, a Jewish worker from the East Side, who wore a rosary around his neck and came to us reciting the Psalms in Hebrew. He stayed with us for weeks at a time, for although mad, he had the gentleness of St. Francis. He helped Hergenhan in our garden on Staten Island, and he liked to walk around in his bare feet. "I can feel things growing," he said. "I look at the little plants, and I draw them up out of the earth with the power of love in my eyes."

He sat at the table with us once and held up a piece of dark rye bread which he was eating. "It is the black bread of the poor. It is Russian Jewish bread. It is the flesh of Lenin. Lenin held bread up to the people and he said, 'This is my body, broken for you.' So they worship Lenin. He brought them bread."

There is nothing lukewarm about such worship, nothing tepid. It is the crying out of a great hunger. One thinks of the words of Ezekiel, condemning the shepherds who did not feed their sheep. I know that my college friend Rayna never heard the word of God preached and she never met a Christian. The failure is ours, and that of the shepherds.

Peter was not so much interested in labor as he was in work and community. He felt that as long as men sought jobs and wages, and accepted the assembly line and the material comforts the factory system brought, they would not think in terms of community, except for that which the union brought them. They might be gathered together in time of crisis, during strikes, but would they listen to what he said about the need for owner-ship and responsibility?

Every talk of Peter's about the social order led to the land. He spoke always as a peasant, but as a practical one. He knew the craving of the human heart for a toehold on the land, for a home of one's own, but he also knew how impossible it was to attain it except through community, through men banding together in farming communes to live to a certain extent in common, work together, own machinery together, start schools together.

He held the collective farms in Palestine up for our consideration. Since Peter's death, Martin Buber's book, *Paths in Utopia*, has told of the experiments in Israel, and Thomas Sugrue has written a book, *Watch for the Morning*, on these great adventures in building up a place in the desert for a dispossessed people. Claire Huchet Bishop has written about the communities in Europe in her books, *France Alive* and *All Things Common*, showing how men can become owners of the means of production and build up a community of work together.

But these books were not written when Peter started to talk, and he knew that people were not ready to listen. He was a prophet and met the usual fate of the prophet. The work of the co-operatives in Nova Scotia had attracted the attention of the world, but Father Jimmy Tomkins said, "People must get down to rock bottom before they have the vision and the desperate courage to work along these lines and to overcome their natural individualism."

Community—that was the social answer to the long loneliness. That was one of the attractions of religious life and why couldn't lay people share in it? Not just the basic community of the family, but also a community of families, with a combination of private and communal property. This could be a farming commune, a continuation of the agronomic university Peter spoke of as a part of the program we were to work for. Peter had vision and we all delighted in these ideas.

"But not a five-year plan," he would say. He did not believe in blueprints or a planned economy. Things grow organically.

A parish priest in Canada, Father John McGoey, had a vision of a community of families. From a poor parish in Toronto, he inspired a number of families who were jobless and living on relief to band together and study the problems of getting back

to the land. He secured a tract of land for them, obtained the
co-operation of the city's relief bureau, and moved the families
out of the slums. A school for the children was started, a weaving
project set up, gardens put in, small animals cared for, and the
families got on their feet again. With the ending of the depression and the beginning of preparations for war, some of them
moved back to the factory neighborhoods again.

Monsignor Luigi Ligutti, head of the Catholic Rural Life
Conference, did the same with a group of unemployed miners
in Iowa. He obtained land and funds from the government,
and the settlement he established has prospered. In both these
cases government help was needed. Peter did not wish to turn to
the government for funds. "He who is a pensioner of the state is
a slave of the state," he felt. Neither Father McGoey nor Monsignor Ligutti felt enslaved, but they did admit there had been
red tape and many headaches involved in getting the help
needed.

Peter's plan was that groups should borrow from mutual-aid
credit unions in the parish to start what he first liked to call
agronomic universities, where the worker could become a scholar
and the scholar a worker. Or he wanted people to give the land
and money. He always spoke of giving. Those who had land
and tools should give. Those who had capital should give. Those
who had labor should give that. "Love is an exchange of gifts,"
St. Ignatius had said. It was in these simple, practical, down-to-
earth ways that people could show their love for each other. If
the love was not there in the beginning, but only the need, such
gifts made love grow.

"To make love." Peter liked to study phrases, and to use them
as though they were newly discovered. (*Honest to God* was the
title of one of his series of essays.)

The strangeness of the phrase "to make love" strikes me now
and reminds me of that aphorism of St. John of the Cross,
"Where there is no love, put love and you will find love." I've
thought of it and followed it many times these eighteen years
of community life.

Peter set much store on labor as a prime requisite for a new order. "Work, not wages." That was an I.W.W. slogan and a Communist slogan too, and Peter liked it. During the days of the depression the Communists and our Catholic Workers often collided in street demonstrations. DOWN WITH CHIANG KAI-SHEK! said one of their posters, when we were demonstrating against evictions. WORK, NOT WAGES was another picket sign, when what the Communists were demanding was more relief, unemployment insurance, and every other benefit they could get from the state. Packed in that one tight little phrase is all the dynamite of revolution. Men wanted work more than they wanted bread, and they wanted to be responsible for their work, which meant ownership.

I know that as this is read, it will be questioned. "This is how people should be, but are they? Give them relief checks and they will sit back and do nothing for the rest of their days. When they do have jobs they see how much they can get away with in giving as little labor as possible for the highest pay they can get." One hears these complaints from householders and even from heads of religious orders, who complain that postulants enter without the slightest knowledge of any skills that will help the order. And girls do not know how to cook or sew or keep house. With the lack of knowledge of how to work has come a failure in physical strength too.

Peter was no dreamer but knew men as they were. That is why he spoke so much of the need for a philosophy of work. Once they had that, once their desires were changed, half the battle was won. To make men desire poverty and hard work, that was the problem. It would take example, and the grace of God, to do it.

The word philosophy is bandied around a great deal today. John Cogley, who formerly headed our house of hospitality in Chicago and is now an editor of *The Commonweal*, told us about one of his professors at Fribourg who lectured on Russian philosophy. "In all their schools, whether of law, medicine, art, engineering or agriculture, philosophy is required study," he said. And that is right, because in order to achieve integration, the whole man, there must be an underlying philosophy that directs and lends meaning to his life.

During World War II, a French Communist wrote an article reprinted in the *New Masses* which emphasized the need for a Communist in the Sorbonne or any other college to teach history or science from a Communist point of view. The party never misses the dominant importance of philosophy.

Peter's Christian philosophy of work was this. God is our creator. God made us in His image and likeness. Therefore we are creators. He gave us a garden to till and cultivate. We become co-creators by our responsible acts, whether in bringing forth children, or producing food, furniture or clothing. The joy of creativeness should be ours.

But because of the Fall the curse is laid on us of having to earn our bread by the sweat of our brows, in labor. St. Paul said that since the Fall nature itself travaileth and groaneth. So man has to contend with fallen nature in the beasts and in the earth as well as in himself. But when he overcomes the obstacles, he attains again to the joy of creativity. Work is not then all pain and drudgery.

All of us know these things instinctively, like Tom Sawyer whose example led others to covet his whitewashing job—or the workman, healthy tired, after a good day's toil like Levin reaping with the peasants in *Anna Karenina*.

Craftsmen, not assembly-line workers, know this physical, but not nervous, fatigue and the joy of rest after labor. Peter was never a craftsman but he was an unskilled laborer who knew how to use an ax, a pick and a shovel, how to break rocks and mend roads.

Peter and his slogans! "Fire the bosses" meant "Call no man master, for all ye are brothers." It meant "Bear ye one another's burdens."

"Eat what you raise and raise what you eat" meant that you ate the things indigenous to the New York climate, such as tomatoes, not oranges; honey, not sugar, etc. We used to tease him because he drank coffee, chocolate or tea, but "he ate what was set before him." Had he been a young husband raising a family he would have done without tea, or coffee, as indeed such a disciple as Larry Heaney did. Larry was in charge of the Holy Family House in Milwaukee until he married and was able with another Catholic Worker family to buy a fine farm in Missouri.

Peter liked to talk about the four-hour day. Four hours for work, four hours for study and discussion; but he didn't practice it. Knowing that people could not fit into neat categories he would seize upon them whenever he could for discussion and indoctrination.

Everyone, of course, wished to indoctrinate. They no sooner had a message than they wished to give it. Ideas which burst upon them like a flood of light made the young people want to get out and change the world.

We always had the war of the worker and scholar when the former accused the latter of side-stepping work. The joke went around the country that the Catholic Worker crowd lived on lettuce one bright summer of discussion at Maryfarm when students from ten universities around the country arrived for long visits. One young politician active in public life in Ohio, spent months with Peter and then returned to the Midwest to teach, eventually starting the Christ the King Center for Men at Herman, Pennsylvania.

Farms like ours began to dot the country. In Aptos, California, in Cape May, New Jersey, in Upton, Massachusetts, in Avon, Ohio, in South Lyon, Michigan—a dozen sprang up as Catholic Worker associates. Many others consisted of young married groups trying to restore the idea of community.

Some were started and abandoned as too isolated, or because of lack of water, lack of funds, lack of people who knew how to work. Men found out the reasons for cities and relief rolls when they ventured onto the land and sought to do manual labor. How to work in industry so as not to compromise oneself and yet earn a living for a family?

The problem did not really become acute until the family entered in. The family thought Peter's farming commune idea was solely for them. The scholars thought the agronomic university idea was for them. The sick and unemployed thought the Catholic Worker farms in general were for women and children and the helpless.

We all wrote a great deal about it in the paper and found interest in the most unlikely places. When I went to visit Tom Mooney, the labor leader who was imprisoned for twenty years for the Preparedness Day bombing in San Francisco, I found him and other prisoners in San Quentin interested in the land. Ramsey, King and Connor—I do not remember their first names—were officials of the Marine Firemen's Union who had also been imprisoned, as all the labor movement believed, on a framed charge of murder. I saw them too at that time and found them interested in the land.

"There's never a seaman wants to settle in the city," one of them said. "What they want is a little chicken farm of their own."

The desire was strong for private property, but even stronger for community. Man is not made to live alone. We all recognized that truth. But we were not truly communitarian, Peter said— we were only gregarious, as most people in cities are. Peter knew that most of us not only had not been trained to disciplined work, but we did not know how to work together. I remember seeing one seaman who was washing our kitchen floor throw down his mop when another man started to help him, saying, "Well, if you want to do it, go ahead and do it. The job is yours."

We had a number of seamen in our first years, so many in fact that one sarcastic sociologist wrote of our efforts on the land as being not farming communes for families but rest houses for celibate seamen. There were many such comments those first few years but the interest was widespread because we actually were trying to put into effect the ideas that Peter talked about. We were learning through grim experience, "the hard way" everyone said, but I never knew any other way. We consoled ourselves that we might not be establishing model communities, but many a family was getting a vacation, many a sick person was nursed

back to health, crowds of slum children had the run of the
woods and fields for weeks, and groups of students spent happy
hours discussing the green revolution.

We write a great deal about the farms in *The Catholic Worker*
to share experiences with our readers and to get their advice.
Realizing that we were poor like themselves, without equipment,
unskilled, floundering along, we have found friends who were
not afraid to tell us of their own poverty and their hard-won
knowledge. We have printed letters from owners of small farms
as well as from farm laborers.

I myself traveled through the Southwest from Arkansas, down
through Texas and Arizona and southern California, and visited
the migrant camps through the state of California. In fact, I
probably covered the route of the Joad family in *Grapes of
Wrath*. After seeing that movie and the dilapidated old car that
carried their poor household things across mountain and desert,
I have never since been afraid to travel in our Catholic Worker
cars, which are mostly discards from our readers. I have had
clutches come out of the floor into my hands, the gas pedal fall
down through the floor board, the battery fall out of the car,
and innumerable tires go flat. And these mishaps always occurred
miraculously enough within a step of home. Often at the end of
a long trip just as I was pulling into the home stretch, the car
would go dead. On one such occasion I was driving a man who
had just been operated on for cancer to our retreat house for a
convalescent period.

With one of these cars, but the best of them, bought for us
by Harold McKinnon, a San Francisco lawyer, I made a trip
down the long valley in California and visited each of the camps
established by the government for the protection of the migrants.
Certainly whenever we have written in *The Catholic Worker*
about the conditions through the country we have tried to see
and study them first hand, and to work out a solution that would
be within the means and the capacities of all.

And what are these means and capacities?

As Peter saw it, to live according to Gospel simplicity meant
that you begged when you were in need and by this you gave

the opportunity to the rich to become poor for Christ's sake. "Appeals, not demands," was another of his slogans.

And since he was most often talking of the destitute, the unemployed, this was the line he usually took. But our young married couples did not fit into this category. "Man should earn his living by the sweat of his brow," Peter repeated, "and a gentleman, truly speaking, is one who does not live on the sweat of someone else's brow." In other words, he worked.

Our Catholic Worker retreats advocated detachment from unnecessary luxuries. The savings of those who do not smoke, drink beer, go to movies, use cosmetics, buy radios, cars, television sets, should be enough to buy a farm to enable them to make a start. And yet it did not always work out in this way. Men might not indulge themselves in any way, and yet be made destitute by sickness and death. And there was many a form of sickness that stalked in our midst.

I wrote one long leading article for *The Catholic Worker* a few years ago which one of the girls in the office entitled, "What Dream Did They Dream—Utopia or Suffering," in which this mystery of suffering is discussed. Recently I have heard from friends in China, missionaries, who asked for more copies of that issue to send to their friends because I emphasized so much the necessity of suffering, and the glory of suffering for a cause. I read over that article recently and I noticed that I left out many of the specific sufferings that our friends in the apostolate have endured, the death of children, the loss of wife or husband, the mental breakdowns.

People tried to save for some purpose. But often their savings had to be spent for doctors or hospital bills, or to help others. How could one save when people were in need? And were not the two ideas contradictory, to perform the works of mercy at a personal sacrifice, and to save to provide for one's own? But one's own family of course came first. These were the arguments of those who wished to marry. They were not the problems of the single.

The Heaney family worked and saved to buy a farm, and joined with the Martin Paul family and Ruth Ann Heaney's brother to make a down payment and to stock the place. Martie Paul had already failed once, because of the war and his years in the army. He had been given a piece of land in northern Minnesota and with the help of Al Reser and his wife from the Chicago *Catholic Worker* had built a few cabins and made a start at a farming commune, calling it after St. Isadore, the patron of farmers. Don Humphrey and his wife from the Milwaukee *Catholic Worker* and their children lived and starved on the place for a while too. It was a grim experience, though all seem now to look back on their days there with nostalgia.

In the case of the St. Isadore's farm, Martie was drafted, the Resers lost a child from some obscure pancreatic disorder, and Al nearly died with asthma. The Humphreys stayed on the farm for a while, Mary with four children and Don away working on the road to Alaska. Later they moved into St. Cloud so that he could make a living for his growing family.

In the case of the Holy Family farm in Missouri, Larry died suddenly after a bout with pneumonia. He had an abscessed lung and died from the anesthetic, leaving a wife and six children. The farm is still in operation, with Ruth Ann's brother and other young men helping Martie with their labor, and contributing financially too.

The Detroit farm was given for our use by a priest's father who lost one son during the war and bore the suffering of his priest son's life for four years in a concentration camp. St. Benedict's farm, at S. Lyon, Michigan, is run for the benefit of the men who live at St. Francis House in Detroit. Produce is raised there, and the hundred acres provide living quarters for a number of the men. There is also Marybrook, a retreat house farm for week-end groups of students and workers.

Our Lady of the Wayside farm in Avon, Ohio, was given to us also, and Bill Gauchat, his wife and their five children share the land and the buildings with another Catholic Worker couple and their children, a Mexican family, and others who fall by the wayside and need help. They have sheltered unmarried girls who were having babies, have cared for sick children, taken in migrant families until they found work and homes, and with the most limited space and facilities have had summer schools and Sunday conferences for the readers of *The Catholic Worker* in that area.

St. Benedict's farm at Upton, Massachusetts was a bargain. We paid a thousand dollars for one hundred acres and an old farmhouse which was big enough to shelter many visitors as well as the families and single people who built it up. It got off to a bad start, with two young men in charge, one of whom wished to have a farming commune and the other a house of hospitality on the land. The farming commune idea won out; then with the first two families there was another conflict over the division of labor. Both men were hard workers. One of them wanted to farm and let the other work in a neighboring institution to raise the cash needed for seed and tools. The one who worked outside St. Benedict's thought that both should share this responsibility. The man who originally wished to remain and farm left to return to Boston. The young man who remained moved not much later for job and health considerations, turning over the house which he had built out of an abandoned schoolhouse to a man whose wife was ill. This schoolhouse home was later leased to a father and seven sons who have lived there for the last ten years.

There are three other families on St. Benedict's now and twenty-five children. The second to settle at Upton was a mother whose artist husband was imprisoned as a conscientious objector during World War II. She had her baby while her husband was in prison and returned to her one-room farmhome to wait patiently for his release some years later. The husband is a fine craftsman. Since his release he has received many a commission for stained glass so that he has been able to employ others on the farm to help him. There are four children in that family now. The chap who returned to the city then came back to the farm, where he now lives with his wife and eight children. Another family in the village of Upton was burned out, and came to live in the original farmhouse, now used for guests. They have decided to join the community and build. The farm is held in the name of Ade Bethune and John Magee, the former head of the Boston Catholic Worker group, as trustees for *The Catholic Worker,* and plots of land of varying sizes are leased for fifty years to the families.

On our Easton farm, where we also had this trustee ownership, deeds of three acres each were given to families until the revolt occurred of the two families who wished twenty acres, not three. This resulted in our deeding them the original farm of twenty-seven acres. When Tamar was married to David Hennessy, they remained there for two years before buying a farm of their own in Stotler's Crossroads, West Virginia, where they lived for three years. This started out to be a community of three families, but that too was a failure, the first two families leaving after a year. One family indeed stayed only a few months and then moved back to the city. Right now Tamar and David are purchasing a farm on Staten Island so they can be near his New York job.

One of the main difficulties of all these farm ventures is the lack of skills, money and equipment; lack of leadership too is a factor. There could be, I believe, groups of families on the land, surrounding a chapel, disciplined by family life and daily attendance at Mass, all subject to one another, with a division of skills and labor and accepting too the authority of one coordinator. Ideally speaking, this should be as successful as any community of monks who maintain themselves by the labor of their hands.

It is no use comparing such a community of families, however, to a community of monks, because the latter are often maintained by the alms of the faithful. Land is often left to a monastery and usually there is income from schools. If lay communities were given the start, if young families were given an initial subsidy, free and clear, and left to work out their way of life, great things could be done.

At Peter Maurin farm, on Staten Island, we have a three-acre asparagus bed which might eventually bring in enough money to pay the taxes of five hundred dollars a year. Our bakery there could make the place self-sustaining if we did not give away all the bread.

Through the skill of David Mason, former head of the house of hospitality in Philadelphia, proofreader and writer by profession, a "surplus commodity" oven from a battleship was set up in a little outer kitchen in the rear of the farmhouse. We can bake a hundred loaves at a time and several of us have learned to bake. Now we have the satisfaction of feeding our two houses, on Staten Island and Chrystie Street, and the breadline of hundreds of men who come twice a day for meals, with the best of whole-wheat bread, made from whole-grain flour which we buy by the half ton.

What a delightful thing it is to be boldly profligate, to ignore the price of coffee and go on serving the long line of destitute men who come to us, good coffee and the finest of bread.

"Nothing is too good for the poor," our editor Tom Sullivan says, and he likes that aphorism especially when he is helping himself to something extra good.

Tom is the "co-ordinator" of the house of hospitality on Chrystie Street, New York, though we never use that title. He is in charge of the house, and his is a gentle and unobtrusive authority. He has won the respect of the men and their co-operation so that many of them take on jobs in the house and kitchen and keep the work going. There are a number who have worked with us in the past, who have been willing to take responsibility but unwilling for others to use initiative. Tom keeps the books, divides the money up in paying the bills, watches every expenditure scrupulously, writes a column for the paper, keeps a quiet eye on the men in the house and does a great deal of praying. People love him because he loves God, and for love of God loves the poor. They feel this in him and trust him.

FAMILY

ONCE a Midwest priest said to me that if I were a woman of family, the things I wrote in *The Catholic Worker* about community and personalism would have more validity. I accepted his criticism at the moment, especially since I was going through a difficult time. I was thirty-eight, wishing I were married and living the ordinary naturally happy life and had not come under the dynamic influence of Peter Maurin. Every now and then I'd look at him and groan, "Why did you have to start all this anyway?"

I thought this criticism of the positions I took in my writing valid because it gave me an excuse to dally with the idea of marriage. Afterward I thought indignantly—"But I *am* a woman of family. I have had husband and home life—I have a daughter and she presents problems to me right now. How can I let anyone put over on me the idea that I am a single person? I am a mother, and the mother of a very large family at that. Being a mother is fulfillment, it is surrender to others, it is Love and therefore of course it is suffering. He hath made 'a barren woman to dwell in a house: the joyful mother of children.' "

I saw the film *Grapes of Wrath* at this time and the picture of that valiant woman, the vigorous mother, the heart of the home, the loved one, appealed to me strongly. Yet men are terrified of momism and women in turn want a shoulder to lean on. That conflict was in me. A woman does not feel whole without a man. And for a woman who had known the joys of marriage, yes, it was hard. It was years before I awakened without that longing for a face pressed against my breast, an arm about my shoulder. The sense of loss was there. It was a price I had paid. I was Abraham who had sacrificed Isaac. And yet I had Isaac. I had Tamar.

She was, of course, everything to me. I have not even to this day ceased to look upon her with wonder. When I looked at her tiny, perfect hands and my own, already worn though I was only twenty-seven, I marveled at her newness. Tamar crowing on the beach, learning to walk on the sands. Tamar at three meeting her father again and saying to me resentfully, "That is *my* father, not your father"—oh, cruel stab! Tamar singing, Tamar praying—"Does the Blessed Mother mind if I say my prayers standing on my head? And how can I pray when I have to keep laughing."

Tamar growing up in community.

But before the Catholic Worker community came about I had to think in terms of a job and rent to be paid, food purchased. There was always a wrench in going away and leaving her with others, whether in a day nursery in New York or with a family in Hollywood. When she was ill I stayed home from work to care for her, and she had the usual run of children's diseases, chicken pox, measles, whooping cough, abscessed ears, bronchitis, in addition to malaria contracted in Mexico. I had her, even in those working years, all to myself evenings and Saturdays and Sundays.

But in community it was another story. With the beginnings of *The Catholic Worker,* my working day began at early Mass with the *Opus Dei,* and ended often at midnight. She was no longer my only one. I should have known what to expect when Peter Maurin stood over her sickbed when she had measles, indoctrinating the doctor. At night when visitors came, workers, scholars, priests, laymen, I left her in her bath and all but forgot her in the heat of discussion. In the delight of staying up late, Tamar stayed in the tub till the water was cold, making boats of the soap and her toys.

There were plenty who laid claim to my sympathy and loving care to the extent of forgetting I had personal family obligations, and there were some who were extremely jealous and found ways of showing it. There was one young woman, sent to us from a hospital for convalescent care, who stayed with us for years, and she was frank in her jealousy to the extent of taking my child's clothes and giving them away, destroying her specimens (she was an avid collector like her father) and venting her petty spite on her in other ways. I had to put up with it, if only for the reason that my daughter did. From her babyhood she had a sympathy for all suffering things and she recognized this poor warped creature as a sufferer.

Probably Tamar enjoyed the freedom my preoccupations gave her. She had playmates in the building on Fifteenth Street, Freddy Rubino, who still comes to *The Catholic Worker* meetings, and the Liguori and Riedel children. When we left Fifteenth

Street she went to an academy on Staten Island, run by the Sisters of St. Dorothy, an excellent teaching order, but she returned home week ends and holidays. She spent her summers on our farm at Easton and her companions were the colored children from Harlem and white children from the lower West Side, none of whom had ever vacationed in the country before. Some of the children were highly intelligent and others were of very low mentality; I learned how hard it is for bright children to play with retarded ones. Tamar and a little boy, Arthur, used to make adobe houses; an entire village was constructed of little mud bricks and it grew to considerable size on a large cement pavement in back of the house out of the way of traffic. A family of feeble-minded children were with us on the farm for several years, and one of the first acts of these children was to destroy this little village. The woman throwing out the terraria and aquaria, the birds' nests and egg cocoons of insects, and the children always on the lookout for something to destroy—these were trials.

Tamar never was very articulate about it. I probably felt it more than she did.

She grew up knowing what she wanted, and that was to make things. She read a great deal. When she was occupied with books on biology or astronomy I knew she was happy, engrossed; but when she read fiction, I knew she was escaping, that she was not as happy as she might be. I transferred her for one brief term to a more fashionable school and here she was so miserable that she read a book a day. It was not the leisurely reading of *David Copperfield* or the Marylea series. It was truly an escape. So I brought her back to St. Dorothy's, where the children took daily walks and helped in Saturday's cleaning, where were only twenty boarders and it was a family.

When she was in first year high school she lived at home. That is, at St. Joseph's House of Hospitality, and left the house at seven-thirty, not returning until four-thirty. There was too much homework—too many activities after school. Life was exciting enough at the Catholic Worker—there were enough extra curriculum lectures, visitors, walks, expeditions with the young people's volunteer group of which she now became a part, so that I felt she was overburdened with her schoolwork.

She was beginning to be interested in the young men who came around, young fellows from Notre Dame or the University of Chicago. She was fourteen then.

She wanted to farm. She wanted to marry young and live on a farm. She was impatient with school. She had a proposal when she was fifteen and we all took it seriously. After all why should she not marry at sixteen, she said. Many peope did.

Eighteen was time enough! I was inexorable. What I did understand, however, was that she wished to fit herself for marriage and I could not see that the school she attended, or any other high school was going to do that.

"Why wasn't I a retarded child," she groaned, "so that I could go to one of these schools where they teach crafts?"

Monsignor Luigi Ligutti heard this pathetic cry and recommended St. Martine's, an *Ecole Ménagère* just an hour's ride out of Montreal. "She can learn spinning and weaving there, and even how to make straw hats," he said enthusiastically. It was a regular high school but all studies were taught in French. Tamar wanted to try it, just to take the crafts, so one miserable fall day we took the bus for Montreal and she was registered at the school where the tuition was only eighteen dollars a month, including board and room.

When I left Tamar that afternoon and went back to Montreal, I never was so unhappy, never felt so great a sense of loneliness. She was growing up, she was growing up to be married. It did not seem possible. I was always having to be parted from her. No matter how many times I gave up mother, father, husband, brother, daughter, for His sake, I had to do it over again.

She enjoyed the school, though she only stayed for the winter term and then returned to Easton to live at Maryfarm for the spring and summer. I had to go to the West Coast for a few months that spring to visit our houses of hospitality there. When I returned I found she was in love, this time most seriously, and determined to marry.

She was not yet seventeen, so in order to continue her schooling I sent her to the home of Ade de Bethune in Newport, where she worked not only with Ade's apprentices, but in her household. She learned to shop intelligently (it was a time of ration books), to buy and cook cheap cuts of meat, to bake and churn, keep a kitchen fire going, care for small animals in a back yard—rabbits, chickens, even white rats and canaries. She learned calligraphy and how to bind a book. There were evenings when one of the monks from a Benedictine priory near by gave talks on philosophy and theology; there were concerts of chamber music at friends' houses, folk dancing on Friday nights, evenings at the marine hospital teaching crafts to wounded sailors. How to take care of the money you earned, how to earn money by caring for children, sitting with invalids, repainting murals in an old church—these too she learned.

When she had spent her year at Ade's, she went for another six months to a school of applied agriculture on Long Island. She would have stayed longer except that her eighteenth birthday came around and she and the young man she loved announced that they would be married as soon as the three Sundays elapsed for the calling of the bans at Sunday Mass.

What a wedding that was! The wedding breakfast was to take place at the Easton farm and Tamar and I spent days beforehand cleaning and scrubbing until it was hard to get the grime out of our hands. It was a wedding in poverty because the young people were to start out in a barracks-like house on the farm, surrounded by a three-acre garden. The house had been occupied previously by a migrant family who left it in anything but appetizing condition. The day before the wedding some homeless dogs killed Tamar's pet goat, leaving two orphan kids, and that tragedy and her care for the little animals cast a shadow on the great event.

It was during the war; there were few volunteers with us, most of the young men were away, and Easton was two hours out of New York. It was a mid-week wedding, so there were not more than a score of guests. Of course Peter was there, thoughtful and happy.

"He is going to make a speech at my wedding breakfast," Tamar said nervously, remembering all the other occasions when Peter delighted in the opportunity to indoctrinate. At the wedding of one of our fellow workers in New York a few years previous Peter had talked so long to the first sitting at the wedding breakfast that the second sitting of our guests in the house of hospitality had a hard time getting anything to eat. Perhaps Tamar was thinking too of the way Peter stood over her bed when she had measles and indoctrinated the physician.

The nuptial Mass was at nine o'clock and it being wartime there was only one car to transport the guests to and from the church. I had to be chauffeur since there was no one else with a license to drive. We got up at six to heat water for bathing (it was a typical old farmhouse with no plumbing) and to get the fire started in the range for the breakfast. Everyone was fasting in order to receive communion at the wedding, but we wanted to have coffee on the stove and the eggs all ready to scramble when we returned. Someone had brought a gigantic ham, and there was an immense cake from an Italian parish in Brooklyn, the remains of an Easter feast there.

Peter was up bright and early. As I bustled Martha-like through the kitchen, putting the finishing touches to the room, he followed me around trying to make a few points, practicing on me for the speech he was about to make at the breakfast. He loved occasions.

With impatience I turned on him. "Can't you see how busy I am!" I cried reproachfully.

With complete meekness, he turned away, and not long after I saw him sauntering down the rocky road which led to the highway. It was very early yet, and I felt guilty, sorry for having repulsed him. It was the first time I had ever spoken so impatiently to *him*. Getting the borrowed car started I hastened down the road after him. "If you are going so early to church, Peter," I called to him, "I will drive you down. Get in." He got in obediently. "I'm sorry I was so rude," I told him. "After all, you must realize that my only daughter is being married. It's a most wonderful day for both her and me. We can't think of anything else but that. I really can't discuss farming for profit on such a morning."

Peter was magnanimous as always. "I knew a man once," he said, trying to be personal to meet me on my plane, "who got so excited on the day his daughter was married that he slapped her." There was no more to the story than that, evidently, and I wondered who the man was, and why the incident had made an impression. But I didn't inquire further. I just tried to hint that Tamar woud prefer no speeches at the wedding breakfast, especially the speech which we knew Peter was dying to make about "pigs for profit." One of the seamen who was in charge of the farm had recently ventured into a partnership with a neighbor and lured by wartime profits, was trying to raise pigs, on our communitarian project, for profit! It was occupying Peter's mind so that he could think of nothing else.

It was a beautiful wedding, simple and happy, and everyone returned to the farm to feast. The married couple were to stay in their new home and spend their honeymoon scraping off whitewash, painting their house and getting a garden in. To supplement his mail-order distributist book business, David was working with a roofer and had little time off from work. There were the baby kids preoccuping Tamar during the breakfast. It looked as though one of them would not live. And then Peter began his speech! We all laughed, but we all had to listen too. After all, it would not have been a Catholic Worker wedding without it. The neighbors were there, some priests were there, the residents of the Catholic Worker farm were there and guests from New York. It was an occasion and occasions called for speeches. And speeches were always affairs of moment with Peter. There were no idle words with him. When he spoke, it was "yea, yea" or "nay, nay." But it took him a long time to say it.

Our poor darling Peter! It was the last speech he made, as a matter of fact, because within a few months, he was stricken down, he lost his memory, and suddenly he could no longer "think," as he tried to tell us sadly.

Joy and sorrow, life and death, always so closely together!

Tamar's family lives near us today, and now there are five grandchildren. God has indeed made me, the barren woman, to dwell in her house, the joyful mother of children. I had always wanted a big family, and here I have them near me. I am seeing my children's children about me.

Tamar is partly responsible for the title of this book in that when I was beginning it she was writing me about how alone a mother of young children always is. I had also just heard from an elderly woman who had lived a long and full life, and she too spoke of her loneliness. I thought again, "The only answer in this life, to the loneliness we are all bound to feel, is community. The living together, working together, sharing together, loving God and loving our brother, and living close to him in community so we can show our love for Him."

RETREAT

THERE is a Jesuit retreat house for men on Staten Island; there is a Passionist house in Jamaica. The Cenacle of St. Regis has one on One Hundred Fortieth Street with a view of the Hudson. There is a retreat house at the Convent of Mary Reparatrix on Twenty-eighth Street across from the Little Church around the Corner. It was to this convent that I went to spend a few days soon after the first issue of *The Catholic Worker* came out. It was my first retreat. I did not enjoy it at all. Perhaps there are those who would say that a retreat is not the time to think of enjoying oneself. It is a time to take stock, to make an inventory, to meditate on one's sins and resolve to do better. It should also be a time of spiritual refreshment.

But I was not refreshed. It was the middle of summer and very hot. There was no garden enclosure in which to wander. It was closed in, this convent, crushed in by the stone walls all about. The church was small. Every day the Sacred Host, the round white disk of bread which had suddenly at the priest's words of consecration become the Body of Our Lord, was enclosed in a

jewel-encrusted ostensorium and placed above the altar, surrounded by candles and flowers. All day long two by two the
white-and-blue-robed nuns knelt, taking turns each hour to
worship in silent adoration. A grill separated them and the sanc-
tuary from the main body of the church, into which shoppers,
tourists, business people and workers came for adoration, contrition, thanksgiving and supplication. Being on retreat, I was
allowed to kneel close to the altar at a little opening in the grill
at the side, having a special *prie Dieu* to myself.

I should not have made a retreat by myself, I felt. I had been a
Catholic only a few years and I was not ready for the long days
of silence, of reading, of intimate colloquy with one of the nuns.
If I had been with a group I might have enjoyed my stay. As it
was I felt stifled, unable to comprehend what I was reading, unable to talk. It was a hard time. I do not remember now how
many days I spent there. But when I left, I felt as though suddenly I was able to breathe again. The atmosphere had been too
rarefied for me. I felt free, released, glad to be away, and yet
guilty because of my gladness. I soon forgot my sense of guilt in
work that was waiting for me. Already, although the paper was
only a few months old, mail from all over the United States was
almost more than three of us could handle, and people came to
the door all the day long, and even far into the night.

A community was growing up. A community of the poor,
who enjoyed being together, who felt that they were embarked
on a great enterprise, who had a mission.

All of them understood the works of mercy—old-fashioned
prayer books list them. The corporal ones are to feed the hungry;
to give drink to the thirsty; to clothe the naked; to harbor the
harborless; to ransom the captive; to visit the sick; to bury the
dead. The spiritual works are to instruct the ignorant; to counsel
the doubtful; to admonish sinners; to bear wrongs patiently; to
forgive offenses willingly; to comfort the afflicted; to pray for
the living and the dead.

Everyone understood, in his destitution, that voluntary poverty on the part of him who possessed some of this world's goods
would enable him to practice these works of mercy—"at a per-

sonal sacrifice," Peter Maurin always added. Eric Gill said that Christ came to make the rich poor and the poor holy.

All of us began to have in some slight way Peter's philosophy of poverty. He told us how Proudhon wrote *The Philosophy of Poverty* and how Karl Marx read it and countered scornfully with *The Poverty of Philosophy*. Peter gave us little lectures about poverty and community as we sat at our meals. He indulged in the first part of his program, these round-table discussions, twice a day. Not at breakfast, because we all went to Mass at different hours, at seven, eight or nine, and so broke our fast at different hours.

I did not think of retreats for a long time again. We were living a retreat, some of us said smugly. Others said scornfully that with all our talk of voluntary poverty, with shelters like our houses of hospitality and with farming communes, we were indeed fleeing to the fields, retreating from the world, living in ivory towers. I wanted to start a farming commune called Tower of Ivory, one of the titles of the Blessed Virgin in the litany dedicated to her.

The first time I heard about what came to be called *the retreat*, was some five years later. Maisie Ward, the wife and business partner of the publisher, Frank Sheed, was telling me of a retreat she had heard of in Canada given by Abbé Saey, in the heart of the slums. "He gives it for workers," she said. "They bring their own lunch and eat it right there in the church and share it with others who come. They spend the day in silence, walk the streets between conferences, go home at night, and come back the next day for more. People are thronging to it. It is an evangelical retreat. I am going to Montreal to make it."

The retreat was in French, and since I could not understand French I did not go. My friend Sister Peter Claver told me of a priest friend of hers who had made a retreat for priests in Baltimore, given by a Father Onesimus Lacouture, a French Canadian from Montreal who had influenced Abbé Saey. She told me that many who heard him changed their lives entirely. She had the retreat notes given to her by her confessor, and gave them to me to read.

I read them and was not much impressed. The written word did not have the life and vitality of the spoken word, and perhaps it was the personality of the retreat master that made the teaching so powerful, I thought. I preferred to go for my spiritual instruction, I told her, to the saints, St. Catherine of Siena, St. Teresa of Avila, St. John of the Cross, St. Francis, and the Little Flower, as well as to the New Testament itself.

Another year passed before Sister Peter Claver came to visit us in New York with Father Pacifique Roy, a Josephite priest from Quebec who was then stationed in Baltimore. He had served as a missionary in Louisiana as well as in Canada, and he had been, he informed us, instrumental in having Father Lacouture give a retreat for priests at Baltimore a few years before.

We were sitting in the dining room having our morning coffee when Father Roy started to talk to us about the love of God and what it should mean in our lives. He began with the Sermon on the Mount, holding us spellbound, so glowing was his talk, so heartfelt. People came and went, we were called to the telephone again and again, but still Father Roy went on talking to all who would listen. The men came in from the soup kettles in the kitchen which were being prepared for the soup line and stayed to listen, tables were set around us and the people came in and were fed and went out again, and still Father talked, and so the day went. It was like the story in the Gospels, when the two apostles were talking on the way to Emmaus, grieving and fearful and lamenting over the death of their Leader; suddenly a fellow traveler came along and began to explain the Scriptures, going as far as the town with them and even going to an inn to break bread with them. They knew Him then in the breaking of bread. They had said to each other, "Was not our heart burning within us, whilst he spoke in the way?"

Father Roy talked to us of nature and the supernatural, how God became man that man might become God, how we were under the obligation of putting off the old man and putting on Christ, how we had been made the sons of God, by the seed of supernatural life planted in us at our baptism, and of the necessity we were under to see that the seed grew and flourished. We had to aim at perfection; we had to be guided by the folly of the Cross.

He not only pointed out to us the obligation we were under by the vows we had taken at our baptism to put off the world, the flesh and the devil, but he pointed out the means to do this, by what he called acting always for the "supernatural motive"— "*moteef*," he pronounced it—in this way supernaturalizing all our actions of every day. If we did our works of mercy to be praised by men, or from pride and vanity and sense of power, then we had had our reward. If we did them for the love of God, in whose image man had been made, then God would reward us; then we were doing them for a supernatural motive. There was little freedom in this life, except in the realm of motive or intention. We could do things either because we were compelled to, or because we loved God and wanted to. And never mind, if we did not by our own sacrifice put off the old man and put on the new; God would see to it that we did so in the natural course of events, just as we grew in age, losing little by little our sense of life, our eyesight, our teeth, our hearing. "Oh yes, we would be stripped," he laughed gaily. "God so loved the world," he cried out with a thrill in his voice. God was that Hound of Heaven who would pursue us, who would not let us go.

His was the kind of talk to which all of us could listen, the men from the soup line, students on vacation or seminarians coming in to help for an afternoon. He had a stock of stories with which we were to become familiar and which he was never tired of telling, nor we indeed of hearing. Sometimes we had not gotten the point and it needed the tenth telling for us to understand, just as it was with Peter's points. As Peter always dealt with the things of this world, so Father Roy always dealt with the things of the next, but the two were interwoven; time and eternity were one. As St. Catherine said, "All the way to heaven is heaven," because He had said, "I am the way." We were like workers for a Utopia already living in their Utopia. We were dying and yet we lived. We were in sorrow yet rejoicing.

He liked to tell of a leper he visited in a hospital in Canada, a huge Russian fellow who was suffering greatly during his slow death. He could not understand why God did this to him, the leper cried.

"I told him about God's love," Father Roy said. "I began with the dirt, and how the flower said to the dirt, 'How would you like to be like me, so pretty, so sweet, waving in the breeze?' And the dirt said, 'Oh, I would like that.' So the roots of the flower assimilated the dirt, and it became a flower. And then the rabbit came along and said to the flower, 'And how would you like to be like me, hopping around, playing in the fields?' And the flower said, 'Oh, yes, I would like to be able to move and to be like you.' So the rabbit assimilated the flower and it became rabbit. And then the man came and said to the rabbit, 'How would you like to be a man, to walk about, to think, to pray?' And the rabbit said, 'Oh, of course, I would like that!' So the hunter killed him and ate him. And do you know that leper grasped my hand, and he lifted his eyes full of tears to me, and he said, *'Oh, Father!'* and there was such a depth of comprehension in the way he said it, that I cried too. 'Though He slay me yet will I trust in Him.' Oh yes, we must die to live; we've got to face it. It is easy to talk about this mystery of suffering but it is hard to take. But what am I talking about. Doesn't God give us strength and grace to bear everything?"

Some years later I read in Louis Fischer's *Life of Mahatma Gandhi* the old Indian poem,

> I died as a mineral and became a plant,
> I died as a plant and became an animal,
> I died as an animal and was a man.
> What should I fear? When was I less by dying?

The doctrine of assimilation is there too.

He certainly filled us with the spirit of joy while he talked. He told us how he had been pastor of a country parish in the bayou region, and how after he had made the retreat under Father Lacouture he had given up cigars, hunting and fishing. "Was I smoking for the love of God, or for myself?" he asked.

And he had had a passion for fishing. "I did not do it for utility," he said humbly.

Father Roy was stationed in Baltimore at that time, and it was but rarely that he was able to get to New York. So we often went to see him. He worked in a Negro parish as a curate, so he could not invite us to stay in the rectory. Our house of hospitality in Baltimore was started by John Doebele, Jim Rogan, and Jon Thornton, three college graduates, and Franklin Smith, who owned a truck and used to peddle sandwiches and doughnuts outside of factory gates. Smiddy, as we called him, would bring his surplus stock to help feed the soup line, but after he listened to Father Roy preach he decided it was not enough to give us the stale goods he could no longer sell. He decided to give himself and his truck to the work, and from then on he collected leftover food from hospitals and restaurants, furniture, and other goods to run the house. Many a time too he picked up sick men in the house and brought them to the hospital, using his little panel truck as an ambulance. He and the others often became vermin-ridden in performing the works of mercy.

Father Roy came to preach to us at the house. The big front room which was formerly a union hall was filled with unemployed longshoremen and seamen and construction workers, colored and white, drunk and sober, sitting on chairs and benches and along the wall on the floor when there were not enough chairs. We did not want the place to have the aspect of a mission, and we did not want to preach to men with empty stomachs. But we wanted to hear Father Roy ourselves and we used the only room we had, which had to accommodate the men in the house too when all the beds were taken.

We often listened to him to the tune of snoring guests. Men crouched and lay around the room in an abandonment of weariness, trying to sit up, propped against each other, against the wall, until sleep overcame them and they slid over against their fellows, their heads on one another's shoulders. And Father Roy talked on, in his gently appealing way, of "the one thing necessary"—love. "Love is the measure by which we shall be judged," he quoted. He always emptied his pockets too of anything he could collect for us.

He had his own work to do of course, and it was in a poor parish with a poor school. There were only outdoor toilets (this in 1939 in Baltimore) and an old hall for recreation, and the parishioners were clamoring for a gymnasium. They openly grumbled at the fact that collections were taken for other parochial schools and nothing was done to improve theirs, so Father Roy began to plan. He came to the house of hospitality and begged some of the men to come to him to work for God. He assembled some carpenters, electricians, plumbers, ditchdiggers, and with the help of these men who lived in the basement of the parish house and were served meals by Mr. Green the janitor, he built a fine gymnasium and shower room. Half of the men would work a few weeks and then succumb to drink, Father put them to bed and cajoled, entreated, rebuked and nursed them back to sanity. When they had recovered, the others were likely to be prostrated. Thus the work was accomplished by the lame, the halt, the blind, the offscouring of all.

In addition to saying Mass every day, preaching, teaching, and doing heavy manual labor (for he directed and joined the men in their work) Father Roy gave us "days of recollection." Usually we had these days at a Dominican convent or a Visitation convent outside of Baltimore. He urged fasting upon us. Prayer and fasting always went together, he said, so he put us on bread and water for the day. It was not literally bread and water. After Mass in the morning we had black coffee, with no sugar in it, and a few slices of bread. At noon we had bread and water. In between we sat and listened to conferences on the love of God, some of us from the house of hospitality, some readers of the paper, students, teachers, workers and unemployed. In the evening we went back to Baltimore to the basement of his rectory and were regaled by Mr. Green with a delicious dish of roast groundhog.

Those were beautiful days. It was as though we were listening to the gospel for the first time. We saw all things new. There was a freshness about everything as though we were in love, as indeed we were. After a day of recollection with Father Roy we went back to New York or Philadelphia refreshed, and "went for forty days and forty nights," like the prophets, on that food. It was good bread. Indeed it was strong meat.

Father Roy hitchhiked often, carrying with him literature by Abbé Longpré, Saint Louis de Montfort, Father Caussade, St. Angela of Foligno, Father Lacouture, the Gospels. In trains and busses he always met someone who was hungering for the Word.

"It was very Providential we met," he ended his stories. Providential was one of his favorite words. He tried to make us cultivate abandonment to Divine Providence.

One time, hitchhiking between Washington and Baltimore, he obtained a ride with several priests who were probably aghast at seeing their fellow cleric hitchhiking, thinking that some accident or illness had overtaken him. He too was abashed on getting into the car to find himself in the company of a bishop. But, "it was very Providential," and even to these he preached the Gospel, the good news, the story of the love of God for men, and how, joyful to relate, we are even now the sons of God and the implications of this profound truth! What a difference it made in our way of looking at other men, and our life here on earth.

His favorite stories, which he told over and over, were the encounter of our Lord with the rich young man and His telling him, "If thou wilt be perfect, go sell what thou hast and give to the poor"; "He who does not hate father, mother, sister and brother, cannot be my disciple"; "Unless the seed fall into the ground and die, itself remaineth alone"; and "Take up your cross daily and follow me."

The twenty-fifth chapter of St. Matthew was his text for the house of hospitality.

He always spoke with such enthusiasm, with such joy, that one could well understand the rejoicing in tribulation that St. Paul talked about. It was just another of those paradoxes, which needed to be experienced to be understood, and one began to experience it in hearing Father Roy.

It was the natural law as well as the supernatural law, he always pointed out. Another favorite tale, which he used not without guile, was from his experience with a pastor who needed a hundred thousand dollars to build a school. (These are general terms, because of course a half a million would be needed now.)

"He had only a thousand dollars," Father Roy would state sadly, "and he knew that was not enough to do anything with. So he sowed it. He threw it into the field as the farmer plants the wheat. He gave it to the poor. And lo and behold, someone presented him with a hundredfold, a hundred thousand dollars!"

There was another story, to bring the same point more into the realm of our experience. "Suppose you want to go to California and it costs a hundred dollars. You have fifteen. It is not enough. So give it away, give it to the poor. Then you suddenly have twenty-five, and that is not enough and the only thing to do is to give it away too. Even seventy-five. That is not enough. Tell the Lord you want more. Throw it away recklessly. You will get back your hundredfold. You will get what you need. Maybe it will come in graces. Maybe it will cover your spiritual needs, not just your physical. But sow, sow! As ye sow, so shall ye reap. He who sows sparingly, reaps sparingly."

Father Roy worked on this principle when he needed funds for materials. He came to us, explained his need, gave us what his pocketbook contained, and the materials somehow arrived by the time he returned home.

He allowed himself an "out," we would tease him, when he said perhaps the reward would be in spiritual gifts, not material. "But the good Lord knows what you need," he assured us. "Maybe you should not go to California. Maybe the train would be wrecked."

The same principle always worked. If we are rushed for time, sow time and we will reap time. Go to church and spend a quiet hour in prayer. You will have more time than ever and your work will get done. Sow time with the poor. Sit and listen to them, give them your time lavishly. You will reap time a hundredfold. Sow kindness and you will reap kindness. Sow love, you will reap love. "Where there is no love, if you put love, you will take out love"—it is again St. John of the Cross.

But Father Roy did get tired, of course. He could give two days of conferences, or perhaps three, but sometimes he would give the same one over with the same enthusiasm and not realize he had repeated himself. He was best at impromptu discussions, at chance meetings.

He antagonized many, as once when he went to a hospital to visit a poor crippled Sister, who had a radio by her bedside. "Sow everything; take up your cross; do not try to escape from it," he urged her. "Mortification, penance, that is what we all need. You are being mortified; you are dying little by little, but not fast enough. Die to the things of sense. Don't use that talcum there; you are indulging your nose. And your ears with the radio, and your taste with that pudding. And when you get rid of mortifying all your exterior senses, there are the interior senses, the memory, the understanding and the will. You should be mortifying your judgment now in regard to me." When he was rebuffed, when he was evicted, he hung his head meekly.

When Father spoke of mortifying, he spoke of putting to death, using the literal meaning of the word. We have been baptized in Christ's death, he reminded us. We are buried with Christ and we will rise with Christ; we must seek the things which are above, not the things which are below. Gospel texts flowed from his lips, but his opponents were not convinced; they had their countertexts.

"Even the devil can quote scripture." "He is a Jansenist." "Grace builds on nature, and he would put nature to death."

I have read Martin Scheeben, that great theologian, and my heart and mind give ready assent to his glowing and beautiful words on the grandeur of the natural man, of natural virtues, of natural life. I could see how theologians would seize upon Father Roy's words to brand him a heretic.

Once a priest said to us that no one gets up in the pulpit without promulgating a heresy. He was joking, of course, but what I suppose he meant was that truth was so pure, so holy, that it was hard to emphasize one aspect of the truth without underestimating another, that we did not see things as a whole, but in part, through a glass darkly, as St. Paul said. I am sure that as a layman, I could be branded for inexactitude of expression over and over again, and I take that risk month after month as I write in *The Catholic Worker,* and as I speak at gatherings and school groups.

Of course Father Roy was never satisfied with his own presentation of what he called *"the retreat,"* differentiating it from all other retreats, and all but branding them as feeble caricatures of the gospel teaching.

"The man who can really give this retreat is Father John J. Hugo," he told me once, and I immediately set out to find Father Hugo. He was a young priest of the diocese of Pittsburgh who amplified the retreat notes of Father Lacouture into a book entitled *Applied Christianity* which has been published with an imprimatur of the archdiocese of New York and which has gone into many editions and been studied by Catholics all over the world. He himself has written a history of this retreat movement in a book called *The Sign of Contradiction.* This was widely circulated among other priests and was regarded as an extreme example of self-criticism, that is, criticism of the clergy in general. At the time that I met him he had written little, but taught and preached a good deal. He was teaching religion in a girls' college in Pittsburgh, and led a street-preaching band in the Hill district of that city. He and Father Louis Farina, who had charge of an orphanage in Oakmont on the outskirts of Pittsburgh, had begun to give the retreat during the summer months at the orphanage when the classrooms could be turned into dormitories and the gymnasium used as a conference room. The Sisters at the orphanage were quite as enthusiastic as the priests and willingly took care of retreatants in addition to the hundred and fifty children who were in their charge.

The first retreat I attended at Oakmont was at the end of a short speaking trip. As I went from Cleveland to Detroit, to South Bend, to Chicago, to Milwaukee, I gathered other members of our Catholic Worker family from our houses of hospitality. Representatives from the New York and the Baltimore houses also came.

In Pittsburgh there had been a slight difference in opinion as to what true Franciscanism was. A few of the young people broke off from the main house of hospitality, which was then housed in a former orphanage on Tannehill Street and seemed to them to be too organized, to start a little house of their own in another section. I disagreed with the small group who felt themselves to be the *spirituals* of the movement, the perfectionists. At St. Francis house they were more truly poor than those at St. Joseph's, they felt. They didn't want to make the retreat because they lived a retreat—they were superior. But they ended up by coming at midnight, after imbibing at a few taverns along the way, but the important thing is that they came. There is a Bohemianism of the religious life among young people as well as Bohemianism in the labor movement, and it too smacks of sentimentality. The gesture of being dirty because the outcast is dirty, of drinking because he drinks, of staying up all night and talking, because that is what one's guests from the streets want to do, in participating in his sin from a prideful humility, this is self-deception indeed!

The five days of complete silence during the retreat were a feast indeed. Every day we had four conferences of an hour each, and after each conference we went to the chapel to pray. Father Hugo was a brilliant teacher and one could see he was taking great joy in his work.

"He who says he has done enough has already perished," he began ominously, quoting the words of St. Augustine. We shivered. How often had we settled back and said that we had done all we could; nothing more could be expected of us.

I have the retreat notes in two little notebooks and I still enjoy taking them to church with me and reading them over for meditation. "Behold I will allure her and will lead her into the wilderness: and I will speak to her heart." These were comforting words, these words from the book of Osee, the words of the prophet who married a harlot and loved her to such folly that when she was faithless to him he said sadly, "She did not know that I gave her corn and wine and oil, and multiplied her silver and gold." She thought they were gifts from her lovers.

This love, this foolishness of love, illustrated in the book of

Osee (Hosea) in the Old Testament and in the story of the prodigal son in the New, this folly of the Cross, was the sum and substance of the retreat. "O taste, and see that the Lord is sweet!" "How precious is the mercy of God; the children of men take refuge under the shadow of thy wings; they are filled with the bounteousness of thy house, and thou givest them to drink of the torrent of thy delights. For with thee is the fountain of life, and in thy light we see light."

We were indeed allured at first. Those first meditations were not the usual meditations on the four last things, heaven, hell, death and the judgment which are given at missions in parish churches. There was not much talk of sin in this retreat. Rather there was talk of the good and the better. The talk was of the choice we had to make and not that between good and evil. We have been given a share in the divine life; we have been raised to a supernatural level; we have been given power to become the sons of God.

Aristotle, Father Hugo explained, wished us to live according to our intellect, but "the just man lives by faith." We had to conform our lives according to faith—that was the teaching of the Jews before Christ. All of the eleventh chapter in the Epistle to the Hebrews is about faith. Abraham had faith when he was told that he was to have a son and the son was to inherit the land. His wife Sara stood in the tent and laughed because she was past the age when women bear children. Even when Abraham was told to sacrifice his son, a mad act, a criminal act, incomprehensible, he had the faith to obey.

"Without faith it is impossible to please God."

Faith that works through love is the mark of the supernatural life. God always gives us a chance to show our preference for Him. With Abraham it was to sacrifice his only son. With me it was to give up my married life with Forster. You do these things blindly, not because it is your natural inclination—you are going against nature when you do them—but because you wish to live in conformity with the will of God.

Love is a commandment, Father Hugo said. It is a choice, a preference. If we love God with our whole hearts, how much heart have we left? If we love with our whole mind and soul and strength, how much mind and soul and strength have we left? We must live this life now. Death changes nothing. If we do not learn to enjoy God now we never will. If we do not learn to praise Him and thank Him and rejoice in Him now, we never will.

Fearful thoughts, but glorious too! Not like that retreat of Daedelus in *A Portrait of the Artist as a Young Man,* which I had read many years before. Grace is a share in the divine life and this idea was the keystone of the retreat. We have been raised above ourselves by baptism, and the law of this supernatural life is love, a love which demands renunciation. This is the official meditation during the paschal season. "Seek the things that are above. . . . For you are dead: and your life is hid with Christ in God." All this is the starting point of Christianity.

Body and soul constitute human nature. The body is no less good than the soul. In mortifying the natural we must not injure the body or the soul. We are not to destroy but to transform it, as iron is transformed in the fire. Most of our life is unimportant, filled with trivial things from morning till night. But when it is transformed by love it is of interest even to the angels.

"Although human nature is essentially good it is infected by original sin, which is forgiven at baptism, but the effects will remain in the soul. We are prone to evil. We have a bias toward evil." These are notes which I took.

In a Jesuit magazine which I read recently there is an article on original sin in which this statement is made:

Man, considered simply as natural man, is as whole today, in intellect and will, as was man regarded in his purely natural endowment when he came from the creative hand of God. In other words, original sin left man in no worse condition on the purely human level of his mind and will, than he was before Adam cast his momentous decision against God. . . . Adam was created not only in a state of natural perfection, but was elevated to the sonship of God by sanctifying grace. . . . Adam's sin did not wreck his nature as such. We are no worse off now than we would have been if God had never elevated Adam to be His adopted son, with this exception; we *ought* to be born with sanctifying grace, and we are not; and so we are born in a state displeasing to God, a state of sin. . . . The statement in the elementary catechism most of us have studied is "our nature was corrupted by the sin of our first parents, which darkened our understanding, weakened our will and left in us a strong inclination to evil." . . . The doctrine taught by the familiar catechism of our childhood is of course true. But the truth admits of better wording; and the recent revision of this catechism puts the matter more clearly; "The chief punishments of Adam which we inherit through original sin are: death, suffering, ignorance, and a strong inclination to sin."

Such a discussion as this in theological journals sometimes becomes acrimonious and such a controversy burst out about the retreat. In Canada, Father Lacouture was charged with inexactitude of expression, causing division among the clergy and causing people to go to extremes in the business of mortification.

When this accusation was brought to the attention of Bishop Hugh Boyle in whose diocese Father Hugo and other young priests who gave the retreat belonged, he said glumly, "I wish someone around here were going to extremes." Nevertheless, within a few years Father Hugo and the others who gave the retreat were refused permission to give it any longer, and were told to take care of their parish duties.

It was the old controversy of nature and grace, and not being a theologian I cannot write about it. I had heard some lay theologians talk about the dangerous teaching in the *Imitation of Christ* in Book Three, Chapter Fifty-three, on the "divers motions of Nature and Grace," and yet on the other hand, Pope Pius XI called it "that incomparable work."

On this side of the Atlantic controversy began and spread through articles in the *Ecclesiastical Review* attacking Father Hugo's teaching. In France there was controversy about the teaching of another Jesuit, Father de Lubac, whom we had read with enthusiasm as a biographer of Proudhon, *The UnMarxian Socialist*, and as the author of *The Drama of Atheist Humanism*. It seemed a wonderful thing to me that priests and laity could still become excited about points of doctrine, about nature and the supernatural, nature and grace, about forces, spiritual capacities far more powerful than the atom bomb.

Not only were many of the young priests told they could no longer give the retreat but two members of an order who gave it were sent to Egypt and the Holy Land, another to Nicaragua, and Father Lacouture himself was sent to an Indian reservation in northern New York where he could administer the sacraments but not teach. He is there today, happy and at peace, sowing, as he terms it, his own interior senses, the memory, the understanding, the will.

"Unless the seed fall into the ground and die," he reminds us.

To us the retreat was the good news. We made it as often as we could, and refreshed ourselves with days of recollection.

The last year of the war, we decided to turn one of our farms into a retreat house where people could come to study and pray, and begin to realize what it meant to be a son of God, what responsibilities such a position entailed. If people did not go away from the retreat examining their consciences as to the work they did in the world, their material goods, their attachments, then it was a failure. Such a retreat should be like a shock treatment, we thought, putting the "old man" to death, bringing us to new life.

Our farms at Easton at this time housed two families and one or two single people. One family living on the upper farm was headed by a man who in himself held two or three heresies, we thought. The heresy of the family, the heresy of the priesthood of the laity, the heresy of the relations of men and women.

We had said the family was the primary unit of society so Victor wished all the work of *The Catholic Worker* to center around the family. The funds should not be used to feed the poor, but to re-establish the family on the land. The man was the head of the house and he emphasized the priesthood of the laity. He made another layman the spiritual adviser of the little community set up and this man imposed penances and insisted on strict obedience. His attitude toward women was that the men were to sit like judges at the gates and the women were to be the valiant women of the Old Testament, hewers of wood and drawers of water, tillers of the field, and clothers of the family. This position was carried to such an extreme on the upper farm that the women were forbidden to speak unless spoken to, and were compelled to knock on the doors of even their own kitchens and dining rooms if there were men present.

Trying to bear with the situation on the upper farm, we started the retreat house on the lower farm, and began having retreats every few months.

Young priests from Pittsburgh, from a Minnesota diocese, and others from the East came to spend time with us. Often they had heavy parish duties and even their vacations were taken up by their own retreats and study. One from Minnesota flew to New York after Sunday morning Mass, began giving our retreat Sunday night, ending it Friday night, returning on Saturday to hear confessions in his own parish.

These were priests who said Mass perfectly, prepared their sermons, "enlightened their minds, inflamed their hearts" by prayer and spiritual reading, and we caught fire from them.

Of course this could not go on. Those who gave us the retreat were given in turn chaplaincies of hospitals or other duties which made it impossible for them to get away. For the last few years, we have not been able to obtain more than one or two priests who could give the course of instruction as outlined by Father Lacouture and Father Hugo. But retreats, given by other priests, go on.

We did not remain at the Easton farm. Life there became too difficult. I have always felt that we had to be most careful about the articles which we printed in the paper. Once when I looked out the farmhouse window during an especially crowded time and saw some footsore travelers coming along the road and sighed, "I suppose they are coming here," one young worker said severely, "You should not write the things you do unless you mean them." In other words—do not write about hospitality unless we are willing to assume the obligations such writings bring with it.

I had recently written a commendatory article about the sit-down householders in Great Britain, who were moving into empty houses and taking possession of them for want of homes. Within the month, we had several experiences which enabled us to take stock of our position.

One group of young men had taken an apartment in our neighborhood in New York and furnished it, to live near us. I remarked to them jokingly one evening that since they were single and could live with us, if a family came they would be forced by their own generous feelings to give the place up to those in need. At once a family arrived asking for help. The young men responded though I think with misgivings. And a week later, the family moved away, taking the furnishings with them.

In Cleveland there was a similar incident. William Gauchat who headed the house of hospitality, furnished an apartment for single women in need, and a married couple arriving first, were sheltered there. But when Bill wanted to put a few single women into the empty bedrooms, the couple announced that they had possession and refused to allow them entrance.

Our guests know that we will not call upon the police to evict them, that we are trying to follow the dear Lord's teachings, "If anyone take your coat, let go your cloak also to him. . . . Give to him that asks of you and from him that would borrow, turn not away. You have heard that it has been said, you shall love your neighbor and hate your enemy. But I say to you, love your enemies, do good to them that hate you, and pray for them that persecute and calumniate you, that you may be the children of your father who is in heaven who makes his sun to rise upon the good and the bad and rains upon the just and the unjust."

When another family came to Maryfarm, we explained that we were trying to open a retreat house and that we did not have room for them. It was the family of one of our own willful leaders who "loved God and did as he pleased." He did not wish to remain on a farm belonging to his father, where he was forced to work too hard. He and his wife refused to listen and unpacked their things to stay with us. First they took over the lower farmhouse. After a few conflicts due to their possessing themselves of retreat house goods (as common goods) they moved to the upper farm to join Victor.

For the following year they continued their guerrilla tactics from the upper farm, coming down to make raids on the retreat house food and furnishings, explaining to retreatants that they were true Catholic Workers and that the retreat house was a perversion of the movement.

If they had worked while making these contentions and so won respect they might have won adherents to their cause. As it was they were classed as a lunatic fringe by our retreatants and when the men from the upper farm came down to indoctrinate our visitors, leaving their wives to the work on the land and with the children, they did not win a hearing. They allowed their goats to run loose to eat the young orchards that had been put in, and this destruction was the final note that brought the situation to a crisis. We decided that if after speaking to one's brother and admonishing him, as St. Paul advised, he refused to listen, then it was time to remove ourselves from him. We deeded the small upper farm to our troublesome families who were living there and sold the lower farm to a neighbor who had been living in a rented house and was looking for shelter. We did not ask a down payment or interest on the mortgage, but arranged that he should make monthly payments like rent to a lawyer friend of ours, who accumulated them for us to make a payment once a year on another farm which we purchased with the help of friends.

The first farm had cost $1,250 for twenty-seven acres; the adjoining which we sold cost $4,000. The new farm we purchased cost $16,000. Miraculously, we were given $10,000 by friends to continue our retreat house work, all the money coming in within a month from a half dozen of our readers.

Our New York retreat farm is five miles west of Newburgh, New York, and is also called Maryfarm Retreat House. Retreatants, including family groups, come for week ends or discussion weeks. Families have vacationed in the barn. Families have come to make retreats together and the place has become a haven of peace in spite of the nearness of Stewart Field down the road and the jet planes overhead.

Usually the "family" there is made up of more than a dozen people, with men coming off the highway for meals and a place to sleep. They, too, often stay for a retreat or to rest up on their way to the mountains to look for work in the resort hotels.

Some farming is done; vegetables are raised for the table, and there are goats, rabbits and chickens in one of the barns. These are a poor man's animals. We don't make ends meet; there is no use keeping accounts. Some retreatants leave something to pay for themselves, and some leave enough to pay for another besides themselves. We always have debts, of course, and there is a mortgage on the farm.

But we never have more than we can care for; we are never overwhelmed as we are in New York by the magnitude of the work to be done. In the cities it is as though we lived in concentration camps. Maryfarm is an oasis in a desert.

It is not only for others that I must have these retreats. It is because I too am hungry and thirsty for the bread of the strong. I too must nourish myself to do the work I have undertaken; I too must drink at these good springs so that I may not be an empty cistern and unable to help others.

"WAR IS THE HEALTH OF THE STATE"

ONE Christmas at the close of World War II, we received a card from the Rochester group saying that they had liked *The Catholic Worker* much better before the pacifists got hold of it. Another letter came from Boston, from an elderly worker who had been responsible for the first house of hospitality in Boston. She too reproached me for the extremism of our revolutionary pacifist position. She was a good trade unionist and was thinking in terms of the immediate steps to be taken, while we tried to keep the vision of a new social order, brought about by peaceful means.

It struck me then how strange a thing it was; here we had been writing about pacifism for fifteen years and members of two of our groups were just beginning to realize what it meant.

We had been pacifist in class war, race war, in the Ethiopian war, in the Spanish Civil War, all through World War II, as we are now during the Korean war. We had spoken in terms of the Sermon on the Mount and all of our readers were familiar enough with that. We had lost subscriptions and bundle orders, but these cancellations came from those who frankly disagreed with us and the matter was settled at once.

But there were a very great many who had seemed to agree with us who did not realize for years that *The Catholic Worker* position implicated them; if they believed the things we wrote, they would be bound, sooner or later, to make decisions personally and to act upon them.

Union workers in steel plants, auto and airplane factories— many in industry and business would have to find other jobs, jobs not tied up with the war effort. And where could they get them? If they worked in the garment factories, they would have to fill government orders for uniforms. Mills turned out blankets, parachutes. Raising food, building houses, baking bread—whatever you did you kept the wheels of industrial capitalism moving, and industrial capitalism kept the wheels moving on war orders. You could not live without compromise. Teachers sold war stamps and bonds. Children were asked to bring aluminum pots and scrap metal to school. The Pope asked that war be kept out of the schoolroom, but there it was.

We wrote as much as we could on the subject, and Father John J. Hugo wrote articles and pamphlets—"The Immorality of Conscription," "Catholics Can Be Conscientious Objectors," "The Weapons of the Spirit," "The Gospel of Peace." The last two were printed as *Catholic Worker* pamphlets under the imprimatur of the Archdiocese of New York.

In Europe, Father Stratman, a Belgian Dominican, wrote *The Church and War* and *Peace and the Clergy*, and Father Ude of Austria wrote a monumental book, *"Thou Shalt Not Kill."* Only the first two appeared in English. All of these set forth our stand.

In addition to the theological articles in our own paper, many young men wrote of war and peace. The most lively articles we published were those of Ammon Hennacy, Christian anarchist, a modern Thoreau in his monthly account of his life on the land. He began with a series on his term, largely spent in solitary confinement, in Atlanta Penitentiary during World War I, where he met Alexander Berkman and studied American history and anarchism with him. Ammon had been a Socialist before he was won by the personalist approach of Berkman. Forced to rely on himself, he recognized the importance of beginning with oneself, starting here and now, and not waiting for someone else to start the revolution. He became a pacifist even in the class war and he came to see the dangers of the modern state, and the inefficiency and waste of bureaucracy.

Reading the Bible while he was in solitary confinement, he was completely won by the Sermon on the Mount and all the teachings of Jesus. Upon reading Tolstoi he recognized himself as a Christian anarchist and from then on, Tolstoi, Gandhi and Jesus became his teachers. Organized religion, as he calls it, he rejects.

"He has seen so great a light, it has blinded him," the rector of a seminary said to me after reading his articles.

(Ammon is not the only non-Catholic contributor to *The Catholic Worker*. Fritz Eichenberg, a Quaker artist, contributes many illustrations, great in their understanding and compassion.)

Ammon's articles were always personal, since he wrote of what he knew, himself and his own experience. His life in jail, his work on dairy farms in Colorado and New Mexico, and on truck farms in Arizona have constituted a moving series about "Life at Hard Labor" and show how a man can live without compromise, and yet earn a living. For years he has paid no income tax. He worked by the day at the "stoop labor" the Mexicans usually performed, at irrigating, at ditchdigging, wood chopping, cotton picking.

He has supported himself and his two daughters, sending both through Northwestern University and in addition to his back-breaking work and his writing, he has found time to sell *The Catholic Worker* at churches and public meetings every week.

He has fasted and prayed for peace; he has picketed the tax collector's office twice a year. For the last few years on the anniversary of the dropping of the atomic bomb he has fasted as penance for six days, picketing the Internal Revenue office at Phoenix while he fasted, and distributing literature. Ammon considers himself a propagandist, an agitator, a one-man revolution. I doubt that he has ever considered himself a sociologist or an anthropologist, yet he could be classed in these categories too. His articles on the Indians of the Southwest, especially the Hopi, who are anarchist and pacifist, are of vital interest.

Ammon is fifty-eight, a tall lank Ohioan of tremendous physical strength and endurance. For all of us at the Catholic Worker headquarters, he epitomizes the positive pacifist. He is trying to change conditions that bring about wars, and as he does not accept from Caesar, he does not render to Caesar. With all his absolutism and certitude, he is friendly and lovable, truly looking upon all as his brothers, overcoming opposition by understanding and affection.

On the other hand, Bob Ludlow, one of the editors of the paper, a convert to the Catholic Church, has been the theorist of our pacifism for the past five years. Son of a Scranton coal miner, educated by the Christian Brothers, he was converted by reading Newman. All his life he has been a student and teacher, and knows little of manual labor. When we have gotten him to work a few hours in our asparagus patch or to mend a leaky faucet, he has felt triumphant for weeks. He has cared for the babies of one of our Catholic Worker families, however, sitting helplessly in the middle of the kitchen while they circled like wild savages around him, and he has walked for miles on picket lines.

During the war, he served as a conscientious objector in the Rosewood Training School at Owings Mills, Maryland, working twelve hours a day, seven days a week, among human monstrosities and idiots as well as "children" with varying degrees of feeble-mindedness. Once every month he had an accumulated four days off which he spent with us in New York, helping us to catch up on correspondence and filing. This went on for three years.

Since the end of the war he has written a monthly article which has aroused our readers to the consciousness that they also are involved in the duty of making moral judgments, that they must begin to think, not only of the pacifism of the Sermon on the Mount, but of the natural law.

Robert is doctrinaire and dogmatic, sometimes belligerent in tone so that we find ourselves in hot water and are forced to re-consider and re-present our position. And yet he is the mildest of mortals, meek and disciplined in his personal life, ready to withdraw or subside, to hold his position alone, if need be, accept-ing without question the authority of the Church, yet determined to call attention to, and take advantage of, the freedom in the Church to discuss, question, and clarify the stand various the-ologians have taken on finance capitalism, the state, and on war and the morality of the means used in war.

His writings have aroused the conscience, have spotlighted attention on the grave questions of freedom and authority.

In the last generation, Chesterton, Belloc, Eric Gill and Father Vincent McNabb were the great distributists who opposed the servile state, the "providential state" as Pius XII recently called it. Of the four only Eric Gill was a pacifist and anarchist. The others would have feared the word, "anarchist," and understood it only in its popular connotation. I myself would prefer the word "libertarian," as less apt to offend. But I do not like to censor the writings of the editors. Peter used to say, "It makes to think." Peter himself liked to shock people, and one article of his entitled "Feed the Poor, Starve the Bankers" did lose us a very good friend. He called himself an anarchist, but privately however. He liked the term Christian Communist, but when that too was misunderstood, he called himself a communitarian.

Bob's anarchism, however, has provoked much thought and has forced many a student to realize that there were other positions on the left besides that of the Marxist.

When correspondents ask him how we can do without government, he says,

Both among Catholics and anarchists in general a great deal of misunderstanding comes about by a confusion of the terms State, government and society. Father Luigi Sturzo's book *Inner Laws of Society* is the best Catholic treatment of the subject I have read. He brings out the point that the State is only *one* form of government. When you analyze what anarchists advocate (particularly the anarcho-syndicalists) it really boils down to the advocacy of decentralized self-governing bodies. It *is* a form of government.

The confusion results because some anarchist writers use the term government as synonomous with the term State and will make the categorical statement that they do not believe in government, meaning by that the State.

The State is government by *representation* (when it is a democracy) but there is no reason why a Catholic must believe that people must be governed by representatives—the Catholic is free to believe one way or the other as is evident from St. Thomas' treatment of law in the Summa Theologica. In Question 90, Art. 3, St. Thomas states: A law, properly speaking, regards first and foremost the order to the common good. Now to order anything to the common good belongs *either* to the whole people, or to someone who is the viceregent of the whole people. Hence the making of law belongs either to the whole people or to a public personage who has care of the whole people; for in all other matters the directing of anything to the end concerns him to whom the end belongs.

Anarchists believe that the *whole* people composing a community should take care of what governing is to be done rather than have a distant and centralized State do it. You can see from the quotation from St. Thomas there is nothing heretical about such a belief. It certainly is possible for a Christian to be an anarchist. As to government proceeding from sin, St. Augustine distinguishes between coercive government and directive government. The former he says is the result of sin. The latter is not, as man is a social being. It could be said that anarchists advocate directive government (mutual aid) but reject coercive government (the State).

Our Lord taught us to pray "Thy kingdom come on earth as it is in heaven"—in other words the nearer earthly government approximates what things are in heaven the more Christian it is. I do believe—whether it can be realized or not—that the anarchist society approaches nearer to this ideal than do other forms of government. As the Christian lives in hope so may we set this as the idea, towards which we work even if it seems as impractical as Calvary.

Bob is one of the most disciplined members of the Catholic Worker family. He needs no rules, no laws—he imposes a very rigid regime on himself. Like Peter Maurin, he follows a rule and it seldom varies. He attends seven o'clock Mass, which means rising a little after six, walks a mile to the post office for the mail and a mile back. His breakfast is a bowl of cereal. From nine until five he is at his desk, aside from half an hour after lunch when he goes to his room to say the Little Office of the Blessed Mother. In the evening he reads from six to ten-thirty, goes out for coffee and a short walk, and is in bed at eleven. You can set your clock by him. Over his desk hangs a picture of the Blessed Virgin and a newsprint photograph of Gandhi.

In stating the Catholic Worker pacifist position, Bob puts it this way:

The question of pacifism may be treated from the natural or supernatural viewpoint. From the natural viewpoint it derives its validity from reason, and natural morality, which is derived from the nature of man, is susceptible of development in that we understand more its implications as we understand more the nature of man. From an ethical and psychological standpoint it seems evident that pacifism, as exemplified in non-violent procedure, is more reasonable than is violent procedure and therefore is more in accord with man's nature which differs from sub-human nature precisely in that man is capable of rationality.

As the Catholic religion is not in opposition to nature but rather completes and confirms nature it would seem then that there could be no opposition between a pacifism basing its validity on man's reason and the official teaching of the Church.

The supernatural viewpoint takes into consideration the revelation of Christ. Here we find that, in the early Church, there was division of opinion. Some of the early saints and Fathers were definitely pacifist. All were critical of the army. The general rule of the early Church was that one who was baptized should not join the army. Those who were already in the army when baptized were admonished to shed no blood even in a war. So there has been a tradition of pacifism in the Church, though this has fallen into obscurity and awaits doctrinal development to become explicit. Some of this tradition survives in canon law wherein the clergy are forbidden to shed blood. The increasing horror and immorality of modern war which, because of the means used, necessitate the slaying of the innocent, should serve to recall this latent pacifist tradition so that the Sermon on the Mount will be seen to confirm and sanction non-violent procedure which is already sanctioned by reason.

If it is remarked that pacifism places too much of a burden on the ordinary Catholic it can then be replied in truth that it places not so much a burden as does Catholic sexual morality with its day to day difficulties and the heroism it requires of many in these days. And yet the Church will not compromise in this regard. It would seem that the day must come when we refuse to compromise on this matter of war—otherwise we will sink to sub-human bestiality and will most certainly stray far from the spirit of Christ.

What would you do if an armed maniac were to attack you, your child, your mother? How many times have we heard this. Restrain him, of course, but not kill him. Confine him if necessary. But perfect love casts out fear and love overcomes hatred All this sounds trite but experience is not trite.

On one occasion an armed maniac did try to kill Arthur Sheehan, one of our editors during the war. A victim of World War I, who had already assaulted several other men in the house and almost broken my wrist one day when I tried to turn off the radio in the kitchen, took a large breadknife and a crucifix and announced he was going to kill Arthur. Another woman and I seized him, forcing him to drop the knife. We could not hold him, however, and after he had hurled a gallon can of vegetables at Arthur and smashed a hole in the wall, we restrained him long enough to allow Arthur to escape. We called the police and asked that Harry be confined to Bellevue for observation, but since we would not bring charges against him, the hospital released him the next day. Later we persuaded them to keep him for a month in the psychiatric ward. He was returned to the hospital, but at the end of thirty days he was out again, and continued to eat on our breadline during the war. Some time later we heard that he had shipped out on an oil tanker.

There were many other incidents that would have resulted in violence if moral force had not been substituted for coercion, which would have resulted in greater trouble.

David Mason was another pacifist member of our group. David came from Philadelphia, where he had been one of the leaders of the house of hospitality there, to work during the war in our New York house. A large stout man, forty-five at that time, with white hair and a peculiar short-stepping gait as though his legs were not properly matched to his big body, he was a paternal figure around the place when most of the young men were called. He served as one of the editors of the paper, took care of the mail, wrote articles, cooked meals. In fact, he was cooking the evening the FBI came to pick him up for failure to report.

I was away on a speaking trip at the time but I can imagine the picture. Two men drove up to the house at Mott Street and stalked in looking very official.

"Where is David Mason?"

"Upstairs in the kitchen. Shall we get him?"

"No, we will get him," and the two agents went through the long hall, the courtyard, up the stairs, and found David, an apron around his large middle, making gelatine for the evening dessert.

"And that night we had gelatine at the Federal House of Detention," he said ruefully, "and it was like leather, not as good as mine."

They kept him only a few weeks, much to his regret. He was obviously not the physical material our infantry needs. "I wanted to write a book," he said as they released him. He came back to the soup kitchen and editorial office instead. Arthur Sheehan, who was exempt as a former tuberculosis patient, is now working for CARE and David for a new Catholic daily.

Younger men, such as Tom Sullivan from our Chicago house, who went to war and served in the Pacific, and Jack English, formerly of our Cleveland house, another veteran, will not call themselves pacifist, though Tom is an editor of our pacifist paper. Tom was brought up on the West Side of Chicago and his heart is always with the underdog. He would scoff at the idea of being called a mystic, but I can only explain his attitude toward war on mystical grounds. He agrees with the condemnation of the means used in modern war. He probably would never lift a hand to injure another man, but his attitude is that if other men have to suffer in the war, he will suffer with them.

He poses the question—how explain the two thousand years of Christianity during which time Crusades were preached, wars were fought with the blessing of the Church, and warriors were canonized?

"I do not consider myself strong enough to court martyrdom," he says, "and that is what it means if atheistic communism wins out. Since nobody seems to be using the spiritual weapons you are always talking about, we may have to use the material ones."

He says nothing about means and ends. He is leaving that to the theologians. And his is the general opinion of the rank and file in the Church today.

It is a matter of grief to me that most of those who are Catholic Workers are not pacifists, but I can see too how good it is that we always have this attitude represented among us. We are not living in an ivory tower.

Jack English suffered more in the war than the others. A gunner on a bomber, he was shot down and spent a year in a Rumanian prison camp. He was rescued by the Russians, only to go through the blitz in London. Jack has theologian friends whose opinions keep him away from the extreme pacifist position.

Tony Aratari, also from a prison camp, Charlie McCormick, Joe Monroe, members of the Catholic Worker group, and younger men in their early twenties just with us to help as long as the draft board permits, talk the issue over constantly. Can there be a just war? Can the conditions laid down by St. Thomas ever be fulfilled? What about the morality of the use of the atom bomb? What does God want me to do? And what am I capable of doing? Can I stand out against state and Church? Is it pride, presumption, to think I have the spiritual capacity to use spiritual weapons in the face of the most gigantic tyranny the world has ever seen? Am I capable of enduring suffering, facing martyrdom? And alone?

Again the long loneliness to be faced.

PETER'S DEATH

"PRECIOUS in the sight of the Lord is the death of his saints," and the details of such a death are precious.

Plato said: "Other people are not likely to be aware that those who pursue philosophy aright study nothing but dying and being dead. But if this be true, it would be absurd to be eager for nothing but this all their lives, and then be troubled when that came for which they had all along been eagerly practicing."

And St. Paul said, "We will not have you ignorant, brethren, concerning them that are asleep, that you be not sorrowful, even as others who have no hope."

So it is with a spirit of joy that I write of Peter as no longer suffering, no longer groaning within himself and saying with St. Paul, "Who shall deliver me from the body of this death?"

No, we are sure that he welcomed Sister Death with joy, and that underneath him he felt the Everlasting Arms.

Up in my room on the third floor, in our house on Mott Street, all the winter of 1947, that hard winter, he waited for the weather to clear so that he could go to the country. He had to lie in bed much of the time, and the plaster was all picked off the wall by the side of his bed. Marge and Joe Hughes, who lived next door, took care of his needs and the children ran in and out of his bedroom. He must have been very weary of lying in bed, he who had traveled north and south, east and west in this vast country. Everybody was always so reassuring, exclaiming how well he looked, how bright he was, but we who had known him these past seventeen years felt only the tragedy of the death in life he was living. Truly he practiced for death a very long time.

Peter was the poor man of his day. He was a St. Francis of modern times. He was used to poverty as a peasant is used to rough living, poor food, hard bed, or no bed at all, dirt, fatigue, and hard and unrespected work. He was a man with a mission, a vision, an apostolate, but he had put off from himself honors, prestige, recognition. He was truly humble of heart. Never a word of detraction passed his lips and as St. James said, the man who governs his tongue is a perfect man. He was impersonal in his love in that he loved all, saw all others around him as God saw them, saw Christ in them.

He never spoke idle words, though he was a great teacher who talked for hours on end, till late in the night and early morning. He roamed the streets and the countryside and talked to all who would listen. But when his great brain failed, he became silent. If he had been a babbler, he would have been a babbler to the end. But when he could no longer think, as he himself expressed it, he remained silent.

For the last five years of his life he was this way, suffering, silent, dragging himself around, watched by us all for fear he would get lost, as he did once for three days; he was shouted at loudly by visitors as though he were deaf, talked to with condescension as one talks to a child for whom language must be simplified even to the point of absurdity. That was one of the hardest things we had to bear, we who loved him and worked with him for so long—to see others treat him as though he were simple-minded.

The fact was he had been stripped of all. He had stripped himself throughout life; he had put off the old man in order to put on the new. He had done all that he could do to denude himself of the world, and I mean the world in the evil sense—that world we pledge ourselves to combat, with the flesh and the devil. There is another sense of the word—"God so loved the world," and "God looked at the world and found it was good"—and Peter was an apostle to this world. He loved people; he saw in them what God meant them to be, as he saw the world as God meant it to be, and loved it.

He had stripped himself, but there remained work for God to do. We are to be pruned as the vine is pruned so that it can bear fruit, and this we cannot do ourselves. God did it for him.

He took from him his mind, the one thing he had left, the one thing perhaps he took delight in. He could no longer think. He could no longer discuss with others, give others in a brilliant overflow of talk his keen analysis of what was going on in the world; he could no longer make what he called his synthesis of cult, culture and cultivation.

He was sick more than five years. It was as though he had had a stroke in his sleep. He dragged one leg after him, his face was slightly distorted, and he found it hard to speak. And he repeated, "I can no longer think." When he tried to, his face would have a strained, suffering expression. He had cardiac asthma, a hernia (as many hard workers have) and he was in pain when he coughed.

For the first couple of years of invalidism, he lived in Easton with us, and the last two at our retreat house at Newburgh, New York. The house was too cold for him in winter as we burned only wood in our furnace, so he lived in a rear house, a house of poured cement built originally as a chicken coop, which was divided into three rooms, one occupied by Father John Faley, our resident priest, another by Alan Bates, and the third shared by Peter with Hans Tunneson. I was thankful that Hans was with him to keep the room warm and clean, and to watch over him at night. Hans was a Norwegian seaman who has worked with us these past years. It was typical of Peter never to ask anything for himself, and, of course, not privacy, that greatest of all luxuries. He had never had a bed of his own, really, until it came to his last illness. He just took what was available in the house of hospitality.

He had always been a meager eater, getting along on two meals a day, never eating between meals. He used to say when he was offered anything, "I don't need it." But toward the close of his life, he was inclined to stuff down his food hastily like a child, and he had to be cautioned to eat slowly. Perhaps this was a hangover from the hunger of a childhood in that large family where there was never too much to eat.

Other habits clung to him. When I'd go in to see if he were warm enough, I'd find him lying in bed with his pants folded neatly and under his head, and his coat wrapped around his feet, a habit I suppose he got from living in flophouses where clothes are often stolen. And once I found him sleeping in the dead of winter with only a spread over him, in a stony cold room. Someone had taken his blankets.

One thing we can be happy about too, and that is that he felt he had finished his work before his mind failed. He used to say, "I have written all I have to say; I have done all I can; let the younger men take over." So he suffered but not with the feeling that there was much still that he could do.

A few months before he died, we attempted to record Peter's voice on wire, and we had him read aloud all his essays on houses of hospitality. His voice strangely enough was louder and clearer as it came over the wire than it had been for a long time. We spent quite a few days over this, Dave Mason and I, because Peter tired easily. Then, after we had triumphantly made a fifteen-minute spool, someone else tried to work the machine and erased it all.

For two months I had been at the farm while Jane O'Donnell who was in charge of Maryfarm, our retreat center, was away at Grailville, and then while returning from the funeral of Larry Heaney, I received a telephone call telling me of Peter's death. Just before I had left, I had told him of Larry's sudden death, and he said yes, to my question as to whether he remembered Larry. He had loved him very much, had sent him his quotations listed as *cult, culture* and *cultivation* over the years, and rejoiced in his total acceptance of his teaching. When I said to him, "Now you will have someone waiting for you in heaven," his face lit up in a radiant smile. He had not smiled for months; there had been only a look of endurance, even pain, on his face.

That was my good-by. Over the telephone in Avon, Ohio, at Our Lady of the Wayside Farm, I heard the news.

It was midnight and I had already fallen asleep. Bill and Dorothy Gauchet were not yet asleep. They had been saying the Rosary for Ruth Ann and Catherine Reser, they said, because Catherine had lost another baby a few months before, and Ruth

Ann had lost her husband. When I hung up the receiver, Bill suggested we say Vespers of the Office of the Dead for Peter, so we knelt there in that farm living room and prayed those beautiful Psalms that are balm to the sore heart. No matter how much a death is expected, no matter how much you may regard it as a happy release, there is a gigantic sense of loss. With our love of life, we have not yet gotten to that point where we can say with the desert father, St. Anthony, "The spaces of this life, set over against eternity, are brief and poor."

Peter had been sitting up for supper that Sunday night, and had been out in the sun all afternoon. There had been visitors from Friendship House, and on Saturday Lydwinne von Kersbergen from Grailville had been at the farm, and had told Peter with love and reverence, all he had meant to the lay apostolate throughout the world. It was like a benediction from Europe. She might indeed have been representing Europe at that moment in saying farewell to him. His writings have been published there; he had been recognized there as perhaps he never has in this, his own adopted country.

John Filliger had shaved him Saturday and Michael Kovalak had dressed and cared for him on Sunday, conducting him to the chapel for Mass that morning, taking him to and from his room to rest. He had looked in again at Peter at nine Sunday night and found him sleeping rather restlessly on his side instead of on his back as he usually did. Eileen had given him, as she did every night, a glass of wine, and I suppose Hans made his usual facetious gesture with the water pitcher, asking her to fill it for him. "It makes me happy to think how everyone cared for him, everyone feeling honored to do so," Jane always said, when she spoke of Peter's needs. He was surrounded by loving care. Father Faley brought him communion the days he could not get up, and it was impressive, day after day at that sick bed, to hear those prayers, to witness that slow dying. A king, a Pope, could have had no more devoted attention, than Father John Faley, who has been with us for a year, gave to Peter.

At eleven that night, Hans said, Peter began coughing, and it went on for some minutes. He then tried to rise, and fell over on his pillow, breathing heavily. Hans put on the light and called Father Faley and Jane. Michael, Eileen and others came too, and there were prayers for the dying about the bedside. He died immediately; there was no struggle, no pain.

He was laid out at Newburgh the first night, in the conference room where he had sat so often trying to understand the discussions and lectures. Flowers were all about him from shrubs in our garden and from our neighbors. He wore a suit which had been sent in for the poor. There was no rouge on his gray face, which looked like granite, strong, contemplative, set toward eternity. There was a Requiem Mass in our chapel sung by Michael and Alan and the rest.

The next morning he was brought to Mott Street and laid out at the end of the store we used as office. Tom Sullivan's desk was moved to make way for the coffin and all the tables taken down at which the paper is usually mailed out. The room had been scrubbed the night before by Rocky and Tony; since they had painted the rooms only a month before, everything was fresh. (Rocky was a seaman, somewhat of a wandering monk, who had been with the Trappists for a while; Anthony Aratari, a writer, painter and craftsman.)

All that day and night people came from the neighborhood, from all over the city, from different parts of the country, and filled the little store and knelt before the coffin. Whenever we were sitting in the room, we saw them quietly, almost secretly, pressing their rosary beads to Peter's hands. Some bent down and kissed him. My daughter came from West Virginia. David, who had accompanied Peter on one of his last trips, stayed home with the children, since Tamar had known Peter the longest; since her sixth year, in fact.

The neighbors sent beautiful floral pieces made up of carnations and gardenias, and all around the coffin were branches of the flowering shrubs the group had sent down from Maryfarm. The sweet smells filled the room and it was hot and fresh outside. Priests came from different orders to lead in the Rosary. And all that night we sat with him.

The funeral was at nine o'clock next morning at the Salesian

Transfiguration Church on Mott Street. Peter always loved the Salesians, and had always urged them to continue opening craft schools and agricultural schools throughout the country.

The pallbearers were John Filliger and Joe Hughes, both of whom had come to us during the seamen's strike in 1936, and had been with us ever since; Bob Ludlow, *The Catholic Worker*'s chief editorial writer; David Mason, who brought out a book of Peter's writings; Arthur Sheehan, former editor of *The Catholic Worker*, and Hazen Ordway, both dear and devoted friends. Arthur had been one of the heads of the Boston group and St. Benedict's farm at Upton; Hazen had been librarian at the Marist Seminary in Washington, when he heard me speak of the work there in 1937 and left immediately to join us, associating himself with us ever since.

Father Francis Meenan, Holy Ghost Father from Norwalk, Connecticut, sang the Mass, with Father Divisio and Father Faley the deacons. They and a group of other priests, headed by Monsignor Nelson, who represented Cardinal Spellman, met the body at the door and ushered it into the church. Everyone sang the Requiem Mass together—the organist, the priests, the seminarians, the parishioners, all of our family from Mott Street and Maryfarm, Newburgh, Ade Bethune, Jane O'Donnell, Serena and Stanley Vishnewsky, and the group from Easton, Victor and Jon and Chris—you could almost hear their individual voices. It was a loud and triumphant singing, with a note of joy, because we were sure Peter heard us in heaven; we were sure that angels and saints joined in.

Peter was buried in St. John's Cemetery, Queens, in a grave given us by Father Pierre Conway, a Dominican.

Peter was another St. John, a voice crying in the wilderness, and a voice too, saying, "My little children, love one another." As the body was carried out of the church those great and triumphant words were sung—the *In Paradisum*.

May the angels lead thee into paradise; may the martyrs receive thee at thy coming and lead thee into the holy city of Jerusalem. May the choir of angels receive thee and mayest thou have eternal rest with Lazarus, who once was poor.

"We need to make the kind of society," Peter had said, "where it is easier for people to be good." And because his love of God made him love his neighbor, lay down his life indeed for his brother, he wanted to cry out against the evils of the day—the state, war, usury, the degradation of man, the lack of a philosophy of work. He sang the delights of poverty (he was not talking of destitution) as a means to making a step to the land, of getting back to the dear natural things of earth and sky, of home and children. He cried out against the machine because, as Pius XI had said, "Raw materials went into the factory and came out ennobled and man went in and came out degraded"; and because it deprived a man of what was as important as bread, his work, his work with his hands, his ability to use all of himself, which made him a whole man and a holy man.

Yes, he talked of these material things. He knew we needed a good social order where men could grow up to their full stature and be men. And he also knew that it took men to make such a social order. He tried to form them, he tried to educate them, and God gave him poor, weak materials with which to work. He was as poor in the human material he had around him, as he was in material goods. We are the offscouring of all, as St. Paul said, and yet we know we have achieved great things in these brief years, and not ours is the glory. God has chosen the weak things to confound the strong, the fools of this earth to confound the wise.

Peter had been insulted and misunderstood in his life as well as loved. He had been taken for a plumber and left to sit in the basement when he had been invited for dinner. He had been thrown out of a Knights of Columbus meeting. One pastor who invited him to speak demanded the money back which he had sent Peter for carfare to his upstate parish, because, he said, we had sent him a Bowery bum, and not the speaker he expected. "This then is perfect joy," Peter could say, quoting the words of St. Francis to Friar Leo, when he was teaching him where perfect joy was to be found.

He was a man of sincerity and peace, and yet one letter came to us recently, accusing him of having a holier-than-thou attitude. Yes, Peter pointed out that it was a precept that we should love God with our whole heart and soul and mind and strength, and not just a counsel, and he taught us what it meant to be sons of God, and restored to us our sense of responsibility in a chaotic world. Yes, he was "holier than thou," holier than anyone we ever knew.

"Do not forget," Mary Frecon, head of our Harrisburg house said before she left, "do not forget to tell of the roots of the little tree that they cut through in digging his grave. I kept looking at those roots and thinking how wonderful it is that Peter is going to nourish that tree—that thing of beauty." The undertaker had tried to sell us artificial grass to cover up the soil, "the unsightly grave," as he called it, but we loved the sight of that earth that was to cover Peter. He had come from the earth, as we all had, and to the earth he was returning.

Around the grave we all said the Rosary and after the Benedictus we left.

CHRYSTIE STREET

BELIEVING as we do that "Life is changed, not taken away," we knew that Peter would continue to be active after death. Within the week following the funeral, we had a notice served on us by a lawyer from the House of Cavalry, our landlord, that 115 Mott Street was up for sale and that we had to find another place to live. The widows were building another wing on their cancer hospital and had to have funds. They had been told by the advisers of the diocese to get rid of the property on Mott Street, which was an expense to them. In principle we agreed with the diocesan authorities. No institutions should own slum buildings, even if they turned them over to people to live in. Such tenements should not exist. I had felt that when we first had been offered the property for our use. So much for theory.

But we had lived there for fourteen years and the house was home and the neighborhood was our village, with its *festas* all summer, its pushcarts, its life on the streets, its little churches where Mass was sung every morning at seven, eight and nine. Tony, the Fordham graduate who ran the grocery store on the corner, let our grocery bill pile up to thousands of dollars on a number of occasions. We charged bread at Pappalardo's, our marriages had been solemnized, our children baptized, our dead buried from either Transfiguration or Precious Blood Church. Our Italian neighbors, though they may have been Fascist during the Mussolini regime, knew what personal responsibility meant. They were anarchists at heart, making their own laws, caring for their own sick, or senile, or feeble-minded, never putting them in institutions. There was always the beggar on those streets and the sick and the maimed. That is the reason why there are so many on the streets of the Italian slums, because the Italians care for their own; they recognize how precious freedom is and all the neighbors help share the responsibility.

We could not believe that we had to move. Hearing nothing further about the proposed sale we went on in our usual routine, housekeeping, cooking, feeding, sheltering, nursing the sick and spending hours besides at correspondence. There was not much time to think or plan. Everyone kept an expectant attitude waiting for Divine Providence to take a hand. "It just can't happen," we all thought. We waited months for further word.

When your day is so fully occupied that you resent the time taken for sleep because life is so full, time flies. A thousand years is as a day. A year flew by before the blow fell. The house had been sold. We had three months to find and purchase another house. There was no question of renting one. Who would rent to such tenants, such disreputable people—the few elderly prostitutes and alcoholics who were always coming back to us to get straightened out far outshone the humble sick and hardworking women who had fallen into misfortune, homelessness and destitution. The long lines of ragged men on the breadline, many of whom came to live with us for months, meant only dissipation, profligacy or idleness to the unthinking. Landlords did not want them. They would soil any house they lived in. Landlords never read Regamey, Léon Bloy or *The Little Flowers of St. Francis;* they knew nothing of St. Vincent de Paul.

But how to buy a house? We had no money, or thought we had none. It was in the early spring of 1950 that we began to give all our nights and days to the problem, searching, praying, pondering. We had just sent out our March appeal and our readers were generous, although we did not have enough to make a payment on a house over and above paying bills. So Tom Sullivan explained the situation to our creditors and they let the bills continue. Our Italian neighbors recognized a crisis when they saw one. We began gathering together every penny.

Every Catholic faced with a great need starts a novena. There is good precedent for this. The apostles stayed in the Cenacle for nine days after the Ascension of Jesus Christ, praying for the descent of the Holy Spirit. That was the first novena. Novenas are started nine days before the feast of some favorite saint or they can be made at any time. My favorite novena is the rosary novena, a devotion during which one recites three novenas in petition and three in thanksgiving. If you don't get what you need by the end of the thanksgiving of twenty-seven days, you begin another series—continuing in prayer with perseverance, with importunity. "Ask and you shall receive," "Knock and it shall be opened to you," and Our Lord tells the story of the unjust judge and the widow, and the weary friend and the neighbor who comes to get a few loaves, to show how importunity and perseverance are rewarded.

I know that we all prayed, coming and going, night and day, sleeping and waking. We cannot abandon a work that is begun; we cannot walk away and leave a family which has grown up around us.

That very conviction made us look in our own neighborhood so that we would not be leaving the Bowery.

I do not know whether we prayed the required fifty-four days, but it was before the three months were up that we found our new home on Chrystie Street, a dozen blocks away. Two Twenty-three Chrystie had been built by a Frenchman from New Orleans; the iron grillwork around the front porch and steps reminds one of the French quarter in that city. Our new house has larger rooms than we had before and there is a large back yard where we can hold our forums. Jim Baker can talk of St. Augustine and the New Man, and Monsignor Hillenbrand can talk of worship. We can wrangle about the state and war, and unions and co-ops, and Helen and Jane and Irene can have folk dancing to ease the strain of nightly thought and talk.

The funds came in to buy the house, supplied by our readers from all over the country in many small sums. There were two large donations of three thousand and two thousand dollars.

We look around us now, at the grove of trees stretching in front of us from Houston Street to Manhattan Bridge, green and gold in the bright sun, and then on our own side of the street there is still the breadline, still the slum, and the Bowery is nearer than ever.

Our work goes on, in surroundings more spacious and comfortable than those on Mott Street, but our poverty is more acute if it is less obvious. We have not yet caught up with the bills of last year. As I write this there is less than a hundred dollars in the bank, the line of men stretches to the corner, and our households here and at Maryfarm and Peter Maurin farm comprise seventy-five people or more. How can we go on? We are as sure as we ever were that God can multiply the loaves, as He has sheltered the homeless these many years.

If it is Peter's intercession which has provided us with a house large enough for craft shop, discussion rooms, library, we thank him from our hearts! He can no longer say to me, "Man proposes and woman disposes."

POSTSCRIPT

WE WERE just sitting there talking when Peter Maurin came in.

We were just sitting there talking when lines of people began to form, saying, "We need bread." We could not say, "Go, be thou filled." If there were six small loaves and a few fishes, we had to divide them. There was always bread.

We were just sitting there talking and people moved in on us. Let those who can take it, take it. Some moved out and that made room for more. And somehow the walls expanded.

We were just sitting there talking and someone said, "Let's all go live on a farm."

It was as casual as all that, I often think. It just came about. It just happened.

I found myself, a barren woman, the joyful mother of children. It is not easy always to be joyful, to keep in mind the duty of delight.

The most significant thing about *The Catholic Worker* is poverty, some say.

The most significant thing is community, others say. We are not alone any more.

But the final word is love. At times it has been, in the words of Father Zossima, a harsh and dreadful thing, and our very faith in love has been tried through fire.

We cannot love God unless we love each other, and to love we must know each other. We know Him in the breaking of bread, and we know each other in the breaking of bread, and we are not alone any more. Heaven is a banquet and life is a banquet, too, even with a crust, where there is companionship.

We have all known the long loneliness and we have learned that the only solution is love and that love comes with community.

It all happened while we sat there talking, and it is still going on.

INDEX

287